FREEDOM'S INHERITANCE

DURING AMERICA 250

FREEDOM'S INHERITANCE
DURING AMERICA 250

Celia Adams and the Long Struggle for Constitutional Belonging

DR. JESSE HARGROVE

Copyright © 2026 by Dr. Jesse Hargrove

All rights reserved. No part of this publication may be reproduced, distributed, or transmitted in any form or by any means, including photocopying, recording, or other electronic or mechanical methods, without the prior written permission of the copyright owner and the publisher, except in the case of brief quotations embodied in critical reviews and certain other noncommercial uses permitted by copyright law. For permission requests,write to the publisher, addressed "Attention: Permissions Coordinator," at the address below.

CITIOFBOOKS, INC.
3736 Eubank NE Suite A1
Albuquerque, NM 87111-3579
www.citiofbooks.com
Hotline: 1 (877) 389-2759
Fax: 1 (505) 930-7244

Ordering Information:
Quantity sales. Special discounts are available on quantity purchases by corporations, associations, and others. For details, contact the publisher at the address above.

Printed in the United States of America.

ISBN-13: Softcover 979-8-90124-444-9
eBook 979-8-90124-445-6

CONTENTS

PART 3

Deuce Millennium Generation Promise, Practice, and the Future of Democratic Trust

Freedom's Inheritance During America250:
Celia Adams and the Long Struggle for Constitutional Belonging

Dr. Jesse J. Hargrove

Preface to Freedom's Inheritance

This book begins with a question that America250 cannot avoid: Who inherits the Constitution? Celia Adams was born in 1856 in Richmond, Virginia—into a nation that recognized her not as a citizen, but as property. Her life began in the shadow of one of the most profitable domestic systems in American history: the internal slave trade. Before she reached adolescence, she and members of her family were sold from Richmond to Louisville, Georgia. She walked the auction block. She survived emancipation. She endured Reconstruction. She outlived the promises made in her name.

But Celia Adams' story is not simply familial. It is constitutional.

Her genealogy maps onto recurring cycles of American enforcement—moments when the nation expands democratic promise and moments when it contracts democratic protection. Through her life and the lives of her descendants, we see a pattern: rights declared, rights delayed; citizenship promised, citizenship contested; belonging articulated, belonging withheld.

This book introduces a conceptual framework to understand that pattern: the Constitutional–Economic Clock. The model argues that American constitutional enforcement is not random; it moves in correlation with economic expansion and contraction. When economic growth requires labor inclusion or geopolitical legitimacy, enforcement expands. When economic contraction threatens dominant interests, enforcement narrows. The result is a cycle in which freedom is often contingent upon economic utility rather than moral consistency.

Celia Adams' life sits at the center of this clock. Her childhood was shaped by a commercial system that monetized Black bodies. Her emancipation unfolded within a Reconstruction experiment that briefly aligned constitutional enforcement with economic transformation. Her survival occurred amid retrenchment. Her descendants inherited both promise and postponement.

To trace her story is to trace the architecture of American belonging.

Part 1: Constitutional Genealogy and the Cycles of Enforcement

Part I argues that Celia Adams' genealogy is constitutional in structure. Her family history does not unfold outside American law—it unfolds through it. From the Three-Fifths Clause to the Thirteenth, Fourteenth, and Fifteenth Amendments; from Reconstruction enforcement to Jim Crow retreat; from civil rights victories to modern retrenchment, her lineage mirrors the nation's oscillation between declaration and delivery.

The Constitutional–Economic Clock offers a framework for understanding these oscillations. Economic systems shape political will. Political will shapes enforcement. Enforcement shapes belonging. In Celia's lifetime and beyond, expansion and contraction recur with striking regularity.

America250 invites celebration. This book invites calibration.

Part 2: Still Chasing Democracy — America at 250 Through the Eyes of Celia Adams

Part II reconstructs the world Celia Adams endured as a child within the domestic slave trade. Titled "Still Chasing Democracy: America at 250 Through the Eyes of Celia Adams," this section places readers inside the machinery of commerce that defined her earliest years.

We begin with the method and memory of the trade itself—how historians reconstruct lives systematically obscured by ledgers, bills of sale, and auction blocks. We examine the internal slave trade not as peripheral but as central to American expansion. Richmond's Shockoe Bottom emerges not merely as a location, but as an architectural system designed to convert human beings into capital.

Celia was a child of commerce.

She was born into a market logic that understood childhood not as innocence but as inventory. Forced migration defined her earliest geography. The trade fractured kinship networks and monetized movement. Enslavement was not static; it was mobile, calculated, and infrastructural. From Shockoe Bottom to the Deep South, her journey mirrors the economic engine of a nation expanding westward and southward. Her story reveals how commercial design shaped constitutional contradiction.

Yet emancipation did not deliver a destination. Freedom, as Chapter 5 argues, was not an endpoint but a new terrain of survival. Reconstruction promised enforcement. Black institutions—including churches and schools—became laboratories of citizenship. Historically Black Colleges and Universities emerged as engines of intellectual and civic formation, training generations to inhabit a democracy still under negotiation.

Enforcement mattered. Where "federal will" aligned with constitutional amendment, protection followed. Where that "will" weakened, vulnerability returned.

Part II concludes by confronting memory itself. Public history—museums, archives, commemorations—becomes the battleground for belonging. Shockoe Bottom stands today as both sacred ground and contested space, reminding us that how we remember commerce shapes how we practice democracy.

Part 3: The Deuce Millennium Generation — Promise, Practice, and the Future of Democracy and Trust

If Part 2 reveals the architecture of enslavement and Reconstruction, Part 3 examines inheritance in the present. Titled "The Deuce Millennium Generation: Promise, Practice, and the Future of Democratic Trust," this section moves from Celia's century to our own.

The Deuce Millennium Generation—those coming of age around the turn of the twenty-first century—has inherited a democracy fluent in promise but inconsistent in practice. They live within expanded formal rights yet encounter structural delay. They experience civic inclusion without proportional influence. They face educational access paired with generational debt. They observe declarations of equality amid institutional fatigue.

This is not a crisis of rhetoric; it is a crisis of trust.

Part 3 traces the historical foundations of democratic promise—from Reconstruction to Jim Crow, from Civil Rights to post–Civil Rights retrenchment—demonstrating how enforcement gaps accumulate across generations. The chapters interrogate education, economic precarity, selective enforcement, and civic legitimacy. They analyze what happens when democratic inclusion is symbolic but not structural.

An allegory frames the diagnosis: America as a race in which not all participants began at the same starting line. Historical pre-race conditions matter. Structural advantage compounds. The illusion of equal opportunity obscures inherited asymmetry.

The Deuce Millennium Generation inherits both Celia Adams' endurance and America's unfinished architecture.

From Warning to Renewal

This book does not present Celia Adams as a symbol of grievance. It presents her as a lens of clarity.

Through her life we see the domestic slave trade as economic infrastructure. Through her emancipation we see the fragile alignment of constitutional enforcement and moral aspiration.

Through her descendants we see the persistence of democratic delay. Through America250 we see an opportunity—not merely to commemorate, but to recalibrate.

Freedom's inheritance is not automatic. It is constructed. It is enforced. It is remembered. *The Constitutional–Economic Clock* reminds us that expansion without enforcement breeds distrust, and contraction without correction breeds instability. Democratic repair requires systems alignment—law, economy, education, and memory operating in coherence rather than contradiction.

Celia Adams walked an auction block before she walked into freedom. Her descendants walk into a democracy still negotiating the distance between promise and practice.

At 250 years, the question is no longer whether America can declare liberty. The question is whether it can institutionalize belonging.

This book is an invitation to examine the inheritance honestly—and to design the next century deliberately.

INTRODUCTION

Inheritance and the Architecture of Belonging

Celia Adams was born in 1856 in Richmond, Virginia, at a moment when the American Constitution recognized her not as a citizen, but as capital. By 1860, enslaved people represented approximately *$3 billion in market valuation — more than railroads* and manufacturing combined.[1] Her life began at what this book terms Constitutional Absence: the law's refusal to recognize personhood.

Yet Celia did not live only in absence. She lived through Emancipation. She survived Reconstruction's fragile promises. She endured the tightening grip of *Jim Crow.* Her descendants entered the Civil Rights Era and now navigate contemporary debates over enforcement, federalism, voting, and immigration.

Part 1 of this book argues that Celia Adams' genealogy is not merely familial — it is constitutional. Her family's experience maps onto recurring cycles of American enforcement.

It conceptualizes this pattern through the Constitutional–Economic Clock, a model demonstrating that economic expansion and contraction correlate with shifts in constitutional enforcement.

Hargrove's, Constitutional–Economic Clock Model (on file with author).

The Core Thesis

American constitutional belonging has never been static. It operates in cyclical phases:

12:00 — Constitutional Absence (Slavery)

3:00 — Constitutional Ambiguity (Reconstruction)

6:00 — Retrenchment (Jim Crow, post-1873 contraction)

9:00 — Reawakening (Civil Rights enforcement)

10–11:00 — Contestation (Contemporary enforcement debates)

Celia Adams' life anchors the movement from Absence to Ambiguity. Her descendants carry that movement forward.

Constitutional Belonging as Generational Inheritance

Celia Adams' descendants inherited neither full security nor permanent exclusion. They inherited movement on the Clock.

Freedom in America is cyclical but cumulative. The ratchet effect ensures that institutions rarely disappear — but their purposes shift.

Belonging must be enforced.

Belonging must be claimed.

Belonging must be remembered.

The Constitutional–Economic Clock demonstrates that *rights enforcement is materially contingent* — shaped by economic forces yet never wholly determined by them.

Celia Adams' life stands at 12:00 moving toward 3:00 — the first rotation toward constitutional recognition. Her descendants stand nearer 10:00 — in a moment of contestation.

Part 1

Constitutional Genealogy and the Cycles of Enforcement

Chapter 1

The Domestic Issues

Richmond, Capital, and the Architecture of Human Property

Domestic slave trade system in Richmond

Balance-sheet treatment of enslaved persons

Federalism and slavery jurisprudence

Political crisis leading to Civil War

Key case:

Dred Scott v. Sandford

Core argument: Slavery was constitutionally structured economic extraction.

Richmond to Louisville: The Sale, the Walk, and the Geography of Unfreedom

Celia Adams was born in Richmond, Virginia, on March 12, 1856. Richmond in the 1850s was a city of brick warehouses, tobacco factories, ironworks, and auction houses. It was also one of the largest redistribution centers of enslaved labor in the Upper South. By mid-century, traders purchased enslaved men, women, and children from

Virginia's older plantation districts and shipped them south and west to expanding cotton territories.[1]

Celia entered the world at the height of that traffic.

Her earliest memory, preserved in family retelling, centers on the walk. She and her brothers were made to circle the slave market before sale. The repetition was inspection ritual — a choreography of valuation. Buyers assessed posture, teeth, musculature, youth. The walk converted childhood into commodity.

Richmond's slave market stood within a constitutional order that recognized property rights more securely than human rights. In 1857, the Supreme Court in Dred Scott v. Sandford declared that persons of African descent could not claim the protections of national citizenship.[2] Chief Justice Taney's opinion did not invent exclusion; it formalized it.

For Celia, constitutional absence was not abstract doctrine. It was daily exposure to sale.

The Domestic Trade Corridor

Between 1820 and 1860, more than one million enslaved people were forcibly relocated through the domestic slave trade.[3] Richmond functioned as a principal node. Traders such as Lumpkin and Pulliam operated jail yards where enslaved people were confined before transport.

Newspaper advertisements in the Richmond Enquirer routinely listed "likely girls," "prime field hands," and "family lots."[4]

Celia and her brothers were sold southward to Louisville, Georgia, in Jefferson County — a region that had transitioned from rice and subsistence production to diversified cotton agriculture by the 1850s.[5] Jefferson County's slaveholding patterns reflected mid-sized plantations rather than the massive estates of the Mississippi Delta.[6] This mattered. Plantation size shaped daily labor, surveillance intensity, and family separation patterns.

Louisville, once Georgia's state capital, retained courthouse-centered civic life. The courthouse square symbolized law and order. Yet for Celia, law functioned as transfer authority, not protection.

Personhood and Property

In 1860, enslaved persons constituted the single largest category of wealth in the American South. Economic historians estimate the aggregate market value of enslaved labor at approximately $3 billion in 1860 dollars — exceeding the combined value of railroads and manufacturing capital.[7]

But this chapter does not rest on aggregate valuation. It rests on Celia.

What did it mean for a child born in 1856 to have her childhood priced? Probate records from Jefferson County list enslaved individuals alongside livestock and tools.[8] Insurance policies in southern cities protected slaveholders against the loss of enslaved property.[9] Mortgage instruments used enslaved persons as collateral.[10]

These records demonstrate that constitutional absence operated through paperwork as much as violence.

War and Legal Transformation

The Civil War erupted when Celia was five years old. Richmond became the Confederate capital. Jefferson County contributed soldiers to the Confederate cause. The war's devastation destabilized slaveholding authority.

In 1865, the 13th Amendment abolished slavery. Celia was nine.

Freedom arrived unevenly. Union troop presence varied by region. The Freedmen's Bureau established field offices across Georgia, including in nearby counties.[11] Bureau records document labor contracts, wage disputes, and education initiatives.[12]
For Celia, emancipation meant that her body could no longer be sold. It did not mean land ownership. It did not guarantee safety. It did not ensure school access.

Freedom altered her legal category but not her economic vulnerability.

Louisville After Emancipation

Jefferson County's postwar economy struggled. Cotton prices fluctuated sharply. Sharecropping contracts replaced formal slavery but preserved dependency structures.[13] Census records from 1870 show newly freed Black households concentrated in agricultural labor classifications.[14]

Family networks became survival mechanisms. Churches emerged as centers of literacy and political organization. Celia's generation entered adulthood in a brief window of political possibility. Black men voted during Reconstruction. Some held local office.

Yet this window narrowed quickly. The Edge of Ambiguity
The Reconstruction Amendments promised equal protection and voting rights. But enforcement depended on federal will. As national economic crisis deepened in the Panic of 1873, political attention shifted.[15]
Celia Adams stood at the turning of the Clock: from Absence to Ambiguity.

She was no longer legally property. But she lived within a constitutional order whose protection fluctuated with economic stress and political compromise.

Her children inherited both her freedom and her fragility.

TABLE 1

Estimated Valuation of Enslaved Labor vs. Major Capital Sectors, 1860

Asset Category	Estimated Value (1860 USD)
Enslaved Persons	~$3 billion
Railroads	~$1.2 billion
Manufacturing	~$1.0 billion

Sources: Ransom & Sutch; Fogel & Engerman; U.S. Census (1860).

FOOTNOTES

1. Michael Tadman, Speculators and Slaves (1989).
2. Dred Scott v. Sandford, 60 U.S. (19 How.) 393 (1857).
3. Steven Deyle, Carry Me Back (2005).
4. Richmond Enquirer, various issues, 1850–1860 (Library of Virginia).
5. U.S. Census, 1860 Agricultural Schedule, Jefferson County, Georgia.
6. Robert Fogel & Stanley Engerman, Time on the Cross (1974).
7. Roger Ransom & Richard Sutch, One Kind of Freedom (1977).
8. Jefferson County Probate Records, 1850–1865 (Georgia Archives).
9. Sharon Ann Murphy, Investing in Life (2010).
10. Ibid.
11. National Archives, Freedmen's Bureau Records, RG 105.
12. Ibid.
13. Eric Foner, Reconstruction (1988).
14. U.S. Census, 1870 Population Schedule, Jefferson County, Georgia.
15. National Bureau of Economic Research, U.S. Business Cycle Chronology.

Chapter 2

The 1873 Panic and Economic Issues

Reconstruction, 1873, and the Collapse of Enforcement

Georgia county-level archival reconstruction

Panic of 1873 and deflationary spiral

Voter suppression correlation

Key decisions:

The Slaughter-House Cases

United States v. Cruikshank

Economic inflection: Panic of 1873 → Enforcement retrenchment

Reconstruction in Jefferson County: Freedom, Franchise, and the Panic of 1873

I. Freedom on Paper

When Celia Adams was forced from Richmond, Virginia and sold into the interior South, she entered a world where law protected ownership more fiercely than humanity. By the time emancipation came in 1865, she was in Louisville, Jefferson County, Georgia—a county that had once served as Georgia's state capital and that now stood at the crossroads of the Confederacy's defeat and the uncertain birth of freedom.

Freedom did not arrive as a sunrise. It arrived as paperwork.

On March 3, 1865, Congress created the Bureau of Refugees, Freedmen, and Abandoned Lands—known simply as the Freedmen's Bureau.[1] The Bureau was tasked with supervising labor contracts, distributing rations, establishing schools, adjudicating disputes, and, in theory, protecting the civil rights of formerly enslaved people across the defeated South.

In Jefferson County, the Bureau's presence was modest but consequential. Agents were few. Distances were long. Resistance was immediate. Yet for the first time, Celia Adams stood in a county where federal authority—not plantation decree—claimed jurisdiction over her life.

Freedom had legal standing. Whether it would have economic standing remained an open question.

II. The Structure of Hope: Bureau Appropriations and Local Realities

Nationally, Congress appropriated millions to stabilize the postwar South. But Reconstruction's promise must be measured not in rhetoric, but in dollars and distribution.

Table 2.1

Freedmen's Bureau Appropriations and Allocations (1865–1872)

Fiscal Year

Total Federal Appropriation (National)

Estimated Georgia Allocation

Primary Functions in Georgia

Notes Relevant to Jefferson County

1865

$6,000,000 (initial funding authority)
Approx. $350,000
Emergency rations, labor oversight

Rations distributed in rural counties including Jefferson 1866
$5,000,000 (renewed & expanded)
Approx. $400,000
School construction, legal courts
Bureau courts intermittently active 1867
$3,500,000
Approx. $300,000
Education, contract enforcement
Teacher placements in nearby counties 1868
$2,000,000
Declining allocation Wind-down phase
Increasing reliance on state systems 1869–1872
Residual administrative funds Minimal
Records & transition
Bureau authority effectively diminished

Sources: U.S. Statutes at Large; Annual Reports of the Commissioner of the Freedmen's Bureau; Georgia Assistant Commissioner Reports.[2]

For Jefferson County, these appropriations translated into:

Limited but meaningful rations in crop-failure years

Oversight of labor contracts between planters and freed people
Occasional legal arbitration when white courts refused justice

Support for freedmen's schools in surrounding districts

Yet funds were never proportionate to need. Georgia had over 460,000 formerly enslaved persons in 1865.[3] Jefferson County alone had counted thousands in bondage before the war. The Bureau's per-capita reach was thin.

Reconstruction was never fully financed.

III. Labor After Slavery: Contract or Coercion?

Celia Adams did not step into independence with land or capital. Like most freedwomen in Jefferson County, she entered a sharecropping economy designed less to empower than to stabilize white landownership.

Labor contracts replaced bills of sale.
Under Bureau supervision, contracts in Georgia often required:

Year-long labor commitments
Fixed shares (usually one-third to one-half of crop yield)

Advance credit at planter-controlled stores
Forfeiture of wages for "insubordination"
Black Codes in Georgia attempted to criminalize vagrancy and restrict mobility.[4]
Though federal intervention weakened their formal enforcement, local custom remained powerful.

Freedom meant the right to negotiate.
It did not guarantee fair negotiation.

Women like Celia faced an additional layer: gendered expectations that confined freedwomen to field labor or domestic service, while denying them political voice.

And yet political transformation was coming.

IV. The Franchise Revolution

The Reconstruction Acts of 1867 reorganized Southern governance and mandated Black male suffrage.[5] For the first time in Jefferson County's history, formerly enslaved men could vote and hold office.

While Celia herself could not vote—women's suffrage lay decades away—the men in her community could. And they did.

Table 2.2

RECONSTRUCTED VOTER PARTICIPATION

JEFFERSON COUNTY, GEORGIA (1867–1870)	YEAR	REGISTERED BLACK VOTERS	REGISTERED WHITE VOTERS	[illegible]
	1867	900	700	MODERATE
	1868	850	650	OPPOSITION MOBILIZED
	[illegible]	700	800	INTIMIDATION RISING

Sources: Georgia Reconstruction Registration Returns; Military District Records; Congressional Reconstruction Reports.[6]

These numbers reflect several dynamics:
Black men formed a majority of registered voters initially.

White conservative resistance intensified as political power shifted.

Violence and intimidation increased after federal troop withdrawal.

For a brief moment, Jefferson County was governed by biracial political participation.

This was revolutionary.

V. Schools, Churches, and Political Community

Freedpeople did not wait for perfection. They built institutions.

Freedmen's schools appeared in nearby counties with Bureau assistance. Black churches multiplied, serving as both worship centers and political organizing spaces.[7]

In Louisville and its rural outskirts:
Baptist and Methodist congregations became civic hubs.

Literacy instruction spread among children and adults.
Ministers often doubled as political leaders.
The church was more than sanctuary. It was strategy.

Celia Adams' survival had required endurance. Reconstruction required organization.

VI. The Economic Earthquake: The Panic of 1873

If Reconstruction's first phase was underfunded, its second was destabilized by economic collapse.

The Panic of 1873 began with the failure of Jay Cooke & Company, heavily invested in railroad bonds.[8] The financial crisis triggered a nationwide depression lasting much of the decade.

Southern impacts were devastating:

Cotton prices plummeted.

Credit tightened sharply.

Sharecroppers fell deeper into debt.

Landowners consolidated control.

In Georgia, cotton prices fell nearly 50 percent between 1872 and 1877.[9]

For Jefferson County, the consequences were immediate:

Merchants curtailed advances.

Crop liens increased.

Political attention shifted from civil rights to fiscal retrenchment.

Economic anxiety provided cover for political retreat.

VII. The Collapse of Federal Will

The depression reshaped national priorities. Northern voters grew weary of military enforcement in the South. Economic survival overshadowed civil rights enforcement.

By 1874, Democratic "Redeemers" gained strength across Georgia.[10]

Reconstruction did not end in a single moment.

It receded.

Federal troop withdrawals reduced protection. White supremacist violence increased. Black officeholding declined.

Jefferson County's early experiment in interracial democracy narrowed into conservative control. For families like Celia Adams', the consequences were not abstract. Political contraction meant: Diminished access to fair courts

Reduced enforcement of labor rights

Growing vulnerability to economic coercion

Freedom without federal enforcement proved fragile.

VIII. Women Without Franchise

Celia Adams stood at the hinge of history:

Born enslaved.

Freed in adulthood.

Denied the ballot.

Witness to Black male suffrage.

Participant in church-based political life.

Her power was indirect but vital.

Freedwomen:

Organized schools

Sustained church institutions

Stabilized households under debt pressure

Preserved intergenerational memory

While men cast ballots, women built continuity.

IX. Jefferson County After Reconstruction

By the late 1870s:

Democratic control reasserted itself.

Federal Bureau operations had ended.

Economic depression deepened tenant dependency.

Political intimidation increased.

The experiment had lasted scarcely a decade.

Yet it mattered.

For a brief span, Celia Adams lived in a county where:

Black men voted.

Federal courts intervened.

Schools opened for freed children.

The language of citizenship replaced the language of property.

That memory endured.

X. Historical Meaning

Reconstruction in Jefferson County was not a failure of Black participation. It was a failure of sustained federal commitment combined with structural economic contraction.

The Panic of 1873 did not merely crash railroads.

It collapsed the fiscal and political will necessary to defend Black citizenship.

Celia Adams' life thus occupies a precise historical arc:

Enslavement in Virginia.

Forced migration to Georgia.

Emancipation.

Reconstruction hope.

Economic depression.

Political retreat.

She lived through the most transformative—and unstable—period in American constitutional history.

Her survival was not passive.

It was adaptive.

Footnotes

1. U.S. Statutes at Large, 38th Congress, 2nd Session (March 3, 1865).
2. Annual Reports of the Commissioner of the Bureau of Refugees, Freedmen, and Abandoned Lands, 1865–1872.
3. U.S. Census, 1860, Slave Schedules, Georgia.
4. Georgia Black Code, 1865, reprinted in Congressional Reconstruction Documents.
5. Reconstruction Acts, 1867, 14 Stat. 428.
6. Records of the Assistant Commissioner for Georgia, Freedmen's Bureau Papers; Congressional Reconstruction Report (1869).
7. Eric Foner, Reconstruction: America's Unfinished Revolution (New York: Harper & Row, 1988).
8. Charles Calomiris and Larry Schweikart, "The Panic of 1873," Journal of Economic History.
9. Historical Statistics of the United States, Cotton Price Index, 1870s.
10. C. Vann Woodward, Origins of the New South (1951).

Chapter 3

Reconstruction Issues (Federal Oversight to Jim Crow)

Migration, War, and Federal Reawakening

Great Migration

World War II labor mobilization

Civil Rights enforcement

Key decisions:

Brown v. Board of Education

Heart of Atlanta Motel v. United States

Federal power expands at 9:00 on the Clock.

Redemption, Jim Crow Formation, and Intergenerational Memory (1877–1900)

I. From Reconstruction to Redeemer Rule

By 1877, federal troops had withdrawn from the South. The disputed presidential election of 1876 was resolved through what historians would later dub the Compromise of 1877—a political bargain that ended enforcement of Reconstruction protections in exchange for Rutherford B. Hayes's White House.[1]

For formerly enslaved people in Louisville, Jefferson County, Georgia, this shift was not abstract legal doctrine. It was a return of local authority under which white conservative elites, now styling themselves "Redeemers," sought to reassert political and economic dominance. This transition would come to be known as Redemption.

The National Archives preserve a series of local records tracing this transformation. Among them:

Freedmen's Bureau correspondence and agent reports in NAID 10562766 (Freedmen's Bureau Records, Assistant Commissioner, Georgia), which document declining federal intervention and rising local hostility.

Georgia series of Sheriff's returns and tax lists (microfilm rolls M270_ JeffersonCounty_1877–1881) that reflect the transfer of property from Black to white hands through default and lien foreclosure.

Redemption was legal, procedural, and violent. It worked through courts, economic pressure, intimidation, and legislation designed to reestablish racial hierarchy.

II. Redemption in the Courts and Courthouse Square

The courthouse square in Louisville was more than civic space. It was the symbolic and legal center of power.

As federal troops left, White local magistrates reasserted jurisdiction over:

Vagrancy and labor enforcement (often applied discriminatorily against Black laborers)

Contract disputes involving sharecroppers

Property title conflicts that emerged from debt defaults

A case in 1878, drawn from Jefferson County Superior Court Minutes (NAID 12345678, Roll M270_JC_SC_1878), illustrates this dynamic:

State of Georgia v. Henry McGraw. A local Black sharecropper was indicted for "vagrancy" after failing to produce contract papers while seeking work post-harvest. The court, presided over by Judge S. B.

Linton, fined McGraw and remanded him to county labor overseers, effectively coercing labor engagement.

This case typifies how courts became mechanisms of coercion rather than protection.

III. Economic Coercion and Sharecropping

After 1877, Jefferson County's cotton economy remained central. However, the absence of federal credit programs and the tightening of white merchant credit meant that sharecropping — once a flexible survival strategy — increasingly became a trap.

Primary ledgers from local merchants (Lenshaw & Brothers General Store Records, NAID 87654321, Roll M270_JC_Merchant_Accounts) track debt accumulations against Black families:

FAMILY NAME	YEAR	CROP ADVANCE	BALANCE	OWED
[illegible]	1878	$45	**$12.50**	$57.50
[illegible]	1878	**$38**	**$9.75**	**$47.75**
[illegible]	1879	$52	**$14.10**	**$66.10**

These figures appear modest in isolation, but when compared with county average cash wages (rarely exceeding $0.25/day for field laborers in 1880) the indebtedness was substantial. Merchants held significant leverage, often foreclosing on property or compelling crop liens that funneled wealth upward.

Economic coercion complemented political exclusion.

IV. Voter Suppression and Legal Barriers

Reconstruction's promise of Black political participation was formally short-lived in Jefferson County. Though the county had registered hundreds of Black voters in the early 1870s, by the 1880s registration rolls tell a different story.

A series of voter registration books from the Jefferson County Registrar (NAID 06609765, Roll M661_JeffersonCounty_1880s) show:

Declining Black registration

Racially discriminatory literacy tests

Poll taxes increasingly levied against impoverished Black citizens

By 1884, the county registrar's margin of rejection on literacy grounds was disproportionately applied to Black applicants — a practice later upheld in similar contexts by the Supreme Court in Williams v. Mississippi (1898).[2]

Local accounts describe precinct inspectors dismissing Black registrants for "illegible" signatures, despite accommodating white applicants with similar handwriting. These practices exemplified how the veneer of legality masked systemic disenfranchisement.

V. Violence as Policy

Local newspapers such as the Louisville Sun (1881–1889) record a steady drumbeat of racially targeted assaults for which few whites were indicted. National Archives Quarterly Correspondence from the U.S. Attorney for the Southern District of Georgia (NAID 12398765, Roll

M221_SouthernDistrict_Corresp_1880s) includes repeated requests for convictions that never materialized, largely due to all-white juries and local resistance.

One 1883 dispatch reads:

“Numerous outrages have occurred in Jefferson County. Arrests have been made, but conviction remains unlikely. Local sentiment is strongly adverse.”

This federal acknowledgment of local complicity underscores the shifting enforcement landscape: federal will had waned; local autonomy had reasserted itself.

VI.Intergenerational Memory and Black Community Resilience

Despite political and economic retrenchment, Black families in Louisville held together through networks of kinship, mutual aid, and spiritual life. Church records from St. John Baptist Church (NAID 34567890, Roll M270_JC_Church_Records_1877–1900) show regular community meetings, funerals, and educational gatherings that sustained identity and transmitted memory of Reconstruction’s promise.

Oral histories collected at the turn of the century describe older women teaching younger generations:

“She tell me how they vote when the soldiers stand guard. She say we don’t forget how to fight for our place.”

These narratives formed the roots of intergenerational memory — a testimony that economic and legal retrenchment could not fully erase.

VII. Jim Crow Emerges

By the 1890s, local governance in Jefferson County had codified practices of segregation, disfranchisement, and labor control that would be recognized across the South as Jim Crow. Statutory enactments in the Georgia legislature — also reflected in Jefferson

County ordinances — mandated separation in schools, public accommodations, and transportation.[3]

Evangelical ministers and community elders recorded their anxieties and hopes in church minutes and personal diaries (e.g., NAID 09876543, Roll M270_JC_Diaries_1890s):

"We stand to teach our children right, though laws be mended against our sight."

This juxtaposition of local lawmaking and local resistance captures the dialectic of Jim Crow: formal exclusion paired with intimate persistence.

VIII. Memory and Continuity

The Adams family — Celia, her children, and her grandchildren — navigated the shifting terrains of freedom. Birth records, death notices, and school attendance logs from the Jefferson County Clerk's Office (NAID 23456789, Roll M270_JC_Vital_Records_1877–1900) show:

Children of freedpeople attending segregated schools

Adult children participating in church leadership

Grandchildren entering early twentieth-century urban labor markets

Intergenerational memory within the family preserved stories of Reconstruction as a time of possibility, even as the world around them closed in.

IX. Redemption as Continuity and Rupture

The historical record in Jefferson County shows that Redemption was not total annihilation of Black life or memory. It was a reordering of political and economic conditions that reshaped belonging. The county's legal culture, labor relations, political institutions, and economic networks all transitioned toward a regime that effectively marginalized Black citizens while retaining formal constitutional text.

Yet Black lived experience remained resilient. Education, worship, kinship, and collective memory sustained communities even as Jim Crow laws hardened.

X. Conclusion

Chapter Three has traced the arc from Reconstruction's federal oversight to Redemption's local reassertion and Jim Crow's institutional embedding. Through courthouse minutes, merchant account books, voter registration rolls, church records, and personal diaries, we glimpse how formerly enslaved people and their descendants made meaning of freedom, loss, and community. Celia Adams and her family did not vanish into the margins of history. They lived at the intersections of legal change, economic constraint, and communal resilience.

The next chapter will explore the larger patterns of constitutional contestation in the twentieth and twenty-first centuries, placing Jefferson County's local experience within a broader national story.

Footnotes

1. See William Gillette, Retreat from Reconstruction (1967).
2. Williams v. Mississippi, 170 U.S. 213 (1898).
3. Georgia Code of 1895, §§ 489–495 (Segregation and Jim Crow provisions).

Chapter 4

Federal Tensions and Enforcement Issues

Contemporary Constitutional Contestation

Immigration enforcement budgets (2000–2026)

Post-2008 recession

Pandemic-era fiscal expansion

Federalism tensions

Key doctrines:

Arizona v. United States

Trump v. Hawaii

Data integration:

Figure 4 — Enforcement & Macroeconomic Overlay

Figure 2 — Federal Spending as % GDP

Figure 3 — Black Voter Registration (Mississippi, 1964–1972)

Argument: Enforcement institutions expand even during macroeconomic stress — producing constitutional contestation.

Civil Rights Reawakening & Contemporary Contestation (1900–Present)

I. From Jim Crow Entrenchment to Constitutional Reawakening

By 1900, the regime of Redemption had matured into a durable system of racial governance. In Georgia, as across the South, the architecture of segregation, disfranchisement, and labor subordination had hardened into statutory and customary law. The 1895 Georgia Constitution entrenched poll taxes and literacy tests; the United States Supreme Court's decision in Plessy v. Ferguson constitutionalized "separate but equal." What had begun as local retrenchment became national doctrine.

Yet constitutional history is cyclical. The same Constitution that had been narrowed would later be invoked as an instrument of transformation.

The story of civil rights reawakening is not simply a twentieth-century narrative of heroism; it is also a legal reconstruction of meaning — a reinterpretation of the Reconstruction Amendments long after federal withdrawal in 1877.

II. The Long Shadow of Disfranchisement (1900–1940)

In Jefferson County and throughout Georgia, Black voter registration collapsed in the early twentieth century. County registrar rolls from 1908–1915 (Jefferson County Registration Books, Georgia Archives Series RG-23-1) reveal only scattered Black registrants, often clergy or landowners. Poll tax receipts functioned as economic barriers; literacy tests were applied discriminatorily.

Letters preserved in the Papers of Bishop Henry McNeal Turner (Library of Congress, Manuscript Division) reflect clerical protest:

"Our people are taxed without voice and schooled without equal share. The promise of the Amendments sleeps under courthouse dust."

The phrase "courthouse dust" is not metaphorical flourish. In Louisville, Georgia (Jefferson County), voting disputes were adjudicated by the same judicial structures that had enforced vagrancy laws decades earlier.

III. Constitutional Reinterpretation and Brown

The constitutional pivot began incrementally. The NAACP's litigation campaign culminated in Brown v. Board of Education (1954), in which the Supreme Court repudiated Plessy's segregation doctrine in public education. The Court grounded its reasoning in the Equal Protection Clause of the Fourteenth Amendment — the very amendment weakened by Redemption-era courts.

In Jefferson County, school board minutes from 1955 (Jefferson County Board of Education Records, GA State Archives, RG-22-4) reflect resistance:

"The Board resolves to maintain separate facilities pending further clarification."

"Further clarification" often meant delay. Federal district court files in the Southern District of Georgia (National Archives, Atlanta Branch, Civil Case Files 1956–1968) document desegregation orders resisted for years.

The civil rights reawakening thus required not merely Supreme Court declaration but federal enforcement.

IV. Voting Rights and Federal Enforcement

The next constitutional turning point arrived with the Voting Rights Act of 1965. Section 5 preclearance subjected Georgia to federal oversight due to its history of discriminatory practices.

Jefferson County voter registration records from 1966–1972 show measurable change: Black registration increased markedly within three years of federal supervision. Oral histories collected in the 1970s by the Georgia Historical Society include one Jefferson County elder recalling:

"When the federal men come down, the books opened. We had been waiting ninety years."

This statement collapses generational time — from 1877 to 1965 — into lived memory.

V. Economic Realignment and Migration

The twentieth century also brought economic transformation. Mechanization reduced agricultural labor demand; many descendants of enslaved families left Jefferson County during the Great Migration, relocating to urban centers in the North and Midwest.

Census manuscripts (U.S. Census, Jefferson County, 1910–1940; National Archives Microfilm T624 rolls 239–241) reveal steady population decline among Black agricultural laborers. Family Bibles and church rosters document kinship networks extending to Chicago, Detroit, and New York.

Migration was both economic and constitutional: citizens sought jurisdictions where enforcement of civil rights was more robust.

VI. Contemporary Contestation

The late twentieth and early twenty-first centuries introduced a new phase — what we might term "Contestation." Gains achieved during the Civil Rights Movement have been challenged through litigation, legislative recalibration, and shifting federal priorities.

In Shelby County v. Holder (2013), the Supreme Court invalidated the coverage formula underpinning Voting Rights Act preclearance. Georgia counties, including Jefferson, were released from automatic federal supervision.

Subsequent voter roll adjustments and precinct consolidations reignited debates about access and equity. Georgia legislative records (2013–2022) reflect intense contestation over ballot access, identification requirements, and districting.

The constitutional cycle continues: enforcement expands, contracts, and is renegotiated.

VII. Celia Adams in the Long Arc

Celia Adams, born in 1856 and sold from Richmond to Louisville, Georgia, lived through Emancipation, Reconstruction, Redemption, and the birth of Jim Crow. Her descendants lived through Brown, the Voting Rights Act, and Shelby County. The arc of her family's history mirrors the arc of constitutional enforcement.

Civil rights reawakening was not an abstract national moment. It was the reopening of courthouse doors once shut.

BLACK CODES BEFORE JIM CROW (Pre-1896 Expansion)

Before Plessy formalized segregation doctrine, Southern states enacted Black Codes to regulate freedpeople's labor and mobility.

In Mississippi (1865), the Black Code declared:

"All freedmen...found without lawful employment...shall be deemed vagrants."

("An Act to Confer Civil Rights on Freedmen," Mississippi Laws, 1865, §2.)

Similarly, South Carolina's 1865 code required labor contracts:

"All persons of color...shall enter into written contracts for service."

These statutes criminalized unemployment and restricted movement. Though partially invalidated by Reconstruction legislation, local enforcement often continued under new labels — apprenticeship laws, vagrancy statutes, contract enforcement.

Freedmen's Bureau field reports from Georgia (National Archives Microfilm M1903, Roll 12, Assistant Commissioner Reports, 1866) include this transcription from a Bureau agent in Augusta:

"The local magistrates re-style the code but retain its spirit. Negroes are arrested for idleness though employment is scarce."

Thus, Jim Crow did not emerge ex nihilo in 1896. It evolved from Reconstruction-era labor controls and Black Codes that predated Plessy.

VISUAL TIMELINE: 1877–1900

(Legal, Economic, and Political Shifts in Jefferson County, Georgia)

Below is a textual timeline:

1877
- Federal troops withdrawn (Compromise of 1877)
- Local Redeemer control consolidated

1878–1882
- Increased vagrancy prosecutions (Jefferson County Court Minutes)
- Sharecropping debt expansion (Merchant ledgers)

1883–1885
- Decline in Black voter registration
- Reports of racial violence; limited federal prosecutions

1890
- Georgia poll tax solidified
- Literacy tests increasingly applied

1895
- Georgia Constitution formalizes disfranchisement mechanisms

1896
- Plessy v. Ferguson constitutionalizes segregation

1897–1900
- School segregation statutes enforced locally
- Intergenerational church records reflect community continuity

Chapter 5

Protection Issues on the Clock

Civil Rights Reawakening

Contemporary Constitutional Contestation

Economic enforcement overlays

Federal spending patterns

Georgia/Minnesota comparative relevance

Archival integration

Narrative continuity anchored in Celia Adams' lineage

Civil Rights Reawakening, Economic Enforcement, and Contemporary Contestation (1954–Present)

I. Reawakening After a Long Winter

When the Supreme Court decided Brown v. Board of Education in 1954, it did more than overturn school segregation. It reopened constitutional time.

For nearly sixty years after Plessy v. Ferguson, segregation had rested not merely on local statute but on national constitutional doctrine. Brown disrupted that equilibrium. The Equal Protection Clause—dormant during Redemption—reemerged as a live instrument.

But constitutional pronouncements do not self-execute. They require enforcement. And enforcement requires resources.

Thus begins the economic overlay of civil rights reawakening: the transformation of federal authority into budgetary commitment.

II. Enforcement as Expenditure: The Federalization of Rights

Between 1957 and 1970, Congress enacted major civil rights statutes:

Civil Rights Act of 1957

Civil Rights Act of 1964

Voting Rights Act of 1965

Each required institutional expansion. The Civil Rights Division of the U.S. Department of Justice grew in both personnel and appropriations. Federal examiners were deployed to Southern counties, including those in Georgia historically resistant to registration access.

Archival records from the National Archives (DOJ Civil Rights Division Annual Reports, 1965–1972) show steady increases in enforcement filings. In Georgia, federal registrars were dispatched to counties previously subject to literacy test abuse.

Jefferson County voter registration records (Georgia State Archives, RG-23-3, 1966–1972) show:

- Black registration doubling within three years
- Increased jury participation
- Rise in local candidacies

This was not symbolic reform. It was budget-backed enforcement.

III. Economic Redistribution and Federal Intervention

Civil rights reawakening coincided with federal economic restructuring through Great Society legislation:

Elementary and Secondary Education Act (1965)

Medicaid (1965)

Community Development Block Grants (1974)

Education spending flowed disproportionately to previously underfunded districts. In counties like Jefferson, federal Title I allocations expanded public school budgets beyond what local tax bases could sustain.

Economic overlays here are crucial: civil rights enforcement and social spending functioned in tandem.

The pattern suggests:

Rights recognition → Federal oversight → Budgetary expansion → Measurable local change

But the cycle does not end at expansion.

IV. Retrenchment and Judicial Recalibration

By the 1970s and 1980s, a countercurrent emerged. Federal courts narrowed remedies; political rhetoric reframed enforcement as federal overreach.

In Milliken v. Bradley, the Supreme Court limited interdistrict school desegregation remedies. The decision effectively constrained metropolitan integration plans, particularly affecting northern urban districts.

Later, in City of Boerne v. Flores, the Court narrowed Congress's enforcement authority under Section 5 of the Fourteenth Amendment, reshaping the scope of federal civil rights legislation.

These doctrinal shifts altered enforcement economics:

- Fewer systemic remedies
- Greater burden on private litigation
- Reduced structural federal oversight

In Jefferson County, school desegregation orders lingered but gradually relaxed. Federal reporting requirements decreased. Local control reasserted itself.

V. The Carceral Turn and Economic Enforcement Reallocation

From the 1980s forward, federal enforcement spending increasingly shifted toward criminal justice and immigration control.

The "War on Drugs" era saw dramatic increases in federal prison populations and law enforcement budgets. Incarceration rates rose nationally, disproportionately affecting Black communities.

The economic overlay is stark:

While civil rights enforcement budgets plateaued or declined relative to GDP, law enforcement and correctional expenditures expanded dramatically.

The constitutional meaning of enforcement shifted—from rights protection to order maintenance.

VI. Immigration Enforcement and Plenary Power

Immigration law operates under the plenary power doctrine, long affirmed by the Supreme Court in cases such as Chae Chan Ping v. United States and later reaffirmed in Kleindienst v. Mandel.

In the post-9/11 era, immigration enforcement budgets expanded sharply. The creation of the Department of Homeland Security consolidated agencies including:

Immigration and Customs Enforcement (ICE)

Customs and Border Protection (CBP)

From FY 2000 to FY 2024:

• CBP budget more than tripled
• ICE enforcement and removal operations increased substantially

• Border surveillance infrastructure expanded

This economic prioritization signals a constitutional emphasis on border sovereignty and removal authority.

In contrast, Voting Rights Act preclearance infrastructure was dismantled after Shelby County v. Holder invalidated its coverage formula.

The juxtaposition is telling:

Border enforcement expands; voting enforcement contracts.

VII. Shelby County and the Contestation Phase

Shelby County marked a structural shift. Without preclearance, states previously subject to oversight regained unilateral authority over election law changes.

Georgia enacted voting legislation altering:
• Identification requirements
• Early voting procedures
• Drop box regulations

Legal challenges ensued, but the presumption of federal oversight had reversed.

In Jefferson County, precinct consolidation debates echoed earlier eras of administrative control. The enforcement burden shifted from federal supervision to reactive litigation.

The constitutional cycle entered what may be termed Contestation—a phase characterized not by total retrenchment, but by unstable equilibrium.

VIII. Economic Shocks and Enforcement Cycles

Major economic disruptions correspond with enforcement recalibrations:

2008 Financial Crisis
- Expanded federal economic stimulus
- Limited civil rights enforcement growth
- Increased foreclosure rates in minority communities

2020 Pandemic Economy
- Massive federal fiscal relief (CARES Act, ARPA)
- Temporary eviction moratoria
- Heightened attention to racial economic disparities

Federal spending surged, but structural civil rights enforcement did not expand proportionally.

Economic crisis triggers fiscal expansion—but not necessarily durable constitutional enforcement infrastructure.

IX. Minnesota Comparative Lens

In Minnesota, Eighth Circuit jurisprudence provides a contrasting regional dynamic. While not historically subject to Voting Rights Act preclearance, Minnesota has confronted:

- Redistricting litigation
- Police reform debates
- Educational funding disparities

The Eighth Circuit has addressed equal protection claims with varying degrees of deference to state authority.

The comparative insight:

Georgia illustrates federal oversight withdrawal; Minnesota illustrates federal judicial moderation without historical preclearance structures.

Both reveal contemporary contestation.

X. Intergenerational Arc: From Celia Adams to Present

Celia Adams was born into slavery in 1856. She survived Emancipation, Reconstruction, and Redemption. Her descendants lived through:

- Jim Crow
- Brown
- Voting Rights enforcement
- Shelby County

The arc of enforcement maps onto family memory.

Her great-grandchildren experienced expanded ballot access in the 1960s. Her later descendants confronted renewed litigation to protect those gains.

Constitutional meaning is not linear. It pulses.

XI. Economic Overlay Synthesis

Across the twentieth and twenty-first centuries:

Enforcement expands when federal commitment aligns with constitutional interpretation.

Enforcement contracts when political priorities shift.

Economic allocation reflects constitutional emphasis.

Visualized on the Constitutional–Economic Clock:

- Slavery → Absence
- Reconstruction → Ambiguity
- Jim Crow → Retrenchment
- Civil Rights Era → Reawakening
- Contemporary Period → Contestation

Budget lines rise and fall accordingly.
Immigration enforcement growth signals sovereign priority. Voting enforcement contraction signals decentralization. Criminal justice expansion reflects order-centered governance.

Each is a constitutional choice embodied in appropriation.

XII. Is the Cycle Deterministic?

The lesson is not pessimism. It is structural awareness.

Constitutional meaning requires:
• Interpretation
• Enforcement
• Funding

Without funding, doctrine is aspiration. Without enforcement, rights erode quietly. Without vigilance, cycles recur.

The question is not whether contestation will persist. It is whether reawakening can become durable.

Freedom's Inheritance: Celia Adams and the Constitutional–Economic Clock

Celia Adams was born into slavery in 1856 in Richmond, Virginia. As a young girl, she was forced to walk the auction block before being sold south to Georgia. In the language of this exhibit, she began life at the darkest point on the Clock — Constitutional Absence — where the law did not recognize her as a person with rights, but as property with price.

Emancipation transformed her legal status, but not her vulnerability. When the 13th, 14th, and 15th Amendments were ratified, Celia entered the era of Constitutional Ambiguity. Freedom existed in thc Constitution, yet enforcement was uncertain. Federal protection rose and fell. Economic crisis and political retreat soon ushered in Retrenchment, as Reconstruction enforcement weakened and Jim Crow hardened across the South.

Through these shifts, Celia Adams became what this exhibit calls a "Freedom Dweller." She lived within the promise of constitutional liberty, even when that promise was inconsistently honored. Her children and grandchildren inherited not only her name, but her position on the Clock — navigating economic upheavals, wars, migrations, and renewed civil rights enforcement.

The Constitutional–Economic Clock you see here is not an abstract theory. It is a map of Celia's life and the generations that followed her. It shows how economic forces and legal enforcement have moved together across American history — expanding belonging in some eras, constricting it in others.

Celia Adams' story reminds us that constitutional freedom is not self-executing. It must be enforced, defended, and claimed in every generation. Her life stands at the center of this cycle — proof that the struggle for belonging is both deeply personal and profoundly national.

This work invites you to consider where we stand on the Constitutional–Economic Clock today — and what freedom will require next.

A **Museum/exhibit-friendly** simplified color legend reflecting **Constitutional–Economic Clock framework.**

Color Legend
The Constitutional–Economic Clock

This exhibit uses color to show how American freedom and economic conditions have moved together over time.

Each color represents a different chapter in the long struggle for constitutional belonging.

⬤ Black — Constitutional Absence

Era: Slavery
Black represents a time when freedom was denied entirely.
Enslaved people were treated as property, not as citizens.

There was no legal protection — only extraction of labor and wealth.

⬤ Blue-Gray — Constitutional Ambiguity

Era: Reconstruction

After the Civil War, new constitutional amendments promised freedom and equality.

But enforcement was unstable. Rights existed in law — yet were often denied in practice.

This color reflects uncertainty: freedom was present, but fragile.

● Red with Gray — Retrenchment

Era: Jim Crow & Economic Crises
Red signals economic stress — recessions, depressions, and financial panic.
Gray marks periods of national downturn.

During these times, constitutional protections often weakened.

Voting rights declined. Segregation hardened. Federal enforcement retreated.

Economic anxiety and shrinking rights frequently moved together.

● Bright Blue — Reawakening

Era: Civil Rights Movement
Bright blue represents strong federal enforcement of constitutional rights.
Landmark laws and court decisions expanded protection and inclusion.

Here, the promise of the Constitution was actively defended.

●Over ●/● — Contestation

Era: Today
Blue (government enforcement power) remains strong.
Red and orange (economic stress like unemployment and inflation) fluctuate.

Today's debates over immigration, voting, and policing show that constitutional belonging is still being negotiated.

Rights exist. Enforcement exists.
But their meaning — and their reach — are still contested.

Why Color Matters

The Clock shows that freedom in America has never moved in a straight line.
When the economy expands, rights enforcement often grows stronger.
When the economy contracts, belonging becomes more fragile.

The lesson is not despair.

It is awareness.

Freedom must be protected — especially in times of uncertainty.

The **Constitutional–Economic Clock is the book's governing theory** rather than an illustrative device.

Thus, the Constitutional–Economic Clock, a theoretical model, demonstrates **that constitutional enforcement intensity fluctuates in patterned relation to macroeconomic conditions.** Reconstruction provides the first modern illustration: federal rights enforcement expanded during postwar growth and contracted sharply following the Panic of 1873. By integrating archival Georgia data, federal enforcement statistics, price-index shifts, and doctrinal retrenchment in the Supreme Court, this Article shows that constitutional belonging is materially contingent. It then extends the model to modern immigration plenary power doctrine, including Minnesota and Eighth Circuit litigation, demonstrating structural continuity between nineteenth-century Reconstruction retrenchment and contemporary enforcement elasticity. The Constitution's text remains fixed; enforcement does not.

I. Introduction: Constitutional Belonging as Economic Function

In 1860, enslaved persons represented approximately $3 billion in capital value—more than railroads, manufacturing, or banking combined.[1] Slavery was not peripheral to the American economy; it was its largest asset class.[2] Emancipation therefore destroyed not merely a labor regime but a capital structure.[3]

The Reconstruction Amendments sought to rebuild constitutional order on a radically altered economic foundation.[4] The Thirteenth Amendment eliminated human property.[5] The Fourteenth nationalized citizenship.[6] The Fifteenth constitutionalized Black male suffrage.[7]

Yet by 1877, federal enforcement had collapsed.[8]

The prevailing explanation is political fatigue or sectional compromise.[9] This Article argues that a deeper structural dynamic was at work: economic contraction following the Panic of 1873 reduced federal fiscal capacity and shifted judicial tolerance toward sovereignty and retrenchment.[10]

The Constitutional–Economic Clock models that relationship.

II. The Constitutional–Economic Clock

The Clock conceptualizes constitutional enforcement as cyclical rather than linear. See infra Appendix Figure A (Hargrove, Constitutional–Economic Clock Model) (on file with author).[11]

At 12:00 — Constitutional Absence (Slavery)

At 3:00 — Constitutional Ambiguity (Reconstruction)

At 6:00 — Constitutional Retrenchment (Jim Crow)

At 9:00 — Constitutional Reawakening (Civil Rights Era)

Returning toward 12:00 — Constitutional Contestation (Modern Era)

Economic conditions map onto this cycle:

Prosperity → expansion of enforcement

Depression → retrenchment

Recession → contestation

Inflationary anxiety → sovereignty hardening

The model does not claim monocausality. It identifies structural correlation between macroeconomic stress and rights enforcement elasticity.[12]

III. 1873 as Structural Pivot

The Panic of 1873 began with the collapse of Jay Cooke & Company, triggering a banking crisis and prolonged depression.[13] Railroad overexpansion, specie contraction under the Coinage Act of 1873, and global capital tightening deepened the downturn.[14]

Wholesale prices fell nearly 30% between 1873 and 1879.[15] Unemployment spiked.[16] Federal revenue contracted.[17]

Simultaneously:

- Enforcement prosecutions under the Enforcement Acts declined.[18]
- Federal troop deployments in the South were reduced.[19]
- Judicial retrenchment accelerated.

In United States v. Cruikshank, the Court limited federal prosecution authority under the Fourteenth Amendment.[20]

In The Slaughter-House Cases, it narrowed the Privileges or Immunities Clause.[21]

In United States v. Reese, it constrained Fifteenth Amendment enforcement.[22]

These cases did not repeal Reconstruction. They hollowed its enforcement capacity.

The Clock identifies 1873 as the pivot from 3:00 (Ambiguity) toward 6:00 (Retrenchment).

IV. Georgia Archival Correlation

County-level Georgia data illustrate the pattern.

Between 1870 and 1880:

• Black voter registration declined sharply in multiple counties.[23]
• Sharecropping tenancy increased.[24]
• Tax delinquency rates rose.[25]
Overlaying price index decline with voter participation suggests correlation between agricultural price contraction and Black disenfranchisement pressure.[26]

Regression modeling (simulated for illustration) indicates that each 5% decline in cotton prices correlates with statistically significant decreases in Black voter registration at the county level ($p < .05$).[27]

The causal pathway is mediated through:
Credit contraction
Labor dependency
White political consolidation

The Constitution remained textually intact. Enforcement collapsed materially.

V. Doctrinal Retrenchment and Sovereignty

Economic contraction corresponded with doctrinal shifts toward sovereignty rhetoric.

In Chae Chan Ping v. United States, the Court articulated immigration plenary power grounded in national sovereignty.[28]

In Fong Yue Ting v. United States, it insulated deportation authority from meaningful judicial review.[29]

These decisions emerged in the same contractionary era that produced Reconstruction retrenchment.
Sovereignty language expands when economic anxiety rises.

DImmigration enforcement functions as the external boundary analogue to Reconstruction's internal boundary crisis.

In Arizona v. United States, the Court reaffirmed federal supremacy amid post–Great Recession anxiety.[30]

In Trump v. Hawaii, it deferred heavily to executive exclusion authority.[31]

Enforcement budgets for ICE expanded significantly during periods of economic uncertainty.[32]

Within Minnesota, litigation in the United States Court of Appeals for the Eighth Circuit reflects limited but meaningful procedural oversight—detention conditions, bond hearings, due process claims—without questioning core removal authority.[33]

This mirrors late Reconstruction:
- Rights formally exist.
- Enforcement discretion dominates.
- Sovereignty rhetoric prevails.

The Clock predicts precisely this pattern.

VII. Federalism Under Economic Pressure

Reconstruction demonstrated that federal supremacy depends on fiscal and political capacity.[34]

Modern immigration federalism similarly oscillates:

- State cooperation agreements fluctuate.
- Sanctuary policies provoke federal responses.
- Courts mediate boundaries but rarely dismantle plenary power.

Federalism tension intensifies at contraction points on the Clock.

VIII. Constitutional Belonging as Materially Contingent

The core contribution of this Article is conceptual:

Constitutional belonging is not self-executing. It is materially sustained.

Economic expansion increases tolerance for inclusive enforcement.

Economic contraction narrows the boundaries of belonging.

Reconstruction was the first modern example. Immigration plenary power is the contemporary analogue.

The Constitution remains constant. Enforcement oscillates.

Conclusion: The Clock as Constitutional Political Economy

The Constitutional–Economic Clock reframes Reconstruction not as a failed moral project but as a structurally vulnerable enforcement regime subject to macroeconomic stress.

It also reframes immigration doctrine as part of a longer enforcement elasticity tradition rather than an exceptionalist anomaly.

The pattern is cyclical:

- Slavery (Absence)
- Reconstruction (Ambiguity)
- Jim Crow (Retrenchment)
- Civil Rights (Reawakening)
- Contemporary Enforcement (Contestation)

The lesson is not pessimism. It is structural realism.

If constitutional belonging is materially contingent, then durable enforcement requires economic stability sufficient to sustain it.

The Clock is not a metaphor. It is a model

that now reads not as narrative history but as a constitutional political economy intervention.

Enforcement as Memory

Celia Adams walked around a slave market before being sold. That was enforcement of property law.

Her descendants voted under federal protection. That was enforcement of constitutional law.

Today's enforcement debates—over voting access, border control, criminal justice—are not new struggles. They are new iterations of the same constitutional negotiation.

The Constitution lives not in parchment but in budget lines and courthouse practice.

Civil rights reawakening was real. Contestation is real. The cycle continues.

But awareness changes trajectory.

And history—carefully preserved, carefully told—anchors the next reawakening.

Four Generations After Celia Adams

Celia Adams walked three times around a slave market before she was sold. That fact alone situates her life inside the harshest enforcement regime the American Constitution ever permitted. Property was protected. Personhood was negotiable.

She survived slavery. She witnessed emancipation. She lived through Reconstruction's hope and Redemption's collapse. Her descendants endured Jim Crow, saw the constitutional dawn of Brown v. Board of Education, registered to vote under the protection of the Voting Rights Act of 1965, and later confronted retrenchment after Shelby County v. Holder.

Her life—and her lineage—trace the Constitutional–Economic Clock.

But history does not turn itself.
Each expansion of liberty required:
Interpretation
Enforcement
Appropriation
Courage

Each contraction followed:

Withdrawal
Fiscal reprioritization
Judicial narrowing
Public fatigue

The next generation inherits not a settled Constitution, but a living negotiation.

I. The Illusion of Permanence

One lesson of the clock is this: no era believes itself temporary.

Reconstruction legislators believed constitutional equality had been secured.

Redeemers believed white supremacy had been restored permanently.

Civil rights reformers believed preclearance would endure indefinitely.

Each was mistaken.

Constitutional rights are durable only when actively maintained. The parchment does not guarantee its own power. Enforcement is the bridge between principle and practice.

The next generation must understand this structural truth: rights without budget are aspiration; doctrine without enforcement is symbolism.

II. The Reallocation Question

Contemporary debates often present civil rights as cultural conflict. But the deeper issue remains economic allocation.

Where does the nation direct its enforcement energy?

- Border control?
- Criminal prosecution?
- Voting access?
- Educational equity?

Every appropriation signals constitutional priority.

The next generation's task is not simply to defend rights rhetorically, but to ensure that enforcement mechanisms remain proportionate to constitutional promises.

III. Intergenerational Responsibility

Celia Adams did not vote. Her daughter likely could not. Her grandsons briefly did under federal supervision. Her great-grandchildren voted under the protection of federal examiners. Later generations faced renewed contestation.

This is not failure. It is civic inheritance.

The work of the next generation is threefold:

Memory Preservation
Without historical memory, cycles appear natural rather than constructed.

Institutional Literacy
Understanding how courts, legislatures, and budgets interact prevents passive retrenchment.

Moral Imagination
Law evolves when citizens insist that constitutional text reflect human dignity.

IV. From Contestation to Stability

Is the Constitutional–Economic Clock destined to spin endlessly?

History suggests oscillation, not inevitability. But oscillation can narrow. Amplitudes can shrink. Stability can deepen.

What stabilizes constitutional rights?

- Durable bipartisan commitment
- Independent judiciary
- Transparent election systems
- Consistent funding for civil rights enforcement

• Civic participation across generations

The next generation must move from episodic reawakening toward sustained equilibrium.

V. The Personal and the National

This manuscript began with one woman—Celia Adams—walking around a market in Richmond, Virginia, before being sold to Louisville, Georgia.

It ends with a question for her descendants and their contemporaries: What will you enforce?

The Constitution has contained:
Enslavement and emancipation
Segregation and integration
Disfranchisement and expanded suffrage
Its meaning has depended on those who interpreted and funded it.

The next generation's work is not to rewrite the Constitution entirely. It is to determine which of its promises receive life.

VI. The Quiet Work

The most transformative changes in American history were often quiet at first:

• A school integrated.
• A voter registered.
• A case filed.
• A budget line approved.

Celia Adams likely never imagined Supreme Court decisions bearing names like Brown or Shelby County. But she understood survival, dignity, and endurance.

Her story does not end in tragedy. It extends into responsibility.

VII. The Clock and the Future

If the Constitutional–Economic Clock teaches anything, it is that time alone does not produce justice. Time amplifies the decisions of each generation.

The next generation stands not at midnight or dawn, but at a point of choice.

They inherit:
A Constitution tested by history.
Institutions reshaped repeatedly.
A record of both retreat and renewal.
They also inherit memory.
And memory is a form of enforcement.

Immigration Enforcement Appropriations and Macroeconomic Conditions, FY 2000–2025

Dark blue line reflects combined appropriations for U.S. Immigration and Customs Enforcement (ICE) and U.S. Customs and Border Protection (CBP). Red line reflects annual national unemployment rates. Orange line reflects annual inflation rates (CPI-U). Gray shaded regions indicate recession periods as determined by the National Bureau of Economic Research (NBER).

Color Key (Constitutional–Economic Clock Framework):

Black (baseline) = Constitutional Absence (Slavery);
Blue-Gray = Constitutional Ambiguity (Reconstruction);
Red/Gray Dominance = Retrenchment (post-1873 contraction; Jim Crow);
Stabilized Blue = Reawakening (Civil Rights enforcement era);
Blue over Red/Orange = Contestation (modern enforcement amid economic volatility).

Blue encodes institutional enforcement capacity; red/orange/gray encode macroeconomic stress. Their interaction visualizes the cyclical relationship between economic contraction and constitutional enforcement described by the Constitutional–Economic Clock. See infra Appendix Figure A (Hargrove, Constitutional–Economic Clock Model).

Suggested Bluebook Source Note (for footnote beneath figure)

Data compiled from U.S. Dep't of Homeland Sec., Budget in Brief (various fiscal years 2000–2025); U.S. Bureau of Lab. Stat., Labor Force Statistics from the Current Population Survey; U.S. Bureau of Lab. Stat., Consumer Price Index Summary; Nat'l Bureau of Econ. Rsch., U.S. Business Cycle Expansions and Contractions (chronology). Author's calculations and visualization.

Hargrove's Constitutional–Economic Clock

It embeds Minnesota/Eighth Circuit relevance in a structurally coherent way for Chapter 4.

Immigration Enforcement Within the Constitutional–Economic Clock

The immigration plenary power doctrine operates on the same structural logic as the Reconstruction retrenchment cases. The Constitutional–Economic Clock predicts that enforcement elasticity—rather than textual amendment—marks the real pivot points in

constitutional belonging. Immigration law provides the modern external boundary analogue to Reconstruction's internal boundary crisis.

1. The Clock Applied to Immigration Doctrine
Under the Clock model, constitutional enforcement strength varies across economic phases:

Expansion (High Growth / Low Anxiety): Broader tolerance for rights enforcement.

Contraction (Economic Stress / Fiscal Anxiety): Heightened deference to sovereignty and enforcement power.

The birth of plenary power in the late nineteenth century occurred in the same contractionary era as Reconstruction rollback. In Chae Chan Ping v. United States and Fong Yue Ting v. United States, the Court framed immigration control as an incident of national sovereignty largely immune from judicial intrusion. This mirrors the narrowing of federal enforcement authority in United States v. Cruikshank.

The doctrinal symmetry is structural:
Reconstruction cases limited federal intervention to protect Black citizens.
Plenary power cases insulated federal exclusion and deportation authority.
Both reflect judicial retrenchment during periods of economic and political strain.

2. Enforcement Intensity and Macroeconomic Anxiety

The Clock's central insight is that rights enforcement is materially contingent. Immigration enforcement demonstrates this vividly.

Modern cases such as Trump v. Hawaii reaffirm deferential review where the executive invokes national security or sovereign authority. Likewise, Kleindienst v. Mandel established that courts will not "look behind" a facially legitimate reason for exclusion.

This doctrinal posture allows enforcement intensity to fluctuate with political economy conditions:

Economic downturn → increased enforcement budgets and removal priorities.
Economic expansion → expanded prosecutorial discretion and humanitarian relief.

The Constitution does not change. Enforcement posture does.

That elasticity is precisely what the Constitutional–Economic Clock predicts.

3. Federalism Pressure and the Minnesota/Eighth Circuit Context

Federalism tension rises at contraction points on the Clock. Immigration provides a contemporary illustration.

In Arizona v. United States, the Court reaffirmed federal supremacy in immigration enforcement while invalidating state-level enforcement expansions. The case reflects a sovereignty consolidation phase during heightened economic and political anxiety following the Great Recession.

Within **Minnesota** and the United States Court of Appeals for the Eighth Circuit, litigation has focused less on *exclusion* power and more on detention conditions, procedural due process, and federal–local cooperation.

For example, detention-related constitutional claims in the Eighth Circuit illustrate the limited but real judicial space available within plenary power. Courts may regulate process, but they rarely question core enforcement authority.

This mirrors Reconstruction's later phase:
Courts did not repeal the Fourteenth or Fifteenth Amendments.

They constrained enforcement scope and federal reach.

Similarly:
Modern courts do not eliminate due process protections for noncitizens.

They defer broadly on removal authority and enforcement discretion.

The result is a system where constitutional belonging remains formally recognized but functionally contingent.

4. Internal vs. External Boundaries of Belonging

Reconstruction addressed the internal boundary—who counts as a full constitutional member within the polity.

Immigration doctrine governs the external boundary—who may enter or remain.

Under the Clock model:

Economic expansion stabilizes belonging.
Economic contraction hardens boundaries.
The 1873 contraction weakened federal enforcement of Black citizenship rights. Post-2008 economic anxiety intensified immigration enforcement debates. COVID-era fiscal strain reshaped detention and border policy. Inflationary cycles correlate with renewed calls for restrictive enforcement.
The pattern is cyclical, not episodic.

5. Why Minnesota Matters Structurally
Minnesota's relevance lies not in immigration exceptionalism but in federalism friction:

Cooperative federalism agreements fluctuate with national administrations.

State political climates influence detention cooperation.

Federal district courts within the Eighth Circuit adjudicate constitutional detention challenges that test the limits of plenary deference.

This places Minnesota within the Clock's mid-cycle institutional tension zone—where federal supremacy is doctrinally clear but enforcement practice remains politically negotiated.

The same was true in Reconstruction-era Georgia:

Federal authority was constitutionally supreme.

Enforcement depended on fiscal capacity, political will, and judicial posture.

Structural Synthesis for Chapter 4
The Constitutional–Economic Clock therefore explains both:

The rollback of Reconstruction enforcement after 1873.

The elasticity of modern immigration enforcement under plenary power.

In both eras:

Economic contraction precedes enforcement retrenchment.

Courts amplify sovereignty rhetoric.

Constitutional belonging becomes materially conditional.

The analogy is not moral equivalence. It is structural continuity.

Reconstruction revealed that citizenship could be constitutionally guaranteed yet practically hollowed.

Immigration law reveals that constitutional process can exist within an enforcement regime defined by broad sovereign discretion.

The Clock captures that recurring dynamic: connecting doctrine, federalism, Minnesota relevance, and ICE. Thus making the model into a coherent constitutional political economy framework.

Modern Comparative Subsection:
Immigration and Eighth Circuit (which includes Minnesota)

Reconstruction enforcement discussion:

F. Modern Comparative Section: Immigration, Plenary Power, and Elastic Enforcement

The Reconstruction enforcement collapse finds a structural analogue in modern immigration law, particularly in the development and persistence of the plenary power doctrine. Just as the Supreme Court narrowed Reconstruction enforcement authority in the 1870s, it constructed a parallel architecture of deference in immigration cases—one that situates immigration control at the apex of federal sovereignty while simultaneously limiting judicial scrutiny.

1. The Birth of Plenary Power

The plenary power doctrine emerged in the late nineteenth century—the same era as Reconstruction retrenchment. In Chae Chan Ping

v. United States (The Chinese Exclusion Case), the Supreme Court upheld broad congressional authority to exclude noncitizens, characterizing immigration control as an inherent sovereign power.[1] The Court reiterated this expansive deference in Fong Yue Ting v. United States, sustaining deportation authority with minimal constitutional constraint.[2]

These decisions coincided chronologically with The Slaughter-House Cases and United States v. Cruikshank. While Reconstruction doctrine narrowed federal enforcement for the protection of Black citizens, immigration doctrine expanded federal authority over noncitizens. Both developments illustrate a structural feature of the period: constitutional belonging was stratified, and judicial doctrine adjusted accordingly.

2. Judicial Deference and Limited Constitutional Review

Throughout the twentieth century, the Supreme Court maintained substantial deference in immigration matters. In Kleindienst v. Mandel, the Court articulated a highly deferential standard when the political branches provide a "facially legitimate and bona fide reason" for exclusion.[3] More recently, in Trump v. Hawaii, the Court reaffirmed broad executive authority in immigration enforcement, applying limited rational-basis review to presidential exclusion authority.[4]

The persistence of plenary power doctrine reflects the elasticity of constitutional enforcement in contexts framed as sovereignty-sensitive. Just as Reconstruction enforcement waned under economic and political pressure, immigration rights protections often fluctuate with national security framing and macroeconomic anxiety.

3. Federalism Tensions: Arizona and Beyond

Immigration enforcement also generates recurrent federalism conflict. In **Arizona v. United States**, the Court reaffirmed federal preemption over state immigration enforcement initiatives, underscoring the federal government's dominant role.[5] Yet this dominance does not eliminate friction. States and localities continue to contest the scope of cooperation and enforcement participation.

Within the Eighth Circuit—which includes Minnesota—litigation has addressed detention standards, procedural due process, and federal-state coordination.[6] While Minnesota itself does not control immigration policy, federal enforcement actions in the state remain subject to constitutional challenge under due process and Fourth Amendment principles. The structural dynamic persists: formal constitutional protections coexist with broad federal enforcement discretion.

4. Structural Parallels to Reconstruction

The analogy is not one of equivalence but of structure.

During Reconstruction:

The Fourteenth and Fifteenth Amendments formally expanded belonging.

Economic contraction and political retrenchment narrowed enforcement.
Judicial doctrine constrained federal intervention in defense of rights.

In immigration law:

Statutory and constitutional protections (due process, equal protection principles as applied to noncitizens) exist.

Enforcement intensity fluctuates with political and economic conditions.

Judicial doctrine affords substantial deference under plenary power.

The central insight of the Constitutional–Economic Clock applies in both contexts:

Rights may be textually articulated, yet enforcement remains materially contingent.

Immigration enforcement intensity often rises during periods of economic insecurity and heightened political anxiety. Budgetary allocations for detention and removal fluctuate with congressional priorities. Prosecutorial discretion expands or contracts across administrations. None of these shifts require constitutional amendment. They occur within elastic enforcement frameworks.

5. Constitutional Belonging and Sovereign Boundary

Reconstruction sought to redefine the internal boundaries of constitutional belonging. Immigration law governs the external boundary. In both contexts, courts have played a decisive role in defining the scope of federal authority and the durability of rights claims.

The late nineteenth century thus produced two simultaneous doctrinal currents:

Narrowing of federal enforcement to protect newly freed citizens.

Expansion of federal authority over noncitizens under plenary power.

The juxtaposition underscores the broader thesis of this Article: constitutional belonging is historically contingent, shaped by institutional capacity, political economy, and judicial posture.

The Constitutional–Economic Clock does not collapse these domains into equivalence. It situates them within a common structural pattern—one in which macroeconomic conditions and political incentives influence the vigor with which constitutional commitments are enforced.

Freedom in Law and in Practice: From Reconstruction to the Present

Celia Adams lived as a “Freedom Seeker” before Emancipation and a “Freedom Dweller” afterward. Her life illustrates that freedom declared is not freedom secured.

Reconstruction proved that constitutional amendments are insufficient without enforcement.

The Panic of 1873 revealed that economic contraction can weaken that enforcement.

Jim Crow institutionalized retrenchment.

The Civil Rights Era reawakened federal commitment.

Today, enforcement persists — but its targets and beneficiaries remain contested.

Immigration enforcement debates echo earlier patterns. Economic anxiety heightens political pressure. Federalism tensions intensify. Constitutional belonging becomes unstable for marginalized groups.

The lesson is not pessimism. It is structural awareness.

Citations

Chae Chan Ping v. United States, 130 U.S. 581 (1889).

Fong Yue Ting v. United States, 149 U.S. 698 (1893).

Kleindienst v. Mandel, 408 U.S. 753 (1972).

Trump v. Hawaii, 138 S. Ct. 2392 (2018).

Arizona v. United States, 567 U.S. 387 (2012).

See, e.g., Ali v. Brott, 770 F. App'x 298 (8th Cir. 2019) (addressing detention and constitutional claims within the Eighth Circuit).

Conclusion

Constitutional Time and Economic Enforcement: Memory, Power, and Generational Inheritance

This study has argued that the life of Celia Adams of Jefferson County, Georgia, cannot be understood solely as a biographical fragment within the archive of American slavery. Her life instead illuminates a broader structural pattern: the cyclical relationship between constitutional promise and economic enforcement. Across five eras—slavery, Reconstruction, Redemption and Jim Crow, Civil Rights reawakening, and contemporary contestation—the American state has repeatedly recalibrated the relationship between rights and resources. The result has not been linear progress but oscillation. Constitutional recognition has expanded and contracted. Economic allocation has followed enforcement priorities. Each generation has inherited not only ideals but fiscal architectures.

The Constitutional–Economic Clock offered in this manuscript is not metaphor alone. It is a structural model derived from the interaction of law, appropriations, administrative enforcement, and political will. Celia Adams' forced sale in Richmond and her relocation to Louisville, Georgia, occurred during a period of constitutional absence: a regime in which Black personhood was denied legal standing and economic extraction was formalized through property law. The clock's first hour is therefore not merely slavery; it is the alignment of constitutional denial with economic exploitation.

Reconstruction marked the first great reset. The Thirteenth, Fourteenth, and Fifteenth Amendments reconstituted the constitutional text. Yet text alone proved insufficient. The Freedmen's Bureau, federal troop deployments, and enforcement statutes represented an attempt to overlay constitutional recognition with material protection. For a brief period, constitutional expansion and economic enforcement converged. But as this manuscript has shown, convergence was politically fragile. The Compromise of 1877 did not repeal the Reconstruction Amendments; it recalibrated enforcement. The constitutional text remained, but the economic overlay receded. Federal withdrawal enabled the rapid consolidation of Jim Crow regimes, whose fiscal architectures—convict leasing, segregated schooling, racially stratified taxation—reproduced subordination through economic design.

The lesson of Reconstruction, then, is not merely that rights were betrayed. It is that rights without sustained economic enforcement prove vulnerable. Constitutional promises require administrative and fiscal commitment. When appropriations decline, oversight weakens. When oversight weakens, constitutional guarantees hollow.

Jim Crow thus represents not constitutional silence but constitutional retrenchment. Courts narrowed the reach of equal protection. Legislatures engineered disenfranchisement. Local economies reorganized around racial hierarchy. Economic enforcement overlays shifted from protection to policing. The clock moved from ambiguity to retrenchment.

The Civil Rights era marks another recalibration. Decisions such as Brown v. Board of Education and statutes including the Civil Rights Act of 1964 and the Voting Rights Act of 1965 reactivated dormant constitutional guarantees. Crucially, these reforms were accompanied by economic enforcement overlays: Department of Justice litigation budgets, federal education funding conditions, and oversight mechanisms. Enforcement once again mattered. Where federal supervision was strong, integration advanced. Where supervision weakened, resistance hardened.

Yet even the Civil Rights reawakening demonstrates the cyclical nature of constitutional time. Enforcement expansions required political coalitions. They depended upon appropriations. They proved subject to retrenchment when judicial interpretation narrowed statutory reach or when congressional will faltered. The contemporary period reveals a familiar pattern: voting rights oversight reduced, regulatory authority contested, educational and social welfare funding politicized. The clock turns not backward in simple repetition, but through patterned recalibration.

This book therefore advances three central claims.

First, constitutional history must be read alongside economic administration. Legal recognition divorced from fiscal enforcement misleads. The question is not only what rights are declared, but what budgets sustain them.

Second, generational analysis matters. Celia Adams' life, her descendants' struggles, and the present-day condition of American democracy exist within a chain of inheritance. Constitutional amendments shape possibilities, but each generation's enforcement choices determine lived reality. The Deuce Millennium Generation framework introduced earlier in this manuscript situates constitutional change within extended planning horizons. Constitutional time exceeds electoral cycles. It unfolds across centuries.

Third, memory functions as structural critique. To reconstruct Celia Adams' forced walk around a slave market three times before sale is not only to narrate cruelty. It is to interrogate the legal and economic order that normalized that cruelty. Memory destabilizes complacent narratives of inevitability. It reminds us that constitutional absence was designed, enforced, and funded.

What, then, does the Constitutional–Economic Clock contribute to historiography?

It reframes the Reconstruction debate beyond the binary of failure versus success. Reconstruction did not fail because constitutional ideals were insufficiently noble. It faltered because enforcement overlays were withdrawn. It reframes Jim Crow as an economic regime, not solely a cultural one. It reframes Civil Rights not as moral awakening alone, but as enforcement architecture.

It also challenges triumphalist narratives of American progress. The clock does not deny advancement. The abolition of slavery, the dismantling of formal segregation, and the expansion of voting access represent substantive transformations. But progress has not been self-sustaining. It has required renewal.

The contemporary period, examined in Chapter Five, demonstrates that constitutional contraction can occur through administrative narrowing rather than overt repeal. Oversight formulas change. Preclearance requirements shift. Budget allocations alter priorities. Courts reinterpret statutory scope. Each of these moves adjusts the enforcement overlay without altering constitutional text. The clock's movement in our time is subtle but discernible.

The implications extend beyond racial history. The model suggests that any constitutional guarantee—environmental protection, labor rights, gender equality—depends upon fiscal and administrative commitment. Rights are durable only when institutionalized within budgets and bureaucracies.

For the scholarly readership, rooted in the serious study of American political development and frontier transformation, this work offers a southern case study with national resonance. Jefferson County, Georgia, becomes a lens through which to examine federalism, enforcement, and memory. Celia Adams' life anchors abstraction in archive.

But this conclusion must also acknowledge limits. The Constitutional–Economic Clock is a model, not a prophecy. It identifies patterned oscillation, not inevitable destiny. Political coalitions can disrupt cycles. Judicial philosophies can alter trajectories. Economic transformations can reconfigure state capacity. The clock is descriptive, not deterministic.

Still, the weight of historical evidence suggests vigilance. When enforcement wanes, vulnerability rises. When budgets shrink, oversight narrows. When oversight narrows, rights erode.

The final question, then, is generational.

What does the present generation inherit? Not only amendments. Not only statutes. It inherits enforcement responsibilities. It inherits administrative institutions built through struggle. It inherits archives filled with testimony and silence.

Celia Adams' descendants—biological and civic—stand within this inheritance. The sale that uprooted her from Richmond to Louisville was lawful within its time. The Reconstruction Amendments that promised equality were lawful within theirs. Jim Crow segregation was enforced through legal regimes. Civil Rights reform was institutionalized through law and funding. Legality has worn many faces.

Thus, legality alone cannot serve as moral compass. Enforcement priorities reveal value hierarchies. Budgets disclose commitments.

The Constitutional–Economic Clock ultimately calls scholars and citizens alike to examine not only what the Constitution says, but what the nation funds. It calls us to track appropriations alongside amendments. It calls us to measure administrative will alongside judicial rhetoric.

This study has attempted to weave archive, theory, and generational reflection into a unified account. Celia Adams' life stands as testimony to the first hour of the clock. Reconstruction's collapse marks the second. Jim Crow's consolidation marks the third. Civil Rights reawakening marks the fourth. Contemporary contestation occupies the fifth.

The clock does not stop. It turns.

Whether the next turn deepens retrenchment or renews enforcement depends upon choices not yet made. Constitutional time remains open.

The work of scholarship is to clarify structure. The work of citizenship is to determine direction.

Celia Adams walked three times before sale. The nation has circled its constitutional promises more than three times since. The question is whether future generations will continue to circle—or finally secure.

Epilogue

The Work of the Next Generation

Constitutions do not move themselves. They are moved by people—by lawmakers and judges, by administrators and advocates, by citizens whose names enter the archive and by those whose names do not. The Constitutional–Economic Clock traced in this book does not tick with inevitability. It advances, retreats, recalibrates because generations choose enforcement or withdrawal, expansion or retrenchment, memory or forgetting.

If the Conclusion has argued that constitutional time is cyclical, this Epilogue turns to inheritance.

Celia Adams did not live to see the Civil Rights Movement. She did not witness the Voting Rights Act or the dismantling of legalized segregation. She lived within a constitutional order that denied her personhood, that classified her as property, that required her to walk around a

slave market three times before she was sold from Richmond to Louisville, Georgia. Yet her life extends beyond the narrow frame of her years. It extends because history does not end with those who endure it. It continues through those who interpret it.

The work of the next generation is not merely to remember Celia Adams as victim. It is to understand the structure that made her sale lawful. It is to recognize how constitutional silence enabled economic exploitation. It is to see how Reconstruction attempted repair, how Redemption withdrew it, how Jim Crow formalized retrenchment, how Civil Rights reopened enforcement, and how contemporary debates continue to recalibrate oversight.

Memory alone is insufficient. Memory must be accompanied by institutional awareness.

Each generation inherits a constitutional architecture and an economic overlay. These are not abstract concepts. They are budgets debated in committee rooms. They are regulatory guidelines drafted in agencies. They are judicial interpretations written in opinions. They are school funding formulas, voting district maps, administrative enforcement priorities. They are decisions about what will be monitored and what will be ignored.

To speak of “the next generation” is therefore not to invoke youth sentimentally. It is to identify a structural reality: constitutional maintenance requires renewal. The Reconstruction Amendments did not enforce themselves. The Civil Rights Act did not supervise its own implementation. The Voting Rights Act did not litigate its own violations. Each required institutional actors willing to fund and defend them.

When enforcement wanes, the clock shifts.

The contemporary moment reveals both fragility and possibility. Legal protections remain on the books, yet their reach depends upon interpretation. Federal oversight expands and contracts. Administrative discretion shapes outcomes. The architecture stands, but its maintenance is uneven.

For the Deuce Millennium Generation—the cohort inheriting twenty-first century institutions—the challenge differs from that faced by those who drafted the Reconstruction Amendments or marched in Selma. The challenge now is less about drafting new constitutional language and more about sustaining enforcement within a complex administrative state. It is about understanding how fiscal decisions shape civic reality.

The work of the next generation, then, includes at least four responsibilities.

First, archival responsibility. Archives are not neutral repositories. They reflect preservation choices. The story of Celia Adams survives because fragments endured—census records, sale documents, family memory. Countless others did not. The next generation must preserve records of enforcement and retrenchment alike. Without archive, there can be no structural analysis.

Second, interpretive responsibility. Constitutional literacy must extend beyond slogans. It must include knowledge of federalism, administrative law, appropriations, and judicial review. If the

Constitutional–Economic Clock teaches anything, it is that rights erode quietly when enforcement mechanisms are misunderstood or ignored.

Third, institutional responsibility. Civic participation cannot end at symbolic affirmation. It must extend to attention to budgets, committee hearings, and regulatory frameworks. The economic overlay—so often invisible in public discourse—determines whether rights remain aspirational or operational.

Fourth, moral responsibility. Constitutional systems can normalize injustice when enforcement aligns with exclusion. Celia Adams' sale was lawful. Jim Crow statutes were lawful. Legality and justice are not synonyms. The next generation must measure enforcement priorities against constitutional ideals, not merely procedural compliance.

Yet this Epilogue does not end in warning alone.

The Constitutional–Economic Clock reveals not only retrenchment but renewal. Reconstruction, though incomplete, demonstrated that constitutional expansion is possible. The Civil Rights era proved that entrenched systems can be disrupted. Enforcement can be strengthened. Budgets can be redirected. Administrative will can be mobilized.

History is cyclical, but it is not static.

Celia Adams' life reminds us that structural transformation often begins beyond the view of power. Those once excluded from the constitutional order become its interpreters and guardians. Descendants of the enslaved testify before Senate committees. Scholars reconstruct suppressed histories. Citizens vote, litigate, organize, and teach.

The movement from absence to ambiguity, from retrenchment to reawakening, depends upon generational continuity. Each cohort inherits both the damage and the design.

To speak of "The Work of the Next Generation" is therefore to speak of stewardship. The Constitution is not self-executing parchment; it is a living framework sustained through practice. Economic enforcement is not an afterthought; it is the operational dimension of rights. Memory is not nostalgia; it is structural insight.

This manuscript began with a woman required to walk in circles before sale. It concludes with a nation that has circled its own promises across centuries. The difference between circling and securing lies in sustained enforcement.

If the next generation understands that rights require resources, that text requires oversight, and that memory requires preservation, then the clock's movement need not repeat earlier contractions. It can stabilize toward durability.

The story of Celia Adams does not close with her death. It continues in courtrooms, classrooms, legislative chambers, and family narratives. It continues wherever constitutional meaning

intersects with economic decision. It continues wherever citizens ask not only what the Constitution declares, but what the nation funds.

The work ahead is neither simple nor finite. It requires scholarship rigorous enough to identify structure, citizenship attentive enough to monitor enforcement, and moral clarity sufficient to distinguish legality from justice.

The Constitutional–Economic Clock will continue to turn. Whether it marks retrenchment or renewal will depend upon those who inherit its hour.

The next generation already stands within it.

Bibliography

Archival Sources

National Archives and Records Administration (NARA).

Freedmen's Bureau Records. Record Group 105. Microfilm Publication M1903.

Records of the Assistant Commissioner for the State of Georgia, 1865–1872.

U.S. Bureau of the Census. Eighth Census of the United States, 1860.
———. Ninth Census of the United States, 1870.
———. Tenth Census of the United States, 1880.

Jefferson County, Georgia. Deed Books and Property Records, 1850–1900.

Jefferson County, Georgia. Voter Registration and Election Returns, Reconstruction Era.

U.S. Congress. Congressional Globe. 39th–45th Congresses.

U.S. Congress. Statutes at Large.

Constitutional and Legal Sources

U.S. Constitution. Amendments XIII, XIV, XV.

Brown v. Board of Education, 347 U.S. 483 (1954).

The Civil Rights Cases, 109 U.S. 3 (1883).

Plessy v. Ferguson, 163 U.S. 537 (1896).

Shelby County v. Holder, 570 U.S. 529 (2013).

Civil Rights Act of 1964. Pub. L. No. 88-352.

Voting Rights Act of 1965. Pub. L. No. 89-110.

Books: Slavery and the Political Economy of Race

W. E. B. Du Bois. Black Reconstruction in America, 1860–1880. New York: Harcourt, Brace and Company, 1935.

Eric Foner. Reconstruction: America's Unfinished Revolution, 1863–1877. New York: Harper & Row, 1988.

Steven Hahn. A Nation under Our Feet. Cambridge, MA: Harvard University Press, 2003.

Walter Johnson. River of Dark Dreams. Cambridge, MA: Harvard University Press, 2013.

Sven Beckert. Empire of Cotton. New York: Knopf, 2014.

Edward E. Baptist. The Half Has Never Been Told. New York: Basic Books, 2014.

Reconstruction and Constitutional Development

Michael W. McConnell. "The Forgotten Constitutional Moment." Columbia Law Review 11 (1995): 115–198.

Akhil Reed Amar. America's Constitution: A Biography. New York: Random House, 2005.

Bruce Ackerman. We the People, Vol. 2: Transformations. Cambridge, MA: Harvard University Press, 1998.

Laura F. Edwards. A Legal History of the Civil War and Reconstruction. Cambridge: Cambridge University Press, 2015.

Pamela Brandwein. Rethinking the Judicial Settlement of Reconstruction. Cambridge: Cambridge University Press, 2011.

Jim Crow, Retrenchment, and Economic Governance

C. Vann Woodward. The Strange Career of Jim Crow. New York: Oxford University Press, 1955.

Douglas A. Blackmon. Slavery by Another Name. New York: Anchor Books, 2008.

Alex Lichtenstein. Twice the Work of Free Labor. London: Verso, 1996.

Michelle Alexander. The New Jim Crow. New York: New Press, 2010.

Civil Rights Era and Federal Enforcement

Taylor Branch. Parting the Waters. New York: Simon & Schuster, 1988.

Ari Berman. Give Us the Ballot. New York: Farrar, Straus and Giroux, 2015.

Charles M. Payne. I've Got the Light of Freedom. Berkeley: University of California Press, 1995.

Mary L. Dudziak. Cold War Civil Rights. Princeton: Princeton University Press, 2000.

Economic Enforcement and American Political Development

Theda Skocpol. Protecting Soldiers and Mothers. Cambridge, MA: Harvard University Press, 1992.

Paul Pierson. Politics in Time. Princeton: Princeton University Press, 2004.

Ira Katznelson. Fear Itself. New York: Liveright, 2013.

Jacob S. Hacker and Paul Pierson. American Amnesia. New York: Simon & Schuster, 2016.

Memory, Allegory, and Historical Interpretation

Hannah Arendt. On Revolution. New York: Viking Press, 1963.

Ralph Ellison. Shadow and Act. New York: Random House, 1964.

James Baldwin. The Fire Next Time. New York: Dial Press, 1963.

George Orwell. Politics and the English Language. London: Horizon, 1946.

SELECT CONSOLIDATED REFERENCES

Ayers, Edward. The Promise of the New South.

Fogel, Robert & Engerman, Stanley. Time on the Cross.

Foner, Eric. Reconstruction: America's Unfinished Revolution.

Keyssar, Alexander. The Right to Vote.

North, Douglass. Institutions, Institutional Change and Economic Performance.

Wright, Gavin. Old South, New South.

U.S. Bureau of Labor Statistics (CPI, unemployment).

National Bureau of Economic Research (Recession chronology).

Department of Homeland Security, Budget in Brief (FY 2000–2026).

Closing Note

This interdisciplinary contribution links constitutional law, economic history, and generational memory through the life of Celia Adams.

PART 2

Still Chasing Democracy: America at 250 Through the Eyes of Celia Adams

Introduction

Introduction

Two hundred-fifty years after Independence, the United States stands at a familiar crossroads—invoking democracy while struggling to fulfill its promise. Still Chasing Democracy reframes the American story through the life of Celia Adams, a Black woman born into slavery in Richmond, Virginia, whose forced journey through the domestic slave trade and lifelong commitment to education reveal the nation's deepest contradictions and its most enduring hopes.

Drawing on archival records, oral history, and public memory, This book traces how Adams's life intersected with the rise of American institutions—from slave markets and church basements to Reconstruction classrooms and the foundations of historically Black education. Her story illuminates how democracy in America was not granted but pursued—carried forward by those denied its protections yet determined to claim its meaning.

Blending family history with national narrative, Still Chasing Democracy challenges celebratory accounts of the American experiment and insists on a fuller reckoning at the nation's semiquincentennial. Through Celia Adams's eyes, democracy emerges not as a settled achievement, but as an unfinished project—shaped by memory, resistance, faith, and the quiet labor of generations who believed America could become what it promised.

At once intimate and expansive, this book offers a vital contribution to American history, African American studies, and public discourse—reminding all that the pursuit of democracy has always depended on those most often excluded from it.

*Slavery, **Memory**, and Geography of Survival*

This book examines the life of Celia Adams as a lens through which to understand the domestic slave trade, enslaved childhood, and the enduring legacy of forced migration in the United States. Born enslaved in Richmond, Virginia, in 1856, Celia entered a world structured by sale, movement, and dispossession. Her life was shaped not by a single plantation or enslaver, but

by a national system that commodified children and relocated families across state lines in service of profit.

At the center of this study is Shockoe Bottom, one of the most significant slave-trading districts in North America. From this site, enslaved people—including children—were sold southward to meet the labor demands of the Deep South. Celia Adams's forced migration from Virginia through South Carolina to Georgia illustrates how slavery operated as an interconnected national enterprise rather than a series of isolated local practices.

This book argues that enslaved childhood must be understood as mobile, precarious, and deeply political. Children were not peripheral to slavery's economy; they were central to it. Their bodies represented future labor and long-term profit, making them especially vulnerable to sale and separation.

Methodologically, this work combines archival research, spatial analysis, and public-history interpretation. It confronts the silences of the archive while refusing to treat absence as erasure. Where direct documentation does not survive, historically grounded inference is employed transparently and responsibly.

By tracing Celia Adams's life from bondage to freedom and beyond, this book seeks not only to recover one woman's story, but to illuminate the structures that shaped millions of lives. It is both a scholarly investigation and a memorial act—an effort to restore dignity, context, and voice to those whom the historical record sought to reduce to property.

Dr. King's voice still echoes in his metaphor usage of the arc of the moral universe is long, but it bends towards justice. This is history, adapted from a 19th Century Abolitionist Minister, Theodore Parker. Let history be the arc of justice as America250 remembers Celia Adams through her generational footsteps.

Chapter 6

The Trade Within: Method, Memory, and the Domestic Slave Trade in American History

Introduction: Seeing the Domestic Slave Trade Clearly

The domestic slave trade was one of the most consequential yet least publicly understood institutions in American history. Between the end of the international slave trade in 1808 and the Civil War, more than one million enslaved people were forcibly relocated within the United States. This movement—by road, river, and rail—reshaped families, regional economies, and the geography of slavery itself. Yet for generations, the domestic slave trade remained obscured, minimized, or rendered abstract in both popular memory and historical scholarship.

This volume begins from a simple but necessary premise: the domestic slave trade was not ancillary to American slavery; it was central to its survival and expansion. It functioned as a system of commerce, governance, and violence that linked northern finance, Upper South

supply regions, and Deep South plantation economies. To understand slavery as a national institution requires tracing the routes, markets, and lives that sustained it.

This chapter establishes the interpretive framework for the book. It explains why descendant-centered microhistory, geographic analysis, and evidentiary transparency are essential to reconstructing lives such as that of Celia Adams—born into the trade in Richmond, Virginia, and sold southward as a child. It also addresses the methodological challenges posed by archival silences and the ethical obligations of writing histories of enslavement.

Historiography and Its Silences

For much of the twentieth century, scholarship on American slavery emphasized plantation life, labor systems, and sectional politics. While foundational, this focus often treated slave trading as episodic or secondary. Early narratives privileged ownership over circulation, obscuring the fact that slavery operated through markets as much as through masters.

Beginning in the late twentieth century, historians began to foreground the domestic slave trade as a system in its own right. Studies revealed how traders, not just planters, shaped enslaved lives; how prices, credit, and speculation structured human movement; and how violence was embedded in commercial exchange. This historiographical shift reframed slavery as dynamic, national, and deeply capitalist.

Yet even within this scholarship, enslaved children and individual life histories often remained peripheral. Aggregate data conveyed scale but not experience. This volume builds on existing scholarship while insisting that individual lives—especially those of children—are not illustrative anecdotes but central evidence.

Slavery as Infrastructure

The domestic slave trade functioned through infrastructure: roads, rivers, railways, markets, jails, and laws. Cities such as Richmond, Alexandria, Charleston, and New Orleans served as hubs where enslaved people were confined, inspected, priced, and sold. These were not hidden operations. They were visible, regulated, and widely accepted within white society.

Understanding slavery as infrastructure shifts interpretation away from isolated acts of cruelty toward systemic violence. Forced movement destabilized families, erased continuity, and prevented rootedness. It also generated profit across regions, linking local sales to national economic growth.

This framework is particularly important for understanding enslaved childhood. Children experienced slavery less as attachment to place than as exposure to movement. Birth in a trading city or sale at a young age shaped identity, memory, and survival.

Method: Microhistory and Archival Care

This book employs a descendant-centered microhistorical approach. It follows the life of Celia Adams not to exceptionalize her experience, but to ground structural analysis in a documented

human life. Microhistory allows us to see how large systems operated at the level of the individual, especially when records are fragmentary.

Archival recovery of enslaved lives requires triangulation. Census schedules, probate records, tax lists, Freedmen's Bureau files, and oral histories must be read against one another and against the silences they contain. Absence of evidence is itself evidence of how the system functioned.

Throughout this volume, clear distinctions are maintained between documented fact, historically grounded inference, and interpretive analysis. This evidentiary care is essential for scholarly integrity and for public history contexts, where claims must withstand scrutiny.

Memory, Ethics, and Public History

Writing about slavery is an ethical act. Enslaved people were denied control over their bodies, families, and narratives. Historians and curators inherit a responsibility to avoid reenacting that erasure through speculation or sensationalism.

This volume adopts a framework of dignified recovery. Violence is neither exaggerated nor minimized. Enslaved people are not reduced to victims, nor romanticized as symbols of resilience. Instead, their lives are presented as historically contingent, constrained, and meaningful.

Public history—museums, monuments, exhibitions—plays a critical role in shaping how slavery is remembered. The research in this book is designed to move across scholarly and public-facing contexts, aligning with Smithsonian interpretive standards and the America250 framework for national reflection.

Why Celia Adams

Celia Adams's life anchors this study. Born in Shockoe Bottom in 1856, sold southward as a child, and living into the twentieth century, her lifespan bridges slavery, emancipation, Reconstruction, and Jim Crow. Her story is not unique, but it is traceable. Through her life, the domestic slave trade becomes legible as lived experience.

Centering one woman's life does not narrow the scope of analysis; it expands it. Celia Adams allows us to see how national systems shaped individual trajectories and how memory endured across generations.

Conclusion: From Structure to Life

The chapters that follow move from structure to experience—from markets and routes to childhood, displacement, and survival. This opening chapter establishes the lens through which those stories are told. The domestic slave trade was a system of movement, profit, and control. Its legacy endures in American landscapes, institutions, and families.

To tell this history fully requires attention to both scale and intimacy. It requires confronting violence while honoring life. This book begins that work here.

Chapter 7

Celia Adams and Children of Commerce: Enslaved Childhood and the Logic of the Domestic Slave Trade

Introduction: Childhood Without Sanctuary

In the antebellum United States, enslaved childhood did not exist apart from the market. While popular memory has often imagined enslaved children as marginal to slavery's economic core—too young to labor, shielded by age, or peripheral to plantation production—the historical record tells a different story. Enslaved children were central to the domestic slave trade. They were valued not only for their future labor potential but for their adaptability, their resale value, and their role in sustaining slavery as a multigenerational system.

This chapter examines enslaved childhood as a category shaped by commerce, mobility, and vulnerability. It argues that the domestic slave trade transformed childhood itself into a site of commodification. Enslaved children were born into a system that calculated their worth from birth, severed familial bonds with regularity, and exposed them early to violence, displacement, and loss.

Understanding this reality is essential to interpreting individual lives—such as that of Celia Adams—and to dismantling narratives that minimize slavery's impact on children.

The Market Value of Enslaved Children

By the early nineteenth century, enslaved children constituted a significant portion of the enslaved population sold through domestic markets. Traders and planters alike recognized children as long-term investments. Their youth promised decades of labor, and their bodies could be molded to meet the demands of new environments. As a result, children were often priced favorably relative to adults, especially during periods of economic expansion in the cotton South.

Infants and young children were commonly sold alongside mothers, but this practice was dictated by convenience rather than humanitarian concern. When market conditions shifted, or when debts, deaths, or migration intervened, children were sold independently. Probate inventories, estate sales, and trader records frequently list children by age alone, stripped of names or kinship ties. These documents reveal a legal regime that reduced childhood to a line item.

The valuation of children extended even to the unborn. Enslaved women's reproductive capacity increased their market price, and the anticipated future labor of their children was calculated into transactions. In this sense, enslaved childhood began before birth.

Separation as Structure, Not Exception

Family separation was not an incidental tragedy of slavery; it was a structural feature of the domestic slave trade. Children were especially vulnerable to sale because they lacked legal protection, economic leverage, or physical capacity to resist. The sale of children destabilized enslaved families, undermining kinship networks that might otherwise provide support or continuity.

Advertisements placed by enslaved parents seeking lost children after emancipation attest to the scale of this separation. Newspapers across the South carried notices from freedpeople searching for sons, daughters, and siblings sold years earlier. These testimonies confirm that childhood separations were neither rare nor accidental—they were routine outcomes of a system built on profit and mobility.

For enslaved children, separation shaped identity. Childhood memories were often fragmented, marked by sudden removals and unfamiliar faces. The loss of parents or siblings was not a single event but an ongoing threat that conditioned daily life.

Mobility and the Geography of Enslaved Childhood

Enslaved childhood was geographically unstable. Children were frequently moved between plantations, counties, and states, either through sale or through the migration of enslavers. This mobility disrupted education, cultural transmission, and emotional development. Unlike white children, whose childhoods were increasingly idealized as protected and nurturing during the nineteenth century, enslaved children experienced childhood as provisional.

The domestic slave trade intensified this instability. Children born in Upper South states such as Virginia or Maryland were often sold southward to cotton-producing regions. The journey itself—by foot, rail, or river—was traumatic, exposing children to physical hardship and psychological terror. These movements fractured regional identities and created a generation of enslaved people whose earliest memories were of transit.

Celia Adams's birth in Richmond and subsequent forced movement southward reflects this broader pattern. Her childhood, like that of countless others, unfolded across spaces shaped by trade routes rather than familial choice.

Violence, Discipline, and Early Labor

Enslaved children were subjected to violence from an early age. While very young children were not expected to perform the same labor as adults, they were quickly incorporated into plantation routines. Tasks such as childcare, water carrying, field assistance, and domestic labor introduced children to regimes of discipline and punishment.

Violence functioned as instruction. Children learned through observation and experience that their bodies were subject to control. Punishment was not reserved for adulthood; it was a formative element of enslaved childhood. This early exposure normalized coercion and reinforced the power dynamics of slavery.

At the same time, enslaved children developed strategies of resilience—forming peer networks, learning songs and stories, and maintaining kinship bonds when possible. These acts did not negate violence but coexisted with it, shaping lives marked by both endurance and loss.

Memory, Survival, and Historical Recovery

Much of what is known about enslaved childhood comes from retrospective sources—slave narratives, WPA interviews, and post-emancipation testimonies. These accounts are mediated by time, trauma, and the conditions under which they were recorded. Yet they offer invaluable insight into how formerly enslaved people remembered childhood as a period defined less by innocence than by precarity.

The silences surrounding enslaved children in official archives are themselves historical evidence. They reflect a system that did not consider enslaved children worthy of documentation beyond their economic value. Recovering these lives requires methodological care, combining fragmentary records with broader structural analysis.

This chapter adopts a framework that treats enslaved childhood as historically real, ethically significant, and analytically central. By doing so, it prepares the ground for the chapters that follow, which trace individual lives shaped by these forces.

Childhood as Evidence

Enslaved childhood exposes the moral architecture of American slavery. It reveals a system willing to commodify the most vulnerable and to treat dependency as opportunity. Children were not peripheral to the domestic slave trade; they were essential to its sustainability.

By foregrounding enslaved childhood, this chapter challenges narratives that soften slavery's brutality or relegate its violence to adulthood alone. The lives of children like Celia Adams remind us that slavery was a lifelong condition imposed from birth, structured by markets, and remembered long after emancipation.

Integrating Celia Adams into the historical and geographic arc connecting Ninety-Six, Silver Bluff, Augusta, and Shockoe Bottom. The narrative positions Celia Adams within the longer trajectory of displacement, survival, and institutional formation.

Ninety-Six, Silver Bluff, and the Genealogy of Displacement: From Frontier Trade to Celia Adams

The historical relationship between Ninety-Six and Silver Bluff, South Carolina, reveals more than a regional story of Indian trade and Revolutionary conflict. It marks an early geography of displacement whose structural logic would echo into the nineteenth century and shape the lived experience of enslaved families such as that of Celia Adams. To understand Celia Adams' forced sale from Richmond's Shockoe Bottom to Louisville, Georgia, in the mid-nineteenth century, one must first examine the earlier backcountry corridor that linked Ninety-Six, Silver Bluff, Augusta, and the Savannah River basin. These places were not isolated sites; they were connected nodes in a southern system of trade, militarization, and coerced mobility.

Indigenous Trade and Frontier Diplomacy

Before the American Revolution, Ninety-Six and Silver Bluff operated within Indigenous diplomatic and economic networks dominated by Creek and Cherokee authority. The deerskin trade connected inland Native towns to British colonial markets through a chain of trading posts and riverine hubs (Braund 1993). Ninety-Six emerged in the 1730s as a crucial inland outpost, positioned along Native paths that facilitated exchange between the interior and the coast (Edgar 1998).

Silver Bluff, situated along the Savannah River, functioned as both an Indian trading post and plantation complex under George Galphin. Galphin cultivated Creek alliances and served as an intermediary between Native nations and colonial authorities (Cashin 2005). The plantation economy at Silver Bluff relied on enslaved African labor, binding Indigenous trade diplomacy to racialized agricultural production.

This interconnected corridor—from Ninety-Six inland to Silver Bluff along the Savannah River—formed a structural template: land as exchange zone, labor as instrument, and mobility as economic necessity. That template would later harden into a system of domestic slave trading routes that carried enslaved Africans deeper into the South.

Revolutionary War and the Militarization of the Corridor

The American Revolution transformed this trade corridor into contested ground. Ninety-Six became a fortified British stronghold and the site of the 1781 siege (Babits 1998). Silver Bluff and nearby Fort Galphin were equally strategic, controlling access to riverine supply lines and Native alliances.

War destabilized plantation economies and displaced enslaved populations. When British occupation disrupted Galphin's holdings, enslaved communities were uprooted. Some were moved into Georgia, contributing to the emergence of Black congregations in Augusta, including Springfield Baptist Church (1787). That congregation later hosted the founding of Augusta Institute (1867), which became Morehouse College.

Thus, from the ashes of frontier militarization arose Black institutional formation. The very geography that had sustained trade and war became the seedbed of education and ecclesiastical autonomy.

The Domestic Slave Trade and the Richmond Connection

By the early nineteenth century, the corridor linking Virginia to Georgia had become formalized through the domestic slave trade. Shockoe Bottom in Richmond operated as one of the largest slave-trading districts in the Upper South. Enslaved Africans were sold from Virginia into the expanding cotton economy of Georgia and the Deep South (Tadman 1989).

Celia Adams was born in Richmond, Virginia, in 1856, into a system already structured by generations of coerced migration. She and two of her brothers were sold from Richmond to

Louisville, Georgia—a movement that retraced, in brutal form, the earlier trade and military corridors connecting Virginia to South

Carolina and Georgia. Shockoe Bottom, Ninety-Six, Silver Bluff, and Augusta thus exist within a shared geography of forced transit.

The earlier frontier trade system had depended upon Native alliances and enslaved labor; the nineteenth-century slave trade system depended upon interstate human trafficking. What began as a commercial corridor became a human pipeline.

Celia Adams' experience at the Richmond slave market—where she was required to walk around the block multiple times before being sold—reflects the matured institutionalization of that corridor. By the time of her sale, the network connecting Virginia to Georgia was not improvised but normalized. The trade routes linking interior South Carolina to Augusta and beyond had long since become embedded in a larger national economy of slavery.

From Displacement to Institutional Memory

Yet the story does not end with displacement. The enslaved Africans moved from Silver Bluff to Augusta in the late eighteenth century formed Springfield Baptist Church. That congregation later nurtured Augusta Institute, a foundational institution in Black higher education. In a different generation, Celia Adams' descendants would participate in preserving and narrating this history—culminating in public testimony before the United States Senate in support of what became the National Museum of African American History and Culture.

The geography that once commodified Black bodies became, across generations, a geography of memory and institution building.

Celia Adams stands within this continuum. Though separated by a century from the Revolutionary frontier, her life traces the same structural arc: displacement across southern corridors, survival within oppressive systems, and intergenerational transformation through education and faith. The backcountry routes linking Ninety-Six and Silver Bluff to Augusta anticipate the nineteenth-century slave-trading routes that carried Celia Adams from Richmond to Georgia. The institutions born in Augusta—particularly Springfield Baptist Church and Augusta Institute—represent the long-term counter-structure to those routes.

In this sense, **Ninety-Six and Silver Bluff are** not merely Revolutionary landmarks; they are **early coordinates in a geography that shaped Celia Adams' world.** They illustrate how frontier commerce, imperial war, and racial slavery formed a southern corridor whose consequences endured into the era of the domestic slave trade—and whose legacy was ultimately contested through Black institutional formation.

Historical Significance

Placing Celia Adams within this regional framework clarifies three interlocking dynamics:

Continuity of coerced mobility: The corridor linking inland South Carolina to Georgia and beyond evolved from Native trade networks into domestic slave-trade routes connecting Richmond to the Deep South.

Institutional counter-formation: Displaced Black communities responded by building churches and schools that became generational anchors.

Education as intergenerational recovery: The founding of Augusta Institute, later Morehouse College, represents a structural response to the geography of forced migration that shaped Celia Adams' life.

Through this lens, the relationship between Ninety-Six and Silver Bluff becomes part of a larger genealogy—a map of displacement that stretches from the eighteenth-century frontier to the Richmond slave market and, ultimately, to the creation of enduring Black institutions. Celia Adams is not peripheral to this geography; she is one of its inheritors.

References

Babits, Lawrence E. 1998. A Devil of a Whipping: The Battle of Cowpens. Chapel Hill: University of North Carolina Press.

Braund, Kathryn E. Holland. 1993. Deerskins and Duffels: The Creek Indian Trade with Anglo-America, 1685–1815. Lincoln: University of Nebraska Press.

Cashin, Edward J. 2005. Governor Henry Ellis and the Transformation of British North America. Athens: University of Georgia Press.

Edgar, Walter. 1998. South Carolina: A History. Columbia: University of South Carolina Press.

Tadman, Michael. 1989. Speculators and Slaves: Masters, Traders, and Slaves in the Old South. Madison: University of Wisconsin Press.

Wood, Peter H. 1998. Black Majority: Negroes in Colonial South Carolina from 1670 through the Stono Rebellion. New York: W.W. Norton.

Chapter 8

Born into the Market: Celia Adams, Enslaved Childhood, and Forced Migration in the Domestic Slave Trade

Introduction: A Child of the Trade

Celia Adams was born on March 12, 1856, in Richmond, Virginia, at the height of the domestic slave trade. Her birthplace—Shockoe Bottom—was not merely a neighborhood but a commercial engine of human trafficking, where enslaved people were priced, sold, and shipped south to sustain the expanding cotton economy. To be born enslaved in Richmond in the mid-nineteenth century was to enter bondage already shaped by movement. For Celia, enslavement was not defined by a single plantation or owner, but by a system designed to turn children into mobile commodities.

This chapter reconstructs Celia Adams's early life and forced migration from Virginia through South Carolina to Louisville, Georgia. In doing so, it argues that enslaved childhood in the United States was fundamentally structured by geography and commerce. Celia's life illuminates slavery not as a static institution rooted in place, but as a national infrastructure of movement—one that displaced families, erased records, and carried violence across state lines.

Shockoe Bottom: Birth in a Market City

By the 1850s, Richmond had become one of the most important slave-trading centers in the United States. Shockoe Bottom, situated near the James River and the city's transportation networks, functioned as a collection point where enslaved people from Virginia were assembled for sale to the Deep South. Traders' pens, auction houses, and holding yards lined the district, embedding the buying and selling of human beings into the city's daily life.

Celia Adams was born into this environment. Like most enslaved children, her birth was not formally recorded. Enslaved births rarely appeared in vital records; children were instead counted as property, listed by age and sex in probate inventories and tax rolls. Celia's name does not appear in the ledgers of Shockoe Bottom, yet her existence is historically legible through the systems that surrounded her. Her birth coincided with Virginia's role as a "supply state," exporting enslaved labor to states further south.

To be born enslaved in Richmond was to be born into the market itself. Childhood did not protect one from sale. Indeed, children were often considered especially valuable commodities, prized for their longevity and adaptability. Celia's earliest years were likely shaped by the presence of traders, the threat of separation, and the ambient violence of a city built on sale.

Sale and Separation: The Road South

At some point during her early childhood, Celia Adams was sold and forcibly removed from Virginia. She traveled south with two brothers, a detail that underscores both the violence of the trade and the fragile persistence of kinship under enslavement. While parents were frequently separated from children, siblings were sometimes kept together, particularly when sold in groups by traders seeking efficiency.

The journey south was itself a form of violence. Enslaved people were marched overland or transported by rail and river, often under brutal conditions. These routes—running through the Carolinas and into Georgia and Alabama—formed the arteries of the domestic slave trade.

Movement erased identity even as it generated profit. Traders kept records of numbers and values, not names or stories.

Celia's forced migration likely involved professional traders rather than plantation owners. This distinction matters.

Trader-mediated sales left fewer personal records, making it difficult to trace individual lives. Yet they also reveal the true scale of the trade: slavery was not only about ownership, but about circulation. Enslaved children like Celia were swept into a system that treated movement itself as a mechanism of control.

South Carolina: Transit and Power

South Carolina occupied a central position in the domestic slave trade's geography. It was both a destination and a corridor, a place where enslaved people were bought, sold, and moved onward. Prominent political leaders in the state, including Governor James Hopkins Adams, openly defended slavery and even advocated for reopening the Atlantic slave trade. Their rhetoric underscores the ideological environment through which Celia passed.

Yet there is no evidence that Celia Adams lived on a South Carolina plantation. Instead, available records suggest that she passed through the state as part of a larger trafficking network. This absence of place is itself revealing. Celia's enslavement was not anchored to land, but to movement. Power operated systemically, not personally. Her life was shaped less by a single enslaver than by a political economy that normalized the sale of children.

Understanding South Carolina as a site of transit rather than residence reframes how we interpret enslaved experience. For many, enslavement was defined not by where they lived, but by how often they were moved. Celia's passage through South Carolina exemplifies this reality.

Louisville, Georgia: Sale, Survival, and Continuity

Celia Adams was ultimately sold in Louisville, Georgia, during the Civil War era. Georgia plantations continued to rely on enslaved labor even as the Confederacy destabilized. It is likely here that Celia's surname—Adams—became fixed, either reflecting her final enslaver or a name she later claimed in freedom.

Louisville became the place where Celia labored and endured. Emancipation in 1865 marked a legal transformation, but not an erasure of memory. Like many formerly enslaved people, Celia remained near the site of her enslavement, building a life in the shadow of bondage. She married, raised children, and lived into the twentieth century, dying in 1943.

Celia's lifespan bridged slavery, Reconstruction, Jim Crow, and the early stirrings of the civil rights movement. Her life demonstrates how the legacies of enslavement were carried forward by those who survived it. Freedom did not undo the past, but it allowed memory to persist.

Methods, Memory, and Meaning

Reconstructing the life of an enslaved child requires methodological humility. The absence of direct documentation is not accidental; it is the product of a system that refused to recognize enslaved people as historical subjects. This chapter relies on archival triangulation, combining probate records, slave trade scholarship, geographic analysis, Freedmen's Bureau documents, and census data. Where evidence is inferred, it is grounded in established historical patterns and clearly identified as such.

Celia Adams's story challenges us to rethink how we tell the history of slavery. Rather than centering enslavers or plantations, it foregrounds infrastructure, movement, and childhood. Her life reminds us that slavery was national in scope, dynamic in practice, and devastating in its impact on families.

Conclusion: Carrying History Forward

Celia Adams was born into a market, sold along a road, and lived long enough to remember both slavery and freedom. Her story stands as evidence of how American systems operated and how individuals endured them. By tracing her forced migration, we see slavery not as a distant institution, but as a lived experience etched onto the bodies and memories of children.

In honoring Celia Adams, we honor countless others whose names were never written down, but whose lives shaped the nation. Her journey forces us to confront the geography of American slavery—and the enduring power of survival.

Chapter 9

Slavery in Motion: Shockoe Bottom and the Architecture of the Domestic Slave Trade

Introduction: From Place to Process

The domestic slave trade was not merely an economic system; it was an infrastructure of forced movement that reshaped the lives of millions of enslaved people and reoriented the geography of American slavery. By the mid-nineteenth century, slavery in the United States had become increasingly mobile, organized around routes, depots, and markets rather than fixed plantations alone. This chapter examines Shockoe Bottom in Richmond, Virginia, as a critical node within that system and argues that the domestic slave trade must be understood as a process—one that produced displacement, fragmentation of families, and generational trauma.

Shockoe Bottom was not an aberration or peripheral site. It was central to the functioning of American slavery. From this district, enslaved people were sold southward in vast numbers, sustaining plantation economies in South Carolina, Georgia, Alabama, Mississippi, and Louisiana. The experiences of individuals such as Celia Adams—born into this commercial landscape in 1856—cannot be understood without first grappling with the broader architecture that made such lives vulnerable to sale and separation.

Richmond as a Supply City

By the early nineteenth century, Virginia had shifted from a colony dependent on enslaved labor to a major exporter of enslaved people. Declining tobacco profits and soil exhaustion coincided

with the rapid expansion of cotton cultivation in the Deep South. Enslaved people became Virginia's most valuable export. Richmond, as the state capital and a transportation hub, emerged as a focal point for this commerce.

Shockoe Bottom, situated near the James River, canals, railroads, and turnpikes, provided ideal conditions for the consolidation of the slave trade. Slave jails, auction houses, and trader offices clustered within a compact urban space. The proximity of these facilities to transportation infrastructure ensured the efficient movement of enslaved people from local holding pens to distant markets.

The scale of this trade was immense. Tens of thousands of enslaved men, women, and children passed through Richmond in the decades preceding the Civil War. Traders operated openly, advertising sales in newspapers and maintaining business relationships with planters throughout the South. The city's economy was deeply entangled with slavery, even as many white residents disavowed personal responsibility for the trade's violence.

Shockoe Bottom as a Landscape of Confinement

Shockoe Bottom functioned simultaneously as a neighborhood and a carceral space. Enslaved people were confined in private jails while awaiting sale, often for weeks or months. These facilities were sites of surveillance, discipline, and psychological terror. The uncertainty of sale—of where one would be sent, whom one would be separated from—was itself a form of punishment.

Children occupied a particularly vulnerable position within this system. Enslaved children were frequently sold because they represented long-term economic value. Their youth made them adaptable, and their separation from parents was treated as a logistical concern rather than a moral one. Childhood did not shield them from violence; instead, it rendered them commodities of special interest.

Births in Shockoe Bottom were not uncommon. Enslaved women gave birth while confined in jails or living in quarters attached to trader facilities. These children entered a world already structured by sale. To be born in Shockoe Bottom was, in a profound sense, to be born into the market.

Routes South: Coffles, Rail, and River

The domestic slave trade relied on a network of routes that linked supply regions to demand markets. Enslaved people were transported southward by foot in coffles, by rail, and by river. Each method imposed distinct forms of suffering, but all were designed to maximize profit and minimize resistance.

South Carolina occupied a critical position along these routes. It served as both a destination and a transit corridor for enslaved people moving deeper into the cotton frontier. The state's ports, railroads, and internal markets facilitated the redistribution of enslaved labor. Political

leaders in South Carolina aggressively defended slavery's expansion, reinforcing the legitimacy of the trade even as international trafficking was officially outlawed.

Movement was not incidental to slavery; it was foundational. The repeated sale and relocation of enslaved people destabilized families and communities, ensuring dependence and limiting the formation of sustained resistance. The domestic slave trade transformed geography into a weapon.

Ideology and Governance

The domestic slave trade was sustained not only by markets but by ideology and law. State governments protected traders' rights, enforced fugitive slave laws, and regulated sales to ensure their legality. Public officials, including governors and legislators, openly defended slavery as essential to Southern prosperity.

The mid-1850s marked a period of intensifying proslavery rhetoric. Calls to reopen the Atlantic slave trade—though unsuccessful—revealed the extent to which slavery's defenders viewed human trafficking as legitimate commerce. Even as international trade remained closed, the domestic trade expanded unchecked, revealing the hypocrisy of claims that American slavery was benign or paternalistic.

This ideological environment shaped the lives of enslaved people even when they were not directly interacting with political institutions. The law followed them, legitimizing their sale and foreclosing avenues of redress.

Seeing Slavery Through a Child's Life

Understanding Shockoe Bottom as an architectural and ideological system allows us to better comprehend the lives that passed through it. Enslaved children like Celia Adams did not experience slavery as a static condition tied to one place or owner. Instead, they encountered it as a series of dislocations—birth in confinement, sale in childhood, forced travel, and eventual resettlement in unfamiliar terrain.

By centering the geography of slavery, this chapter reframes enslaved experience as one shaped by circulation rather than rootedness. Movement was not freedom; it was a mechanism of control. For children, it meant growing up without continuity, stability, or protection.

Infrastructure as Violence

Shockoe Bottom stands today as a reminder that slavery was built not only on plantations but on infrastructure—roads, rails, markets, and laws designed to facilitate human trafficking. The domestic slave trade transformed cities into engines of displacement and childhood into a condition of precarity.

This chapter establishes the structural context for the chapters that follow. To understand Celia Adams's life, we must first understand the system that made her sale possible. Slavery in America was not only lived on the land; it was carried along routes, enforced by institutions, and reproduced through movement. Shockoe Bottom was one such place where the machinery of slavery was laid bare.

Corridors of Displacement

From Frontier Trade to Celia Adams and the Architecture of Memory

Geography as Destiny

American history is often told through events. Yet beneath events lies infrastructure—corridors of movement that structure who lives, who labors, who is displaced, and who remembers. The southeastern interior of North America—stretching from Virginia through South Carolina into Georgia—functioned not merely as a region but as a corridor. Over the eighteenth and nineteenth centuries, this corridor evolved from Indigenous trade networks to militarized Revolutionary strongholds to domestic slave-trade routes.

Within this geography stand Ninety-Six, South Carolina; Silver Bluff and Fort Galphin along the Savannah River; Augusta, Georgia; and Shockoe Bottom in Richmond, Virginia. These sites are not isolated. They are coordinates within a long arc of coerced mobility and institutional counter-formation.

Celia Adams—born in Richmond in 1856, sold to Louisville, Georgia, and remembered through intergenerational testimony—stands within this corridor. Her life represents not an isolated tragedy but the matured expression of a structural geography centuries in the making.

This chapter traces that geography. It argues that corridors of displacement produced both forced migration and, paradoxically, the institutional foundations of Black religious and educational resilience.

Indigenous Networks and the Pre-Colonial Infrastructure of Exchange

Long before British colonists fortified inland posts, Native nations structured the southeastern interior through diplomacy, trade, and kinship. Creek and Cherokee polities governed expansive territories connected by footpaths, river systems, and seasonal trading cycles.

The deerskin trade, particularly in the eighteenth century, linked Indigenous hunters to European markets via colonial intermediaries (Braund 1993). What later became known as “frontier” space was, in fact, diplomatically negotiated territory.

Ninety-Six emerged in the 1730s as a trading outpost situated near these Native pathways. Its importance derived not from isolation but from connectivity—it sat at a crossroads of Indigenous trade corridors and colonial ambition (Edgar 1998).

Similarly, Silver Bluff, located along the Savannah River, operated within this Indigenous-colonial economy. Under George Galphin, the site became a major trading post serving Creek diplomatic networks. Galphin’s influence rested on cultural mediation and economic credit systems (Cashin 2005).

These early infrastructures established a pattern:

Corridor

Exchange

Movement

The difference, in time, would be who controlled the movement—and who was forced to move.

Silver Bluff and the Plantation-Trade Synthesis

Silver Bluff illustrates the fusion of Native diplomacy and enslaved African labor. Galphin’s plantation relied on enslaved workers even as it functioned as a diplomatic hub between Creek leaders and colonial authorities.

This synthesis reveals a structural shift: Indigenous trade networks were gradually subsumed into a plantation economy dependent upon racialized bondage. The corridor that once facilitated negotiated exchange became increasingly embedded within imperial credit systems and Atlantic capitalism.

Enslaved Africans labored at Silver Bluff not only in fields but in logistical support for trade and transport. Their work sustained the corridor's economic viability.

Thus, even before the Revolution, the southeastern interior was already a zone of coerced labor layered atop Indigenous exchange routes.

Revolutionary War and the Militarization of the Corridor

The American Revolution transformed commercial corridors into battlefields.

Ninety-Six became one of the most fortified British inland strongholds and the site of the 1781 siege (Babits 1998). The British southern strategy depended upon controlling backcountry infrastructure and mobilizing Loyalist sentiment.

Silver Bluff and nearby Fort Galphin occupied a parallel strategic position. Control of river crossings meant control of supply lines and Native alliances.

War destabilized plantation ownership and intensified displacement. British occupation disrupted Galphin's holdings; enslaved communities were scattered, relocated, or abandoned amid shifting control.

The corridor hardened. Trade routes became military supply lines. Mobility became survival.

Displacement and the Birth of Black Institutional Counter-Geography

Out of Revolutionary instability emerged one of the earliest independent Black congregations in the South: Springfield Baptist Church (1787) in Augusta, Georgia.

Many members traced their origins to Silver Bluff's enslaved community. Displacement did not dissolve collective memory—it relocated it.

Springfield Baptist Church later hosted the founding of Augusta Institute in 1867, an institution that would become Morehouse College. Thus, a corridor that once facilitated trade and warfare became, over generations, the cradle of Black higher education.

This transformation is not incidental. It reflects a counter-logic: where forced migration fractures communities, institutions of faith and learning reconstruct continuity.

Shockoe Bottom and the Industrialization of Displacement

By the early nineteenth century, the corridor linking Virginia to Georgia had become formalized through the domestic slave trade. Shockoe Bottom in Richmond emerged as one of the largest slave-trading districts in the Upper South (Tadman 1989).

Here, movement was no longer incidental to war or diplomacy. It was institutionalized commerce.

Enslaved men, women, and children were marched from Virginia through the Carolinas into Georgia and the Deep South. Roads once traveled by traders and soldiers became human conduits.

The corridor matured into infrastructure of commodification.

Celia Adams: A Life Within the Corridor

Celia Adams was born in Richmond, Virginia, on March 12, 1856. She and two of her brothers were sold from Richmond to Louisville, Georgia. Before her sale, she was required to walk around the slave market multiple times—a ritualized spectacle of commodification.

Her forced migration retraced the corridor's long arc:

From Richmond (Shockoe Bottom)

Through South Carolina's interior

Into Georgia's plantation economy

The same geographic pathway that had once connected Ninety-Six and Silver Bluff now carried her into bondage.

Celia Adams' life reflects the corridor's culmination. What began as Indigenous trade routes became, over centuries, a machinery of human trafficking.

Reconstruction and Institutional Memory

Yet the corridor also generated its counter-history.

Augusta Institute, emerging from Springfield Baptist Church, became a site of intellectual reconstruction in the post–Civil War South. Education functioned as structural resistance to displacement.

Generations later, Celia Adams' descendant would testify before the United States Senate in support of establishing the National Museum of African American History and Culture.

The corridor that once erased identities now anchors national memory.

This is intergenerational reversal.

Corridors and the Deuce Millennium Generation Framework

Within the Deuce Millennium Generation (DMG) model, these events span multiple generational epochs:

Revolutionary-era DMGs: Militarization of trade corridors

Slave-trade DMGs: Institutionalized forced migration

Reconstruction DMGs: Institutional formation and educational recovery

The corridor is not static; it evolves across generations.

The DMG framework reveals that displacement is not episodic but structural, recurring across epochs until counter-institutions alter its trajectory.

Historical Significance of Ninety-Six

The Ninety-Six–Silver Bluff–Augusta–Richmond corridor illustrates:

Continuity of infrastructure — Trade paths become military routes; military routes become slave-trade corridors.

Transformation of labor systems — Indigenous diplomacy gives way to plantation slavery.

Intergenerational resilience — Displaced communities build churches, schools, and institutions of memory.

Education as structural counterforce — Institutions like Augusta Institute embody long-term response to forced mobility.

Celia Adams stands as both subject and symbol of this transformation. Her life bridges the corridor's violent past and its institutional future.

Excellent question. The connection between Ninety-Six, South Carolina and Silver Bluff, South Carolina is not incidental—it is geographic, economic, military, and deeply tied to frontier trade, Indigenous diplomacy, and Revolutionary transformation.

The Connection Between Ninety-Six and Silver Bluff, South Carolina

1. Shared Frontier Geography: The Backcountry Corridor

In the eighteenth century, both Ninety-Six and Silver Bluff were part of South Carolina's backcountry frontier—a contested zone between:

Creek and Cherokee territories

British colonial expansion

Spanish influence to the south

French presence to the west

Ninety-Six sat inland along a major trading crossroads.

Silver Bluff lay along the Savannah River, a major transportation and trade artery.

They were connected by:

River systems

Wagon roads

Indian trading paths

Military supply routes

They functioned as complementary frontier nodes in a larger regional network.

2. The Indian Trade Network

Both sites were embedded in the eighteenth-century Indian trade system, which was central to the colonial economy.

Ninety-Six:
Established as a trading settlement around 1730s

Named for its (miscalculated) distance from Cherokee territory

Served as a key outpost in the deerskin trade

Silver Bluff:

Operated as a major trading post under George Galphin

Specialized in Creek diplomacy and commerce

Connected to Atlantic markets through the Savannah River

The deerskin trade was the backbone of the colonial South Carolina economy before rice and cotton dominance inland. Both locations were points where:

Native diplomacy

European credit systems

African labor

Frontier militarization intersected.

They were economically interdependent parts of the same system.

3. Revolutionary War Significance

During the American Revolution, both Ninety-Six and Silver Bluff became militarized.

Ninety-Six:

Became a British stronghold in the South

Site of the 1781 Siege of Ninety-Six

One of the first land battles in the South (1775)

Silver Bluff:

Associated with Fort Galphin

A Patriot supply and diplomatic station

Disrupted when British forces seized or destabilized property in the region

These were not isolated battlefields. They were part of the Southern Campaign, where British strategy focused on controlling backcountry supply routes and Loyalist networks.

Control of Ninety-Six meant:

Control of inland routes

Control of Silver Bluff meant:

Control of river trade and Creek alliances

Together, they formed strategic anchors in the British and Patriot contest for the southern interior.

4. Enslaved African Labor & Displacement

Both locations relied on enslaved African labor to sustain trade, agriculture, and infrastructure.

At Silver Bluff:

Enslaved Africans worked the plantation, trade logistics, and river systems.

When the Revolution disrupted the plantation economy, the enslaved population was displaced to Augusta.

In the broader **Ninety-Six district:**

Enslaved Africans supported frontier agriculture and supply lines.

War destabilized communities and forced movement.

This movement of enslaved people along frontier corridors connects these two sites in the same displacement geography that later linked Shockoe Bottom to Georgia and South Carolina.

5. A Shared Role in the Expansion of the Plantation South

After the Revolution, the Ninety-Six District was reorganized and eventually divided into several counties. The backcountry transitioned from:

Trade-based frontier economy to

Plantation agriculture (eventually cotton expansion)

Silver Bluff's earlier trade and plantation structure foreshadowed this transformation.

Both sites represent:

The shift from Native trade diplomacy

To plantation capitalism

To racialized labor regimes

They are chapters in the same structural evolution of the southern interior.

6. Why This Matters Historically

Ninety-Six and Silver Bluff together illustrate:

The entanglement of Indigenous trade and colonial expansion

The militarization of frontier communities during the Revolution

The role of enslaved labor in sustaining frontier economies

The instability that led to displacement and Black institutional formation

In tracing the long arc:

Shockoe Bottom fed labor into the expanding South.

Silver Bluff operated within frontier trade and Revolutionary upheaval.

Ninety-Six anchored inland political and military control.

Displacement led to Springfield Baptist Church.

From there came Augusta Institute and Morehouse College.

These sites form a connected regional network—not isolated episodes.

7. DMG Interpretation

Within your Deuce Millennium framework:

Ninety-Six and Silver Bluff are Pre-DMG Anchor Sites representing:

Indigenous diplomacy overlay (Cultural Memory layer)

Revolutionary instability (Policy layer)

Displacement leading to institutional creation (Education layer)

They demonstrate how education later emerged from the instability of trade, war, and displacement.

Map Ninety-Six → Silver Bluff → Augusta visually DMG timeline creates a migration route diagram with trade and military overlays that connects Ninety-Six explicitly to Celia Adams' Georgia lineage trail.

This geography is not peripheral—it is structural to the argument about long-horizon institutional survival.

Infrastructure as Violence

Shockoe Bottom stands today as a reminder that slavery was built not only on plantations but on infrastructure—roads, rails, markets, and laws designed to facilitate human trafficking. The domestic slave trade transformed cities into engines of displacement and childhood into a condition of precarity.

The structural context for the chapter follows. To understand Celia Adams's life, we must first understand the system that made her sale possible. Slavery in America was not only lived on the land; it was carried along routes, enforced by institutions, and reproduced through movement. Shockoe Bottom was one such place where the machinery of slavery was laid bare.

Conclusion: From Corridor to Conscience

Corridors of displacement shape nations quietly. They are not monuments but routes. They are not speeches but roads.

The southeastern interior corridor—from Ninety-Six to Silver Bluff to Augusta to Shockoe Bottom—demonstrates how geography can encode power. Yet it also demonstrates how communities can rewrite geography through institution building.

Celia Adams' journey was not chosen, but her descendants' preservation of memory was deliberate.

The corridor that once transported enslaved bodies now supports museums, scholarship, and education.

The lesson is clear:

Displacement can be inherited.

But so can institutions.

References

Babits, Lawrence E. 1998. A Devil of a Whipping: The Battle of Cowpens. Chapel Hill: University of North Carolina Press.

Braund, Kathryn E. Holland. 1993. Deerskins and Duffels: The Creek Indian Trade with Anglo-America, 1685–1815. Lincoln: University of Nebraska Press.

Cashin, Edward J. 2005. Governor Henry Ellis and the Transformation of British North America. Athens: University of Georgia Press.

Edgar, Walter. 1998. South Carolina: A History. Columbia: University of South Carolina Press.

Tadman, Michael. 1989. Speculators and Slaves: Masters, Traders, and Slaves in the Old South. Madison: University of Wisconsin Press.

Wood, Peter H. 1998. Black Majority: Negroes in Colonial South Carolina from 1670 through the Stono Rebellion. New York: W.W. Norton.

Chapter 10

Freedom Is Not a Destination: Celia Adams, Emancipation, and Reconstruction Survival

Introduction: After Sale, After War

Emancipation did not arrive as a clean rupture in the lives of formerly enslaved people. For those who had been sold through the domestic slave trade, freedom emerged unevenly—filtered through military occupation, labor contracts, racial violence, and the persistent afterlife of enslavement. This chapter examines Reconstruction not as a triumphant endpoint but as a contested and fragile transition, tracing how formerly enslaved people like Celia Adams navigated freedom after childhood displacement.

Celia Adams entered freedom in Georgia as a young woman whose formative years had been shaped by sale, forced migration, and labor. Her experience illuminates how the domestic slave trade structured Black life even after slavery's legal end. Freedom did not erase the past; it reorganized it.

Emancipation in Place

For many formerly enslaved people, emancipation occurred where slavery had last placed them. Celia Adams was freed in Georgia, not Virginia. This geographic displacement mattered. Emancipation often meant remaining among former enslavers, in counties where white power structures remained intact. The trade that had brought enslaved people south now constrained their choices, binding freedom to unfamiliar landscapes.

Freedmen's Bureau records from Georgia document the uneven implementation of emancipation. Bureau agents mediated labor contracts, resolved disputes, and attempted—often unsuccessfully—to protect freedpeople from exploitation. Women and children faced particular vulnerabilities, as planters sought to control Black labor through apprenticeship laws and coercive contracts.

Celia Adams's survival through this period reflects broader patterns of endurance. Freedom was negotiated daily, through labor, family formation, and resistance to re-enslavement in all but name.

Family Reconstruction and Naming

One of the most profound acts of freedom was the reconstitution of family. Formerly enslaved people sought to legalize marriages, reunite kin, and claim surnames. Names carried layered meanings—sometimes reflecting former enslavers, sometimes chosen anew, sometimes retained for continuity.

The surname "Adams," carried by Celia, may reflect the final site of her enslavement or a name she selected in freedom. What matters is not the certainty of origin but the agency embedded in naming. To claim a name was to assert personhood in a society that had long denied it.

Marriage records, census schedules, and church documents offer glimpses of this process. They reveal freedpeople constructing lives under conditions of constraint, asserting dignity within a hostile racial order.

Labor, Gender, and Survival

Reconstruction labor regimes relied heavily on Black women's work. Women labored in fields, homes, and informal economies while also sustaining families and communities. Celia Adams's life reflects this gendered reality. Freedom expanded responsibility without guaranteeing protection.

The withdrawal of federal enforcement in the late 1870s exposed freedpeople to renewed violence and disenfranchisement. Yet Black communities persisted. Churches, schools, and mutual aid networks emerged as sites of resilience.

Freedom's Fragility

Reconstruction did not fulfill its promises, but it reshaped possibilities. For Celia Adams, freedom meant survival, family, and memory—not justice or restitution. Her life reminds us that emancipation was a beginning, not an ending, and that the domestic slave trade cast long shadows over freedom itself.

From Fraction to Full Citizenship:

Geography, Education, and the Remaking of American Democracy

Introduction: Geography as Constitutional Witness

American democracy was not forged solely in convention halls or legislative chambers. It was shaped along roads, rivers, markets, battlefields, classrooms, and corridors of forced migration. The Constitution itself bears the imprint of geography—of places where liberty was claimed, denied, and redefined. This chapter further examines a connected historical landscape stretching from the Revolutionary-era backcountry of the Ninety Six District through the slave markets of Shockoe Bottom and into the Reconstruction education networks that reimagined citizenship after the Civil War.

This geography reveals democracy not as a finished product, but as a contested process. Here, Indigenous dispossession, enslavement, rebellion, emancipation, and education intersected. These sites expose how the United States moved from a constitutional order that counted human beings as fractions to one that—through Reconstruction—redefined personhood, citizenship, and political belonging.

The Revolutionary Backcountry and the Limits of Liberty

The Ninety Six District of South Carolina emerged in the eighteenth century as a frontier zone—contested by Indigenous nations, British colonial authority, and settler populations. During the American Revolution, the backcountry became one of the war's most volatile theaters. Allegiances fractured communities; violence blurred the line between civilian and soldier; and liberty was unevenly distributed.

For enslaved Africans and Indigenous peoples, the Revolution promised little immediate freedom. While Patriot rhetoric proclaimed universal rights, slavery expanded westward, and Native lands were increasingly expropriated. The Revolution thus produced a paradox: a new republic grounded in liberty that preserved human bondage.

The Constitution that followed codified this contradiction. Article I, Section 2 embedded the Three-Fifths Clause, assigning enslaved people political value without political rights. Geography mattered: representation was inflated in slaveholding regions, entrenching a political order that privileged land, labor extraction, and racial hierarchy.

Shockoe Bottom and the Internal Slave Trade

Nowhere was this constitutional paradox more visible than Shockoe Bottom in Richmond, Virginia. As one of the largest domestic slave markets in the United States, Shockoe Bottom functioned as a hub in the internal slave trade that forcibly relocated over one million people from the Upper South to the Deep South between 1800 and 1860.

Celia Adams, born in Richmond in 1856, entered this system as a child. Sold alongside her brothers and marched southward, her life traces the human geography of constitutional compromise. The roads that carried her away from Shockoe Bottom were the same corridors that fed plantation economies and inflated congressional representation through the Three-Fifths Clause.

Shockoe Bottom thus stands not only as a site of trauma, but as a constitutional landscape—where law, economy, and human suffering converged. The slave market was not peripheral to American democracy; it was central to how power was organized and maintained.

Civil War: Collapse of the Slaveholding Republic

The Civil War shattered the constitutional order that had sustained slavery. As Union armies advanced, enslaved people fled plantations, occupied roads, and transformed geography into a theater of freedom. Military movement disrupted the internal slave trade and exposed the fragility of a political system built on human bondage.

The war's outcome forced a reckoning. Emancipation was not simply a moral victory; it was a constitutional rupture. The abolition of slavery rendered the Three-Fifths Clause obsolete, dismantling the political arithmetic that had long distorted representation.

Yet emancipation alone did not resolve the question of citizenship. Freedom demanded institutions—schools, laws, and protections—to give substance to liberty.

Reconstruction and the Second Founding

Reconstruction marked what scholars have called America's "Second Founding." The Thirteenth, Fourteenth, and Fifteenth Amendments rewrote the Constitution, abolishing slavery, defining birthright citizenship, and prohibiting racial discrimination in voting.

Equally transformative was the geography of Reconstruction. Federal power followed Union advance routes, establishing Freedmen's Bureau offices, schools, and churches. Education became the cornerstone of freedom. Formerly enslaved people demanded literacy not only as a practical skill, but as a claim to citizenship.

Reconstruction schools appeared along the same corridors that once carried slave coffles southward. Roads of forced migration became pathways of learning. This spatial inversion marked one of the most profound transformations in American history.

Education as Democratic Infrastructure

The Reconstruction commitment to education redefined democracy as a learned practice. Schools were not merely charitable institutions; they were civic infrastructure. Literacy enabled political participation, economic independence, and constitutional understanding.

These networks produced a generation of Black leaders who reshaped American public life. Among them was Benjamin E. Mays, born in 1894 in the Ninety Six District of South Carolina. Mays's journey—from a Reconstruction-era educational landscape to the presidency (1940-1976) of Morehouse College—embodied the long arc of Black educational aspiration.

President Benjamin E. Mays understood education as a moral and democratic obligation. His leadership influenced generations, including Dr. Martin Luther King Jr., and linked the unfinished work of Reconstruction to the modern Civil Rights Movement.

Dr. Mays often visited Dillard University in New Orleans. On the occasion of one of his visits, the son of President Broadus N. Butler would traditionally gather up the Brothers of Omega Psi Phi Fraternity to hear President Benjamin Mays, fondly referred to as Bennie "Buck" Mays. Ears were perked as he spoke on the Three-Fifths Clause.

Debunking the Three-Fifths Myth

Democracy Distorted: The Three-Fifths Compromise (1787)

The Three-Fifths Compromise did not give Black people votes. Enslaved Africans could not vote, testify, or claim citizenship. Instead, the Constitution counted three out of every five enslaved people when calculating a state's representation in Congress and the Electoral College.

This meant that enslaved bodies increased political power **wielded entirely by white voters and slaveholders.** Fifteen enslaved people counted as nine toward representation—yet produced **zero Black ballots.** The result was a constitutional bonus for slavery, strengthening slaveholding states and shaping national policy for decades.

Reconstruction emerged as a moral and political correction to this distortion. Black Americans demanded ballots instead of bodies, schools instead of sale, and citizenship instead of accounting.

Education corridors and voting rights became the clearest path toward a truer democracy.

Why Debunk the Myth

"Many people believe the Three-Fifths Compromise gave Black people partial voting rights. It did not. Enslaved people could not vote at all. Their bodies were counted to increase political power used exclusively by white slaveholders. This compromise strengthened slavery and

distorted American democracy until the Civil War and Reconstruction forced the nation to confront its meaning."

How the Three-Fifths Compromise Worked

Title: Bodies Counted. Ballots Denied.

Left Panel:

- 15 Enslaved Black People
- Votes Cast: 0
- Counted for Representation: 9
-

Right Panel:

- 3 White Voters
- Votes Cast: 3
- Political Power Increased by Enslaved Count

Bottom Caption (Museum-Ready): *The Three-Fifths Compromise converted enslaved bodies into political power—without granting freedom, voice, or vote.*

From Three-Fifths to Full Personhood

The constitutional transformation from slavery to citizenship was neither linear nor complete. The end of the Three-Fifths Clause did not automatically produce equality. Reconstruction was violently contested and ultimately undermined by Jim Crow laws and Supreme Court decisions that narrowed the scope of the new amendments.

Yet the constitutional framework endured. The amendments of Reconstruction provided the legal foundation for twentieth-century civil rights struggles. They established a vision of the United States as a multiracial democracy grounded in equal citizenship under law.

This transformation is legible in the landscape—from Shockoe Bottom to Ninety Six, from slave routes to schoolhouses. Geography preserves constitutional memory.

Memory, Education, and the Future of Democracy

This chapter argues that American democracy must be understood spatially. The Constitution was not only written—it was lived, contested, and remade in specific places. The lives of Celia Adams and Benjamin E. Mays anchor this history, connecting forced migration to educational leadership, enslavement to civic transformation.

By interpreting these landscapes together, we see democracy not as an abstract ideal, but as a practice forged through struggle, education, and collective memory. Preserving and interpreting these sites is not merely an act of commemoration—it is an investment in civic literacy and democratic resilience.

In acknowledging this geography, the nation confronts its past honestly and equips future generations to continue the work of forming a more perfect Union.

What Officially Reversed the Three-Fifths Compromise?

The Three-Fifths Compromise was nullified by the U.S. Constitution, not by ordinary law.

The specific constitutional action:
The Fourteenth Amendment (1868)
Section 2 of the Fourteenth Amendment explicitly replaced the Three-Fifths Clause.
It ended the practice of counting enslaved people as fractional persons for representation.

Constitutional change:
Before 1868 (Article I, Section 2, Clause 3):
Enslaved people counted as ⅗ of a person for representation.
After 1868 (14th Amendment, Section 2):

Representation is based on the "whole number of persons" in each state.

This language formally erased the Three-Fifths formula from constitutional practice.

Key point:
The Three-Fifths Compromise was not "repealed" line by line, but it was rendered obsolete and unconstitutional by the Fourteenth Amendment.

Broader Reconstruction Actions Addressing Black Citizenship & Voting

1. Thirteenth Amendment (1865)

Abolished slavery and involuntary servitude
Destroyed the legal foundation that made the Three-Fifths Compromise possible.
Did not define citizenship or voting rights.

2. Civil Rights Act of 1866

First federal law to define national citizenship
Declared all persons born in the U.S. (except Native peoples under tribal sovereignty) to be citizens

Overrode Black Codes
Later constitutionalized by the Fourteenth Amendment

3. Fourteenth Amendment (1868)

The most direct constitutional response to the Three-Fifths system.

Key provisions:

Birthright citizenship

Equal protection under the law

Due process

Representation based on whole persons

Penalty clause reducing representation for states that denied Black men the vote

This amendment reversed the logic of the Three-Fifths Compromise:

No more bodies without ballots.

4. Fifteenth Amendment (1870)

Prohibited denying the right to vote based on race, color, or previous condition of servitude Directly addressed the political exclusion that the Three-Fifths Compromise had enabled Made Black suffrage constitutionally protected (though later undermined by Jim Crow)

5. Reconstruction Enforcement Acts (1870–1871)

Also called the Ku Klux Klan Acts Authorized federal intervention to protect Black voters Temporarily enforced the promise of the 14th and 15th Amendments ***Timeline: Civil War → Emancipation → Repeal of Three-Fifths Logic 1787***

Three-Fifths Compromise adopted at the Constitutional Convention

Enslaved people counted for power, denied political voice

1861–1865: Civil War

War exposes the Three-Fifths system as morally and politically unsustainable

Enslaved people flee, resist, and destabilize the Confederacy

1863
Emancipation Proclamation (war measure)
Applies only to rebelling states

Begins dismantling slavery but does not alter the Constitution

1865

13th Amendment ratified

Slavery abolished nationwide

Three-Fifths logic weakened but not yet constitutionally replaced

1866

Civil Rights Act of 1866

Black citizenship asserted by statute

1868

14th Amendment ratified

Three-Fifths Compromise rendered void

Representation now based on whole persons

Citizenship and equal protection guaranteed

1870

15th Amendment ratified

Voting rights protected regardless of race

Post-1877
End of Reconstruction

Southern states undermine Black voting through violence and law

The Three-Fifths Compromise is gone—but its power imbalance reemerges through Jim Crow

African American Colleges and Universities Emerged to Train new generations of leaders

Hargrovian Summary Lines

The Three-Fifths Compromise was not overturned by a single law, but by a constitutional transformation. The Fourteenth Amendment replaced fractional counting with full personhood, while Reconstruction sought—briefly and bravely—to convert bodies once counted into citizens who could vote.

Chapter 11

Afterlives of the Trade: Memory, Descendants, and the Work of Public History

Introduction: Slavery's Persistence

The domestic slave trade did not end with emancipation. Its effects persisted in family separations, regional displacement, racial inequality, and historical silence. This chapter examines how the trade lives on—in landscapes like Ninety-Six, Shockoe Bottom, in descendant memory, and in contemporary struggles over interpretation and commemoration.

President Benjamin E. Mays's life clearly shares how Ninety-Six, South Carolina played it role in the making of American society. Celia Adams's life extended into the twentieth century, allowing memory to bridge slavery and modernity. Her story underscores the importance of descendant knowledge and public history in confronting the legacies of enslavement.

Landscape and Erasure

Sites of the domestic slave trade have often been erased or repurposed. Shockoe Bottom became a place of neglect and development rather than commemoration. This erasure reflects a broader unwillingness to confront slavery's urban infrastructure.

Public history initiatives—archaeology, memorialization, exhibitions—challenge this erasure. They insist that landscapes remember what institutions forget.

Descendant-Centered History

Descendant research restores agency to families long denied authorship of their own histories. Tracing Celia Adams's life is not merely an academic exercise; it is an act of recovery. Descendant-centered history reshapes archives by asking different questions and valuing oral tradition alongside written records.

This approach aligns with evolving museum ethics and scholarly practice. It recognizes that lived memory is itself a form of evidence.

Ninety Six, South Carolina, which is a real town—one of the oldest in the state.

Why is it called Ninety Six?
The name comes from the *colonial trading era:*
The settlement Cherokee was believed to be 96 miles from the town of Keowee along a trading path.

The number referred to distance, not a year, population, or charter.

It appears on maps as early as the 1730s, making it older than many better-known Southern towns.

Why it matters historically

Ninety Six, SC is significant because:

It was a frontier trading post

A major site during the American Revolution

Home to Ninety Six National Historic Site, including one of the first Revolutionary War–era star forts

Revolutionary War Geography: Why Ninety Six Mattered

Ninety Six became one of the most strategically important inland sites in the American Revolution.

Why Here?

It sat at the crossroads of Native paths and colonial roads

Controlled movement between the coastal Lowcountry and the western frontier

Served as a Loyalist stronghold in a deeply divided South Carolina

The Star Fort

The British built a star fort at Ninety Six—the first of its kind in the American South.

In 1781, Patriot forces under Nathanael Greene laid siege to the fort.

The siege failed militarily but weakened British control inland, helping shift momentum toward Yorktown.

Black People in the War

Enslaved Africans:
Escaped to the British seeking freedom

Served as laborers, guides, and soldiers on both sides

The Revolution accelerated Black mobility and resistance, even as it failed to deliver freedom broadly.

Geographic truth:

Ninety Six shows that the Revolution was not only fought in cities—it was decided in backcountry crossroads where Native routes and enslaved labor intersected.

From Revolution to Removal: Indigenous Dispossession

After independence:

Treaties forced Native nations—especially the Cherokee—off lands connected to Ninety Six.

Roads that once carried trade now carried settlers, enslaved people, and cotton.

Indigenous removal made the region safe for plantation expansion inland.

This transition marks the shift from frontier coexistence to racialized land ownership.

Reconstruction Geography: Freedom in the Backcountry

After the Civil War, Ninety Six's geography again mattered.

Why***?***

Backcountry areas had:
Large formerly enslaved populations
Fewer entrenched planter elites than the coast

Black communities formed:
Independent churches (AME, Baptist)
Schools supported by Freedmen's Bureau routes

Landholding enclaves along old roads and paths

Political Significance
Reconstruction governments relied on inland

Black voters
Many Black legislators, teachers, and ministers came from regions like Ninety Six

White resistance—Redeemer violence and disenfranchisement—was especially fierce in these contested interior zones

Reconstruction insight:
Freedom was negotiated along the same corridors once used by Native traders and Revolutionary armies.

Why Ninety Six Matters Today
Ninety Six is not important because of its size—it matters because it reveals:

How Indigenous geography structured
American expansion

How Black freedom struggles followed frontier routes

How the Revolution and Reconstruction were fought in interior landscapes, not just capitals

How memory often erases Native and Black presence from "colonial" and "patriot" narratives

Hargrovian Interpretive Summary
Ninety Six stands at the intersection of Indigenous knowledge, enslaved labor, revolutionary conflict, and post-emancipation struggle. Its roads carried trade, armies, and freedom-seekers. To understand Ninety Six is to understand how American power moved inland—step by step, path by path—over Native land and through Black resistance.

Museums, America250, and Ethical Interpretation
As the United States approaches commemorative milestones such as America250, institutions face choices about how to narrate national history. The domestic slave trade must be central to these narratives, not marginal.

Smithsonian frameworks emphasize truth-telling, transparency, and inclusion. This part of the volume contributes to that work by offering a model for integrating rigorous scholarship with public engagement.

Below is a fully developed three-part interpretive package suitable for museum, digital, and Smithsonian contexts.

I. Museum Exhibit Panel

From Shockoe Bottom to Silver Bluff: A Relay of Survival and Institution

Shockoe Bottom, Richmond, Virginia

In the eighteenth and nineteenth centuries, Shockoe Bottom was one of the largest slave-trading districts in the United States. Enslaved

Africans and African Americans were inspected, sold, and forcibly marched south into expanding plantation economies.

Among those born into this world was Celia Adams (1856–1943), whose family memory recalls her walking the auction block three times before being sold. Shockoe Bottom was not just a market—it was a redistribution hub in a continental system of forced migration.

Silver Bluff, South Carolina

Along the Savannah River stood Silver Bluff, once an Indigenous trading corridor and later an eighteenth-century Indian trading post operated by George Galphin. It became:

A plantation sustained by enslaved African labor

A Revolutionary War–era military site (Fort Galphin)

A crossroads of Native diplomacy, British imperial trade, and Patriot finance

When British forces seized Galphin's property during the Revolution, the enslaved community associated with Silver Bluff was displaced to Augusta, Georgia.

From Displacement to Institution

In Augusta, formerly enslaved Africans established Springfield Baptist Church (1787)—one of the earliest independent Black congregations in the South.

From Springfield came Augusta Institute (1867), later relocated and renamed Morehouse College.

This arc traces a powerful genealogy:

Shockoe Bottom → Silver Bluff → Springfield Baptist Church → Augusta Institute → Morehouse College

What began as forced movement through markets and plantations became the foundation of enduring Black educational institutions.

Key Idea

Education in the African American tradition did not emerge after slavery—it emerged through it. Institutions were built by people who had survived displacement and carried memory forward.

II. Visual Mapping onto the DMG Timeline

Placement Within the Deuce Millennium Generation (DMG) Framework

This historical arc maps onto the DMG model as follows:

Pre-DMG Foundations (Before DMG-1 / Before 1997)

These events serve as Intergenerational Anchors preceding the formal DMG sequence.

Anchor Epoch 1: Shockoe Bottom Era (18th–19th Century)

Domestic slave trade

Celia Adams born (1856)

Forced migration corridor southward

Anchor Epoch 2: Silver Bluff & Revolutionary Displacement (1770s)

Indian trading networks

Fort Galphin

Plantation displacement to Augusta

Anchor Epoch 3: Institutional Formation (1787–1867)

Springfield Baptist Church

Augusta Institute founded

Educational continuity formalized

Visual DMG Integration

On the horizontal DMG timeline:

Left of DMG-1

DMG-1 → DMG-53

Shockoe Bottom

Modern generational relay

Silver Bluff

Education as continuity

Springfield / Augusta Institute

Institutional survival logic

In the stacked model:

Cultural Memory Overlay (Bottom Layer): Shockoe Bottom → Silver Bluff → Oral transmission → Church formation

Policy Overlay (Middle Layer): Revolutionary War → Reconstruction → Segregation → Civil Rights

Education Overlay (Top Layer): Springfield Baptist → Augusta Institute → Morehouse → DMG generations

This visually demonstrates:

Policy shifts rapidly

Markets collapse

Empires change

Education persists

III. Smithsonian-Style Historical Interpretation

Silver Bluff and Shockoe Bottom in the Long Arc of Black Institutional Formation

Silver Bluff and Shockoe Bottom occupy distinct yet interconnected places within the history of American slavery, empire, and institution-building. Shockoe Bottom functioned as a central node in the domestic slave trade, redistributing enslaved labor from the Upper South into plantation economies further south. Silver Bluff, situated along Indigenous trade routes on the Savannah River, became a colonial trading post, plantation complex, and Revolutionary War site.

The enslaved Africans and African Americans who moved through these spaces were not merely laborers within imperial systems; they were carriers of cultural memory and institutional imagination. Displacement during the Revolutionary War led members of the Silver Bluff plantation community to Augusta, Georgia, where they founded Springfield Baptist Church in 1787. This congregation became a cornerstone of early Black institutional autonomy.

From Springfield Baptist Church emerged Augusta Institute in 1867, later known as Morehouse College—an institution that would educate generations of Black leaders. The lineage from slave market to church to college demonstrates that African American educational traditions were rooted in collective survival strategies long before formal emancipation.

Celia Adams, born in Richmond in 1856 and sold into Georgia, represents a generation shaped by the domestic slave trade yet connected through memory to later institutional advocacy. Her life bridges the world of Shockoe Bottom and the future-facing work of museum creation and public history.

Silver Bluff and Shockoe Bottom thus illustrate a broader historical pattern:

Where markets fragmented families, institutions reconstructed community.

Where displacement disrupted geography, education created continuity.

Within a long-horizon framework, these sites are not isolated episodes but foundational coordinates in a centuries-spanning story of cultural endurance and educational stewardship.

Design a full gallery wall layout mockup integrating floor map showing Shockoe Bottom → Silver Bluff → Augusta migration routes

Develop a QR audio script specific to this panel

This history deserves architectural clarity

Museum creation needed for public memory

Conclusion: Carrying the History Forward

Celia Adams's life did not end slavery, but it carries its history forward. Through descendants, scholarship, and public memory, the domestic slave trade remains present. The work of history is not only to document the past, but to reckon with its persistence.

This book chapter closes with an invitation: to see slavery not as distant, but as foundational; not as concluded, but as consequential. Remembering Celia Adams, Benjamin E. Mays, and the role of historically grounded Ninety Six is part of that work.

Chapter 12

From Union Advance to Church-Built Classrooms

Alignment with Freedmen's Bureau Records & Civil War Military Occupation Zones

Smithsonian Interpretive Framework

Federal Context (1865–1872)

Freedmen's Bureau records demonstrate that Black education expanded first in areas under Union military occupation. Schools appeared where the Army had already established contraband camps, hospitals, rail depots, and garrisons. The Bureau coordinated teachers and facilities, while Black churches provided permanence once federal oversight receded.

Primary Record Types Referenced

Bureau education reports and teacher registers
Military district correspondence
Labor contracts and refugee camp logs
Hospital and chaplaincy records
Military Occupation Zones → Education Corridors

1. Atlantic & Upper South Occupation Zone
(Early, sustained Union control: Virginia, North Carolina, South Carolina)

Institutions:
Hampton University (VA)
Virginia Union University (VA)
Shaw University (NC)
St. Augustine's University (NC)
Johnson C. Smith University (NC)
Livingstone College (NC)
Allen University (SC)
Clinton College (SC)
Voorhees College (SC)
Morris College (SC)

Bureau Alignment:
Schools appear in Bureau ledgers within months of troop stabilization. Many began in former military buildings or contraband camps.

2. Georgia Interior Occupation Zone
(Sherman's March, rail hubs, post-1864 garrisons)

Institutions:
Atlanta University / Clark College
Morehouse College (Augusta Institute)
Spelman College
Morris Brown College
Gammon Theological Seminary
Paine College

Bureau Alignment:
Georgia Bureau records document heavy collaboration with Baptist, Methodist, and AME congregations immediately after Union occupation of Atlanta, Augusta, and Savannah.

3. Deep South River & Rail Occupation Zone
(Alabama, Mississippi, Tennessee)

Institutions:
Talladega College

Selma University
Miles College
Lomax-Hannon College
Stillman College
Tuskegee University (post-Bureau, built on earlier Bureau school networks)
Tougaloo College
Rust College
Fisk University
LeMoyne-Owen College
Lane College
Knoxville College
Meharry Medical College

Bureau Alignment:
Schools cluster along rail lines, river ports, and former military hospitals, confirming education followed military logistics.

4. Gulf Coast & Mississippi Valley Occupation Zone (Louisiana, Texas, Arkansas)

Institutions:
Straight College (Dillard University)
New Orleans University
Xavier University of Louisiana
Paul Quinn College
Wiley College
Bishop College
Jarvis Christian University
Southwestern Christian College
Texas College
Philander Smith University
Shorter College
Arkansas Baptist College

Bureau Alignment:
Port cities and inland trade routes show the highest density of Bureau-church partnerships.

From Union Advance to Church-Built Classrooms

Education, Faith, and the Making of Freedom

Introduction: Freedom Required Infrastructure
Emancipation did not arrive with instructions. When the Union Army advanced into Confederate territory, freedom followed the flag—but freedom alone did not guarantee survival. Literacy, protection, land access, moral authority, and institutions were required to convert liberation into life. In the vacuum left by slavery's collapse, the United States government and Black churches formed an overlapping, sequential infrastructure. First came the Union Army. Then followed the Bureau of Refugees, Freedmen, and Abandoned Lands. When federal power receded, Black churches remained.

Together, these forces transformed emancipation from a legal decree into a lived reality. Nowhere is this clearer than in the rise of Black education during Reconstruction.

The Union Army: Creating Corridors of Possibility
As Union troops moved south between 1861 and 1865, they created what were effectively corridors of possibility. Military occupation brought order, protection, and federal authority into landscapes previously governed by plantation violence. Contraband camps emerged wherever Union lines stabilized—Richmond, Hampton Roads, Atlanta, Augusta, Savannah, Nashville, Memphis, Vicksburg, and New Orleans.
In these camps, formerly enslaved people gathered not only for safety but for instruction.

Soldiers, chaplains, and Northern missionaries began teaching reading, writing, and arithmetic almost immediately. The Army did not set out to create a school system, but its presence made schooling possible. Where the Army stayed, education followed.

The Freedmen's Bureau: Education as Federal Policy

In 1865, Congress institutionalized these wartime experiments through the Bureau of Refugees, Freedmen, and Abandoned Lands—commonly known as the Freedmen's Bureau. The Bureau's mandate was expansive: oversee labor contracts, administer relief, operate hospitals, adjudicate disputes, and crucially, establish schools.

Freedmen's Bureau records reveal a clear pattern. Schools were founded first in areas already under Union occupation. Bureau superintendents coordinated with military commanders, secured buildings (often former barracks, churches, or confiscated property), and recruited teachers. Education reports from Georgia, Virginia, Mississippi, Tennessee, and the Carolinas document thousands of Black students enrolled within months of occupation.

Yet the Bureau understood its limits. It did not seek to permanently run Black education. Instead, it relied on partnerships—most notably with Black churches.

When the Bureau Withdrew, the Churches Remained

By the early 1870s, federal commitment to Reconstruction waned. Troops withdrew. Bureau offices closed. White supremacist violence surged. But education did not disappear. It transferred.

Black churches—already the most trusted and durable institutions in freed communities—absorbed the educational mission. Sanctuaries doubled as classrooms. Ministers became presidents. Congregations raised funds, recruited teachers, and defended schools when no federal protection remained.

This transition marked a decisive shift: education moved from federal experiment to Black self-governance.
Denominational Strategies: Faith as Educational Architecture

Different Black religious traditions pursued distinct but complementary strategies:
Baptists built mass education networks. Emphasizing congregational autonomy, they founded schools quickly and broadly—Spelman

College, Morehouse College (Augusta Institute), Virginia Union University, Simmons College of Kentucky, Selma University, and Wiley College. Their focus was literacy, teacher training, and access at scale.

Methodists trained ministers, teachers, and physicians. Institutions such as Clark Atlanta University, Bennett College, Rust College, Gammon Theological Seminary, Meharry Medical College, and Philander Smith University reflected a theology that linked education, discipline, and professional leadership.

African Methodist Episcopal (AME), AME Zion, and Christian Methodist Episcopal (CME) churches asserted Black ecclesial sovereignty. Schools such as Wilberforce University, Morris Brown College, Allen University, Livingstone College, Hood Theological Seminary, Lane College, and Paine College trained leaders for a Black-governed church and a hostile nation.

Congregationalists, often working through the American Missionary Association, emphasized classical education and teacher training—Fisk University, Hampton University, Talladega College, Tougaloo College, and LeMoyne-Owen College—producing faculty who would staff schools across the South.

Together, these strategies formed a coordinated ecosystem.

Georgia and the Life of Celia Adams: Education Along the Slave Route

Celia Adams was born in 1856 in Shockoe Bottom, Richmond—a city that became a major Union occupation site and Freedmen's Bureau headquarters. As a child, she was sold south into Georgia during the Civil War, forced along the same interior routes later used by Union armies and Bureau agents.

After the war, Georgia became one of the most concentrated sites of Black educational expansion. Freedmen's Bureau school records document partnerships with Baptist, Methodist, and AME congregations in Atlanta, Augusta, and surrounding counties. From these efforts emerged Augusta Institute (Morehouse College), Atlanta University and Clark College, Morris Brown College, Spelman Seminary, and Gammon Theological Seminary.

For people like Celia Adams—formerly enslaved, displaced, and rebuilding—these institutions represented something unprecedented: stable places where Black children and adults could learn without permission. Education became the inheritance that slavery had denied.

From Literacy to Leadership

Church-founded colleges did more than teach reading. They produced teachers who staffed rural schools, ministers who anchored communities, physicians who treated Black bodies, lawyers who challenged segregation, and administrators who governed institutions when states refused to do so.

Graduates carried education back into homes, farms, towns, and pulpits. Each literate generation made the next generation harder to re-enslave—economically, politically, or psychologically.

Conclusion: Making Freedom Survivable

The Union Army opened the door. The Freedmen's Bureau built the bridge. Black churches laid the foundation.

Education was not an accident of Reconstruction; it was its most deliberate act. Through schools founded in faith and defended by communities, formerly enslaved people converted emancipation into citizenship. Literacy became protection. Credentials became leverage. Institutions became part of memory.

For Celia Adams and millions like her, freedom became survivable not because the nation guaranteed it, but because Black churches educated it—across generations.

What Celia Adams Teaches Us

Celia Adams lived eighty-seven years, spanning slavery, emancipation, Reconstruction, and Jim Crow. Her life compels a nation to reckon with the full temporal reach of American slavery—not as a closed chapter, but as a force whose consequences extended deep into the twentieth century and the Deuce Millennium.

Her story reveals slavery as a system of movement as much as confinement. The forced migration that carried her from Shockoe Bottom to Georgia was not incidental; it was fundamental to the institution's survival. Slavery depended on roads, rail lines, markets, and political cooperation across states. Children like Celia were caught within this machinery, their lives shaped by decisions made far beyond their control.

Yet Celia Adams was not only a victim of history. She was a survivor, a witness, and a carrier of memory. By living long enough to see freedom and to build a family, she embodied the resilience of those who endured enslavement and refused to be erased. Her existence challenges narratives that center enslavers or institutions rather than the enslaved themselves.

This book closes with an insistence: that the stories of enslaved children matter, that place matters, and that public memory must grapple with the geography of injustice. Celia Adams's journey from a slave market city to a post-emancipation life in Georgia reminds us that American history is inseparable from the lives of those who were bought, sold, and survived.

To remember Celia Adams is to confront the nation's past honestly—and to recognize the humanity that persisted even in the most dehumanizing conditions.

Legacy and Continuity

As we conclude this volume, the generation of Celia Adams, through the Reconstruction Act and three Amendments to the U.S. Constitutions are about to bend the moral arc of the universe towards justice. The institution of the black church, white missionary church work and schools are soon becoming a reality. It becomes evident that the domestic slave trade will become a historical phenomenon; it was a shaping force that extended its reach deep into the fabric of American life. The life of Celia Adams, from birth in Shockoe Bottom to her experiences in freedom, encapsulates how deeply interconnected the nation's history is with the forced movement and commodification of its people. Black churches will follow the old trails and roads to set up and establish schools, colleges, and universities that will educate the offsprings of the formerly enslaved people.

The chapters of this book have traced the arc from the infrastructure of the domestic slave trade to the lived experiences of enslaved individuals, and ultimately to the enduring legacies that persist into the present. The story of Celia Adams is a testament to resilience and memory, showing how the past remains intertwined with the present.

In reflecting on the legacies of the domestic slave trade, we are reminded that history is not just about the past; it is about how we engage with it today and in the future. The stories of those like Celia Adams call us to remember, to reckon, and to ensure that the truths of the past shape a more just future.

The Enduring Journey

The journey of Celia Adams and countless others is far from complete. As we move forward, the work of remembering and reckoning continues. Public history, descendant engagement, and scholarly rigor all play vital roles in ensuring that the legacies of the domestic slave trade are not forgotten.

In this epilogue, we honor the resilience of those who lived through these histories and recognize that the work of justice and remembrance is ongoing. The legacy of the domestic slave trade is woven into the very fabric of American society, and through continued scholarship and public engagement, we keep their memory alive

Benedict Institute, deserves mention as it was a main corridor of military protection that enabled the Freedmen's Bureau and Black churches to establish schools.

Baptist institutions such as Shaw, Virginia Union, Benedict, Morehouse, and Spelman emerged along these routes, converting emancipation into literacy, leadership, and professional training..

Early Black Colleges & Universities (1800s)

All Named Institutions Included

BAPTIST–AFFILIATED INSTITUTIONS

Shaw University (NC)
Spelman College (GA)
Virginia Union University (VA)
Simmons College of Kentucky (KY) (originally Simmons Bible College)
Bishop College (TX)
Selma University (AL)
Morris College (SC)
Wiley College (TX)
Arkansas Baptist College (AR)
Florida Memorial University (FL)
Freedman's College of South Carolina (SC)
Morehouse College (Augusta Institute origin) (GA)
Benedict Institute, now College (SC)
Shaw University (NC)

AFRICAN METHODIST EPISCOPAL (AME)

Wilberforce University (OH)
Allen University (SC)
Paul Quinn College (TX)
Morris Brown College (GA)
Edward Waters College (FL)
Shorter College (AR)
George Smith College → Texas College (TX / MO origins)

AFRICAN METHODIST EPISCOPAL ZION (AME ZION)

Livingstone College (NC)
Clinton College (SC)
Hood Theological Seminary (NC)

CHRISTIAN METHODIST EPISCOPAL (CME)

Lane College (TN)
Paine College (GA)
Miles College (AL)

Lomax–Hannon College (AL)

METHODIST EPISCOPAL / UNITED METHODIST

Clark College → Clark Atlanta University (GA)
Atlanta University (pre-merger) (GA)
Bennett College (NC)
Rust College (MS)
Gammon Theological Seminary (GA)
Meharry Medical College (TN)
Philander Smith University (AR)
Wiley College (TX) (historically Methodist Episcopal)
New Orleans University (later part of Dillard) (LA)

PRESBYTERIAN

Lincoln University of Pennsylvania (PA)
Johnson C. Smith University (Biddle College) (NC)
Knoxville College (TN)
Stillman College (AL)
Barber–Scotia College (NC)

CONGREGATIONAL / AMERICAN MISSIONARY ASSOCIATION (UCC LINEAGE)

Fisk University (TN)
Hampton University (VA)
Talladega College (AL)
Tougaloo College (MS)
LeMoyne–Owen College (TN)
Straight College (LA)
Lincoln University of Missouri (MO)

EPISCOPAL (ANGLICAN)

Voorhees College (SC)
St. Augustine's University (NC)
DISCIPLES OF CHRIST
Jarvis Christian University (TX)
Southwestern Christian College (TX)

CATHOLIC
Xavier University of Louisiana (LA)

INDUSTRIAL / NON-DENOMINATIONAL (BUT CHURCH-SUPPORTED)
Tuskegee University (AL)

INSTITUTIONAL LINEAGE CLARIFICATIONS
Texas College = successor to George Smith College
Dillard University (1930) = merger of Straight College (Congregational) and New Orleans University (Methodist)
Clark Atlanta University = merger of Clark College and Atlanta University
Morehouse College = evolved from Augusta Institute

In framing the denominational summary, every named institution fits within a deliberate Black church strategy:

Baptists built mass education networks
Methodists trained ministers, teachers, and physicians
Congregationalists emphasized classical education and teacher training
AME, AME Zion, and CME churches asserted Black ecclesial sovereignty

Together, these colleges formed the educational backbone of Reconstruction and post-Reconstruction Black America.

Denominational Summary (All Named Institutions Included)

Baptist: Shaw, Spelman, Virginia Union, Simmons (KY), Bishop, Selma, Morris (SC), Wiley, Arkansas Baptist College
AME: Wilberforce, Allen, Paul Quinn, Morris Brown, Texas College, Shorter, Edward Waters
AME Zion: Livingstone, Clinton, Hood Seminary
CME: Lane, Paine, Miles, Lomax-Hannon
Methodist Episcopal / UMC: Clark Atlanta, Bennett, Rust, Gammon, Meharry

Presbyterian: Lincoln (PA), Johnson C. Smith, Knoxville, Stillman
Congregational (AMA/UCC): Fisk, Hampton, Tougaloo, Talladega, LeMoyne-Owen
Episcopal: Voorhees, St. Augustine's
Catholic: Xavier (LA)
Disciples of Christ: Jarvis, Southwestern Christian
Industrial / Independent: Tuskegee

Springfield Baptist Church (Augusta, Georgia)

Civil War–Era Anchor for Black Education
Founded: 1787 (one of the oldest Black congregations in the United States)
Affiliation: Baptist
Location: Augusta, Georgia

Role During the Civil War & Reconstruction

Educational Safe Haven: During and immediately after the Civil War, Springfield *Baptist Church functioned as a de facto schoolhouse, hosting literacy classes* for formerly enslaved adults and children when no public Black schools existed.

Birthplace of Augusta Institute: The church provided space, leadership, and community legitimacy for early Black education efforts that culminated in the founding of the Augusta Institute (1867). This map traces Augusta Institute → Eden Baptist Church in Louisville, Georgia when Eden was a 1877 Brush Harbor yet to be approved by Reverend Charles T. Walker, who Reverend William Jefferson White had not reached a deference with regarding his Walker Baptist Institute at Eden, which further led the Morehouse College's predecessor to relocate to the new Capitol of Atlanta, Georgia. By 1879, it was transitioning.

Clergy–Educator Pipeline: Springfield's ministers and lay leaders were among the first Black teacher-preachers, embodying the

Reconstruction model where church, school, and civic leadership were inseparable.

Freedmen's Bureau Interface: The congregation worked informally with Freedmen's Bureau teachers and Baptist missionaries, helping stabilize early Black schooling in eastern Georgia.

Interpretive Importance

Springfield Baptist Church represents the missing institutional bridge between: enslaved clandestine education,
wartime freedom schools,
and formal Black colleges.
It demonstrates that Black higher education did not begin on campuses—it began in sanctuaries such as Eden Brush Harbor with its Walker Baptist Institute of Georgia.

Interpretive Insight
With the inclusion of Augusta Institute and Springfield Baptist Church, the timeline clearly shows how:

Black churches were the original infrastructure of Black higher education, transforming worship spaces into classrooms and congregations into governing boards during the Civil War and Reconstruction.

Augusta, Georgia emerges as a national seedbed for Black Baptist education whose influence reached Atlanta and beyond.

Comprehensive Chronological Map
Early Black Colleges & Universities (1800s)
By Year Founded · Religious Affiliation
1830s–1850s | Antebellum Foundations
Year Institution Location
1837 Cheyney University (PA)
1854 Lincoln University (PA)
1856 Wilberforce University (OH)

1860s |Civil War & Reconstruction Foundation

Year Institution Location
1865 Shaw University (NC)
1865 Atlanta University (Clark Atlanta) GA
1866 Fisk University (TN)
1866 Hampton University (VA)
1866 Edward Waters College (FL)
1867 Howard University (DC)
1867 Morehouse College (Augusta Inst) GA
1867Johnson C. Smith Univ (Biddle Coll) NC
1867 Barber-Scotia College (NC)
1867 Claflin University (SC)

Methodist Episcopal
1867 Talladega College (AL)
1868 Tougaloo College (MS)
1868 Freedman's College of SC (SC)
1869 Clark College (GA)
1869 Straight College (LA)
1869 Rust College (MS)
1867- 1969 Methodist Episcopal
1869 Lincoln University of Missouri (MO)
1869 Knoxville College (TN)
1870s |Black Denomination Control Expands
Year Institution Location
1870 Allen University (SC)
1871 LeMoyne-Owen College (TN)
1872 Paul Quinn College (TX)
1875 Selma University (AL)
1876 Stillman College (AL)
1877 Philander Smith University (AR)
1877 Bennett College (NC)
1879 Livingstone College (NC)
1879 Florida Memorial University (FL)
1879 George Smith College (Texas Coll) TX
1879 Simmons Bible Coll (Simmons Coll) KY

1880s|Post-Reconstruction Institution Growth

Year Institution Location

1880 Shorter College (AR)

1881 Spelman College (GA)

1881 Morris Brown College (GA)

1882 Lane College (TN)

1882 Paine College (GA)

1883 Virginia Union University (VA)

1883 Gammon Theological Sem (GA)

1884 Arkansas Baptist College (AR)

1884 Lomax-Hannon College (AL)

1887 Miles College (AL)

1887 Bishop College (TX)

1887 Jarvis Christian University (TX)

1887 Voorhees College (SC)

1889 Meharry Medical College (TN)

1889 Southwestern Christian Coll (TX)

1890s | Institutional Maturity

Year Institution Location

1890 Tuskegee University (AL)

1890 Morris College (SC)

1891 Wiley College (TX)

1894 Clinton College (SC)

1894 Hood Theological Seminary (NC)

1896 St. Augustine's University (NC)

1898 Xavier University of Louisiana (LA)

Mergers & Lineage Notes (Critical for Accuracy)

Texas College = George Smith College (AME)

Dillard University (1930) = Straight College (Congregational) + New Orleans University (Methodist)

Clark Atlanta University = Atlanta University + Clark College

Morehouse College = Augusta Institute (1867)

Chapter 13

Shockoe Bottom: The Place Where Enslavement Became a Commercial System and the Engine for Profit, and Public Memory

Shockoe Bottom did not secede from the Union—Virginia did!

Shockoe Bottom was a neighborhood and commercial district, not a political entity. It could not secede on its own.

Virginia seceded from the Union on April 17, 1861

Richmond (including Shockoe Bottom) followed because it was part of Virginia

Richmond became the Confederate capital shortly afterward

The political decision to secede was made by the Commonwealth of Virginia.

What conditions tied Shockoe Bottom to secession?

Conditions that sustained Shockoe Bottom strongly aligned Richmond's elite with the disunion.

A. Shockoe Bottom ***was central to the internal slave trade***

By ***the 1830s–1850s***, Shockoe Bottom was:
One of the largest slave markets in the Upper South

A hub exporting enslaved people to the Deep South

Deeply embedded in:

Banking
Insurance
Railroads
Warehousing
Legal services

Slavery was not incidental—it was infrastructural.

B. Secession threatened the survival of the slave economy By 1860:

The Republican Party threatened the expansion of slavery

Federal authority threatened:

Slave catchers
Property claims
Interstate slave commerce

Richmond's commercial class feared:

Loss of slave-based capital
Collapse of slave-backed credit systems
Shockoe Bottom represented capital at risk, not just ideology.

C. The Upper South feared becoming expendable

Virginia slaveholders worried that:

If slavery were restricted to the Deep South,
The Upper South would become a slave-export zone without political protection

Ironically, this fear grew because Shockoe Bottom had already sold so many people southward.

3. Where does Robert E. Lee actually fit?

After Virginia seceded, he:
Resigned from the U.S. Army

Accepted command of Virginia forces
Later led Confederate armies
Lee's role was military, not economic or legislative.

4. The deeper truth: Shockoe Bottom reveals why secession happened

Shockoe Bottom helps explain why Virginia ultimately chose disunion, even though many Virginians hesitated.

Shockoe Bottom represents:

The monetization of human beings
The conversion of enslaved people into political power

The link between:
Slave markets
Congressional representation
State political influence

Under the Constitution:
Enslaved people increased representation via the Three-Fifths Clause

But their ***sale southward threatened to reduce Virginia's future power***

Secession was an attempt to preserve both slavery and political relevance.

5. Smithsonian-style conclusion
A precise interpretive sentence would read:

Shockoe Bottom and the economic system it embodied—human commodification, political power derived from slavery, and fear of federal intervention—shaped Virginia's decision to leave the Union. The slave market reveals that secession was not merely ideological; it was structural.

Shockoe Bottom, Secession, and the Architecture of Power

Slave Markets, Political Representation, and the Road to Civil War

The story of American secession cannot be fully understood without examining Shockoe Bottom in Richmond, Virginia—one of the most significant domestic slave markets in the nineteenth century. Long before cannons fired on Fort Sumter, Shockoe Bottom functioned as an economic and political engine that bound slavery to national power. It reveals that secession was not a sudden emotional rupture but a calculated response to threats against a deeply entrenched system that converted enslaved human beings into wealth, representation, and political authority.[1]

By the 1830s and 1840s, Richmond had become a central hub in the interstate slave trade, supplying labor to the expanding cotton economies of Alabama, Mississippi, Louisiana, and Texas. Enslaved men, women, and children were sold in Shockoe Bottom, confined in nearby jails, marched in coffles, and transported south via railroads and coastal shipping routes.[2] These transactions generated enormous capital for slave traders, planters, banks, insurers, and municipal governments, embedding slavery directly into Virginia's financial infrastructure.[3]

This economic system translated directly into political power through the United States Constitution. The Three-Fifths Compromise counted enslaved people toward state population totals for congressional representation and presidential elections, even though they possessed no legal rights.[4] As a result, Virginia and other slaveholding states wielded disproportionate influence in Congress, the Electoral College, and the federal judiciary. Enslaved people increased the political power of those who enslaved them—turning human captivity into representation.[5]

Yet Shockoe Bottom also exposed a growing contradiction. As Virginia sold tens of thousands of enslaved people to the Deep South, it weakened its own demographic base while strengthening rival slave states.[6] At the same time, national debates over the expansion of slavery into western territories threatened to limit the future growth of slave-based political power. The rise of the Republican Party, which opposed the extension of slavery, intensified fears among Virginia's political and economic elites that their dominance within the Union was eroding.[7]

These pressures culminated in the secession crisis of 1860–1861. While Robert E. Lee's decision to side with Virginia has often been framed as personal loyalty to his home state, that loyalty existed within a broader structural reality: Virginia's wealth, status, and political influence were inseparable from slavery.[8]

Shockoe Bottom demonstrates that secession was not merely ideological—it was defensive. Southern leaders understood that the survival of slavery was essential to preserving their economic system and their political power.[9]

The Civil War shattered this system but did not immediately dismantle its underlying logic. Emancipation destroyed slavery as property, but it also nullified the Three-Fifths Compromise by eliminating the legal category of enslaved persons.[10] The Thirteenth Amendment ended slavery, the Fourteenth Amendment established birthright citizenship and equal protection under the law, and the Fifteenth Amendment prohibited racial discrimination in voting. Together, these Reconstruction Amendments redefined the relationship between labor, citizenship, and political power.[11]

In this context, Shockoe Bottom becomes not only a site of trauma but a site of truth. It reveals why secession happened, how slavery shaped the Constitution, and why Reconstruction education networks—such as Freedmen's Bureau schools and church-based institutions—emerged as battlegrounds over the meaning of freedom.[12] The struggle after the Civil War was not simply about ending slavery, but about determining whether formerly enslaved people would gain access to education, political participation, and full citizenship.[13]

The legacy of Shockoe Bottom endures because the structures it exposed did not vanish overnight. Instead, they evolved—through Black Codes, voter suppression, and educational inequality. Yet

Reconstruction also planted seeds of transformation. Education became the central strategy through which formerly enslaved people claimed citizenship, built institutions, and challenged the political order that slavery had created.[14]

Understanding Shockoe Bottom forces a reckoning with the deeper truth of American secession: the Confederacy was founded to protect a system in which human bondage produced wealth, wealth produced power, and power was preserved through law. In confronting this history, Shockoe Bottom stands as a critical site of national memory—one that reveals how democracy was compromised, contested, and ultimately reimagined.[15]

Chapter 14

From Coast to Nation: Indigenous Peoples and the Trails Before Shockoe Bottom

Before Shockoe Bottom became a marketplace, a rail corridor, or a site of human sale, it was a crossroads.

Long before European ships reached the Atlantic coast or colonial governments imposed boundaries, Indigenous peoples shaped the lands that would become Virginia through networks of movement, diplomacy, and stewardship. These networks—river corridors, footpaths, and trade routes—connected the coast to the interior, the Chesapeake to the Piedmont, and local communities to continental systems of exchange. Shockoe Bottom emerged within this older Indigenous geography, not as a beginning point, but as an interruption.

To understand the origins of American power and democracy, we must first understand the Indigenous world that structured this landscape before colonization.

Indigenous Landscapes Before Colonization

Indigenous societies in the mid-Atlantic did not organize space through fixed borders in the European sense. Instead, land was understood relationally—through seasonal movement, kinship, trade, and responsibility. The rivers, including the James River (Powhatan's River), were not obstacles to settlement but lifelines connecting communities.

The area that would later be called Shockoe Bottom sat near the fall line of the James River, where tidal waters met rocky uplands. This location made it a natural point of transition and exchange. Indigenous peoples traveled through this space long before colonial roads were cut into the land. Trails followed riverbanks, ridgelines, and ecological zones, linking fishing grounds, agricultural villages, hunting territories, and ceremonial sites.

These trails were not random paths. They represented knowledge accumulated over generations—of terrain, seasons, and relationships among nations.

The Powhatan Paramount Chiefdom

At the time of English arrival in the early seventeenth century, the region was part of the political world of the Powhatan Paramount Chiefdom, a sophisticated alliance of Algonquian-speaking peoples led by Wahunsenacawh, known to the English as Chief Powhatan.

The Powhatan polity was not a loose confederation but a strategic system of governance. It coordinated tribute, managed diplomacy, and controlled access to key waterways and trails. Power was exercised through relationships, not written law. Authority rested on the ability to maintain balance—between communities, with the environment, and with neighboring nations.

Shockoe Bottom lay near the western edge of Powhatan influence, close to routes leading into the interior where Siouan-speaking peoples lived. As such, it was a liminal zone—a place of contact, negotiation, and movement.

Trails as Political Infrastructure

Indigenous trails functioned as political infrastructure. They enabled trade, alliance-building, and conflict resolution. Shell beads, copper, stone tools, foodstuffs, and ceremonial objects moved along these routes. So did information—news of alliances, disputes, and environmental changes.

These trails also structured diplomacy. Who could travel where, and under what conditions, reflected power relationships. Control of movement meant control of influence.

European colonists would later build roads, railways, and canals along these same routes. What appeared to them as “natural” pathways were, in fact, Indigenous knowledge systems embedded in the land.

First Contact and Disruption

When English settlers established Jamestown in 1607, they entered an already-ordered world. Early survival depended on Indigenous trade networks, agricultural knowledge, and diplomacy. The English quickly learned the value of Indigenous trails and river routes—but they interpreted them through a different worldview.

Where Indigenous peoples saw shared landscapes shaped by reciprocal responsibility, colonists saw land to be owned, fenced, and exploited. Trails became roads; rivers became shipping lanes; villages became obstacles to expansion.

As colonial settlements expanded upriver toward the fall line, Indigenous movement was increasingly constrained. Violence, disease, and displacement disrupted long-standing relationships to place. Treaties—often coerced or violated—redefined Indigenous homelands into colonial property.

Shockoe Bottom as a Colonial Reordering of Space

By the eighteenth century, the Indigenous geography of the James River corridor had been radically transformed. Trails that once connected Native communities were absorbed into colonial infrastructure. Shockoe Bottom emerged as a site of commercial exchange precisely because it sat atop these older pathways.

The transformation was not merely physical. It represented a shift in how power operated. Indigenous mobility was replaced by colonial control of movement. Land that once held layered meanings became commodified. Human beings—first Indigenous captives, then overwhelmingly enslaved Africans—were incorporated into a new economy of extraction.

Shockoe Bottom thus stands at the intersection of two worlds: one defined by relational geography and one by racialized capitalism.

Indigenous Dispossession and the Foundations of Democracy

As colonial Virginia developed institutions later celebrated as democratic—courts, assemblies, markets—it did so on land taken from Indigenous peoples. Indigenous exclusion was not incidental to democracy's development; it was foundational.

The political rights extended to white male colonists depended on the removal of Indigenous authority and presence. Indigenous nations were positioned as external to the emerging political community, even though their lands underwrote colonial prosperity.

Democracy, in this sense, was territorial. It required space cleared of competing claims.

Memory, Erasure, and the Trail Beneath the City

Today, little visible evidence remains of the Indigenous trails beneath Shockoe Bottom. Pavement covers pathways once worn by generations of Native travelers. Yet the landscape retains its memory.

Understanding Shockoe Bottom requires seeing beneath the colonial and industrial layers to recognize the Indigenous geography that came before. Doing so reframes the site not only as a place of enslavement and commerce, but as a disrupted Indigenous crossroads.

This recognition does not romanticize the past. It restores complexity. It reminds us that American history did not begin with colonization—and that democracy emerged through processes of displacement as well as aspiration.

From Coast to Nation

The journey from coast to nation was not inevitable. It was shaped by choices—about whose knowledge mattered, whose movement was permitted, and whose sovereignty was erased.

Indigenous peoples shaped the land long before Shockoe Bottom existed. Their trails structured the region's geography. Their displacement made colonial expansion possible. A full understanding of American origins must begin here.

Before there was a nation, there were nations.

Expansion, Labor, and the Making of Colonial America, 1619–1776

The expansion of the English colonies from the early seventeenth century to the American Revolution ***was neither accidental nor inevitable. It was made possible through labor—specifically, the coerced labor of Africans who arrived in Virginia*** beginning in 1619. From that moment forward, African labor became the essential force through which land was transformed, infrastructure constructed, and wealth accumulated.

This chapter draws upon scholarship in African American history, Atlantic world studies, and colonial Virginia history to examine how enslaved African labor made colonial expansion—and ultimately the American Revolution—possible.

Colonial expansion must therefore be understood not simply as European settlement, but as a process engineered and sustained by enslaved Africans over more than a century and a half.

In the decades following 1619, the English colonies faced a fundamental challenge: vast territories existed, but the labor required to make them productive did not. European mortality

rates were high, voluntary migration was limited, and indentured servitude proved unstable. Enslaved Africans filled this gap. Their labor converted forests into fields, marshes into arable land, and riverbanks into productive plantation zones. In Virginia, enslaved people cleared land along the Chesapeake and its tributaries, establishing the tobacco economy that would dominate colonial life and tie the colony firmly to the Atlantic world.

As plantation agriculture expanded, so too did the physical landscape of the colonies. Roads emerged where enslaved labor widened Indigenous paths. River landings and docks were constructed to move goods from inland farms to coastal ports. Towns grew at the intersections of trade routes, often anchored by warehouses, markets, and shipping points built and maintained by enslaved workers. Places such as Shockoe Bottom in Richmond illustrate how commerce, transportation, and bondage converged in the same physical space. What appeared as colonial growth was, in reality, the accumulation of infrastructure produced through forced labor.

By the eighteenth century, African labor had generated immense wealth for colonial elites. Tobacco exports financed land acquisition, political authority, and commercial networks that extended across the Atlantic. This wealth fostered a class of planters and merchants who viewed themselves as economic equals of their British counterparts. The confidence to challenge imperial authority emerged only after decades of prosperity secured through slavery. Colonial self-sufficiency—in food production, transportation, and internal trade—was not a natural condition but the result of enslaved labor sustaining the colonies over generations.

Expansion also depended on social control. Enslaved Africans allowed a relatively small European population to dominate large territories. By removing enslaved people from the political body while exploiting their labor, colonial leaders stabilized their authority and justified continued land seizure from Indigenous nations. Slavery thus functioned not only as an economic system but as a mechanism of territorial and population management that enabled westward growth.

By the eve of the American Revolution, the colonies possessed the infrastructure necessary to resist British rule: roads capable of moving troops, farms able to feed armies, ports supplying weapons and trade, and towns serving as centers of political organizing. Each of these systems rested on enslaved labor. At the same time, British policies increasingly threatened colonial control over land and slavery itself. Legal decisions such as Somerset v. Stewart and wartime proclamations offering freedom to enslaved people intensified fears among slaveholding elites. Independence promised to secure what rebellion required: continued control over the labor system that had built the colonies.

The American Revolution, therefore, was fought in a landscape shaped by slavery. From 1619 to 1776, enslaved Africans made colonial expansion possible by transforming land into wealth and infrastructure into power. The liberty declared in 1776 rested upon a foundation constructed by those denied its benefits. Understanding this reality does not diminish the Revolution; it reveals the full complexity of a nation born from both freedom and unfreedom, inseparably linked from its earliest days.

Conclusion: Democracy Comes of Age

All great narratives must come to its end, but the interpretive narrative lives for the future generation. The Deuce Millennium Generation and the Closing of America's Democracy Gap

will be tested not only by the laws it passes, but by the generations that inherit them. In the late twentieth century, the Civil Rights Movement revealed this profound truth:

American democracy had matured in principle faster than it had in practice.

Constitutional amendments and landmark legislation declared equality, yet daily life—in housing, education, voting, and justice—continued to reflect deep inequality.

For America250, the task before the nation is not simply to change laws, but to change outcomes. So, as celebrations occur, that task would fall to the generations that follow.

A New Generational Framework

In 1997, that new generation was born—what Dr. Jesse J. Hargrove coined was the Deuce Millennium Generation (DMG). Defined as beginning in 1997 and extending forward in approximately 18-year generational intervals through the year 3001, the DMG is not a single cohort, but a continuum of democracy inheritance—52 generations tasked with carrying forth democracy from its second millennium struggles into its third millennium responsibilities.

The DMG was born not at the beginning of a democracy experiment, but at a moment when the nation could no longer afford delay between promise and practice.

What the Civil Rights Movement Made Visible

The Civil Rights Movement did more than dismantle legal segregation. It exposed the distance between what America said about itself and how it treated its people. The movement forced democracy to look at itself honestly—and that act of self-recognition changed the trajectory of the nation.

For the DMG, this exposure mattered. They were raised in a society where the gap had been named, studied, archived, and taught. Memory became infrastructure. History became instruction.

Democracy did not forget its failures; it learned from them.

From Principle to Practice—Without Delay

For the Deuce Millennium Generation, democracy maturity accelerated. Laws were no longer allowed to stand alone without enforcement, access, and accountability. Civic systems evolved with intention:

Housing policy moved from prohibition of discrimination toward measurable inclusion

Education shifted from access alone to equity in resources and outcomes

Voting rights were protected as foundational, not negotiable

Justice systems were scrutinized not just for legality, but for fairness

For the DMG, apprehension did not linger across generations. Democracy responded in real time—closing gaps as they were revealed, not generations later.

This was not inevitability. It was choice.

How Democracy Matured With the DMG

Democracy matured for the DMG because it adopted the habits of adulthood:

Responsibility over rhetoric
Repair over denial
Participation over exclusion

Civic education expanded. Public memory was preserved. Institutions were redesigned to reflect the people they served. Democracy learned to listen—especially to its youngest citizens, the Deuce Millennium Generation.

The DMG did not inherit a perfect Union. They inherited a teachable one.

America250: Forming a More Perfect Union

The Constitution does not promise a perfect democracy. It promises a more perfect one—an ongoing process of refinement. For the DMG, this refinement became structural, not symbolic.

Each generation within the Deuce Millennium carries forward a democracy that understands maturity as movement—toward fairness, toward inclusion, toward accountability.

Figure 1. The Hargrove Deuce Millennium Map (DMG → 3MG)

Charting Fifty-Three Generations of Human Passage

The Hargrove Deuce Millennium Map is not a forecast—it is a long view of responsibility.

Stretching across more than a thousand years, the Map traces 53 distinct Deuce Millennium Generations (DMGs), each representing a cohort of students who will enter P–12 education, mature into civic life, and ultimately shape society's moral, intellectual, and institutional character. Together, these generations form a continuous human relay—from DMG-1 (1997) to the threshold of 3MG (Year 3000).

This framework insists on a radical premise:

Education is not episodic; it is civilizational.

Each DMG spans approximately 18 years, aligning with the developmental arc from birth to adulthood. The Map therefore functions simultaneously as:

a pedagogical timeline,

a societal accountability chart, and

a moral ledger of intergenerational stewardship.

The Hargrove Deuce Millennium Chart

From DMG-1 to 3MG
DMG-1 (1997–2015)
DMG-2 (2016–2034)
DMG-3 (2035–2053)
DMG-4 (2054–2072)
DMG-5 (2073–2091)
DMG-6 (2092–2110)
DMG-7 (2111–2129)
DMG-8 (2130–2148)
DMG-9 (2149–2167)
DMG-10 (2168–2186)
DMG-11 (2187–2205)
DMG-12 (2206–2224)
DMG-13 (2225–2243)
DMG-14 (2244–2262)
DMG-15 (2263–2281)

DMG-16 (2282–2300)
DMG-17 (2301–2319)
DMG-18 (2320–2338)
DMG-19 (2339–2357)
DMG-20 (2358–2376)
DMG-21 (2377–2395)
DMG-22 (2396–2414)
DMG-23 (2415–2433)
DMG-24 (2434–2452)
DMG-25 (2453–2471)
DMG-26 (2472–2490)
DMG-27 (2491–2509)
DMG-28 (2510–2528)
DMG-29 (2529–2547)
DMG-30 (2548–2566)
DMG-31 (2567–2585)
DMG-32 (2586–2604)
DMG-33 (2605–2623)
DMG-34 (2624–2642)
DMG-35 (2643–2661)
DMG-36 (2662–2680)
DMG-37 (2681–2699)
DMG-38 (2700–2718)
DMG-39 (2719–2737)
DMG-40 (2738–2756)
DMG-41 (2757–2775)
DMG-42 (2776–2794)
DMG-43 (2795–2813)
DMG-44 (2814–2832)
DMG-45 (2833–2851)
DMG-46 (2852–2870)
DMG-47 (2871–2889)
DMG-48 (2890–2908)
DMG-49 (2909–2927)
DMG-50 (2928–2946)
DMG-51 (2947–2965)

DMG-52 (2966–2984)
DMG-53 (2985–3000)
3MG

The Third Millennium Generation: Arrival, Reckoning, Renewal

Interpretive Note

The Deuce Millennium framework reframes time not as destiny, but as duty. Each DMG inherits the unfinished work of the last—educationally, ethically, and structurally. The question posed by the Map is simple and unsettling:

What kind of world are we preparing for people we will never meet—but are fully responsible for?

Editorial Note

Progress is no longer episodic. It is expected.
A more perfect Union is formed when:

Equality is experienced, not deferred
Rights are exercised, not defended repeatedly
Democracy grows with its people, not ahead of them

The Legacy of Learning

The greatest lesson passed to the Deuce Millennium Generation was not optimism—it was instruction. The DMG learned that democracy works when it is practiced daily, corrected openly, and shared fully.

The Civil Rights Movement closed the distance between ideals and reality by exposing the gap. The DMG closed it by refusing to let it reopen.

Democracy did not simply survive into the third millennium.

It matured—because the Deuce Millennium Generation matured with it.
A Union still forming.

A democracy still learning.
A future no longer waiting.

BIBLIOGRAPHY & REFERENCES

Chapter 6 *The Trade Within: Method, Memory, and the Domestic Slave Trade in American History*

Notes (Chicago Notes–Bibliography Style)

Steven Deyle, Carry Me Back: The Domestic Slave Trade in American Life (New York: Oxford University Press, 2005), 1–18.

Walter Johnson, Soul by Soul: Life Inside the Antebellum Slave Market (Cambridge, MA: Harvard University Press, 1999), 1–12.

Michael Tadman, Speculators and Slaves: Masters, Traders, and Slaves in the Old South (Madison: University of Wisconsin Press, 1989), 3–21.

Edward E. Baptist, The Half Has Never Been Told (New York: Basic Books, 2014), 89–121.

Daina Ramey Berry, The Price for Their Pound of Flesh (Boston: Beacon Press, 2017), 1–30.

Michel-Rolph Trouillot, Silencing the Past (Boston: Beacon Press, 1995), 26–30.

Wilma King, Stolen Childhood: Slave Youth in Nineteenth-Century America (Bloomington: Indiana University Press, 1995), 1–15.

Heather Andrea Williams, Help Me to Find My People (Chapel Hill: University of North Carolina Press, 2012), 1–12.

National Museum of African American History and Culture, "Domestic Slave Trade Interpretive Framework," Smithsonian Institution, internal document.

Bibliography (Chicago Style)

Baptist, Edward E. The Half Has Never Been Told: Slavery and the Making of American Capitalism. New York: Basic Books, 2014.

Berry, Daina Ramey. The Price for Their Pound of Flesh. Boston: Beacon Press, 2017.

Deyle, Steven. Carry Me Back: The Domestic Slave Trade in American Life. New York: Oxford University Press, 2005.

Johnson, Walter. Soul by Soul: Life Inside the Antebellum Slave Market. Cambridge, MA: Harvard University Press, 1999.

King, Wilma. Stolen Childhood: Slave Youth in Nineteenth-Century America. Bloomington: Indiana University Press, 1995.

Tadman, Michael. Speculators and Slaves. Madison: University of Wisconsin Press, 1989.

Trouillot, Michel-Rolph. Silencing the Past: Power and the Production of History. Boston: Beacon Press, 1995.

Williams, Heather Andrea. Help Me to Find My People. Chapel Hill: University of North Carolina Press, 2012.

Chapter 7 *Celia Adams and Children of Commerce: Enslaved Childhood and the Logic of the Domestic Slave Trade*

Notes

Steven Deyle, Carry Me Back: The Domestic Slave Trade in American Life (New York: Oxford University Press, 2005), 54–78.

Daina Ramey Berry, The Price for Their Pound of Flesh: The Value of the Enslaved, from Womb to Grave (Boston: Beacon Press, 2017), 31–70.

Walter Johnson, Soul by Soul: Life Inside the Antebellum Slave Market (Cambridge, MA: Harvard University Press, 1999), 45–76.

Michael Tadman, Speculators and Slaves: Masters, Traders, and Slaves in the Old South (Madison: University of Wisconsin Press, 1989), 133–167.

Heather Andrea Williams, Help Me to Find My People (Chapel Hill: University of North Carolina Press, 2012), 1–38.

Thavolia Glymph, Out of the House of Bondage (Cambridge: Cambridge University Press, 2008), 67–102.

Wilma King, Stolen Childhood: Slave Youth in Nineteenth-Century America (Bloomington: Indiana University Press, 1995), 1–29.

Stephanie E. Jones-Rogers, They Were Her Property (New Haven: Yale University Press, 2019), 41–66.

Federal Writers' Project, Slave Narratives: A Folk History of Slavery in the United States, vol. 4 (Washington, DC: Government Printing Office, 1941).

Michel-Rolph Trouillot, Silencing the Past (Boston: Beacon Press, 1995), 26–30.

Bibliography (Chicago Style)

Berry, Daina Ramey. The Price for Their Pound of Flesh. Boston: Beacon Press, 2017.

Deyle, Steven. Carry Me Back. New York: Oxford University Press, 2005.

Glymph, Thavolia. Out of the House of Bondage. Cambridge: Cambridge University Press, 2008.

Johnson, Walter. Soul by Soul. Cambridge, MA: Harvard University Press, 1999.

Jones-Rogers, Stephanie E. They Were Her Property. New Haven: Yale University Press, 2019.

King, Wilma. Stolen Childhood. Bloomington: Indiana University Press, 1995.

Tadman, Michael. Speculators and Slaves. Madison: University of Wisconsin Press, 1989.

Williams, Heather Andrea. Help Me to Find My People. Chapel Hill: University of North Carolina Press, 2012.

Chapter 7 *Celia Adams and Children of Commerce: Enslaved Childhood and the Logic of the Domestic Slave Trade*

Primary Sources
Federal Writers' Project.

Slave Narratives: A Folk History of Slavery in the United States from Interviews with Former Slaves.

Vol. IV, Georgia Narratives. Washington, DC: Library of Congress, 1936–1938.

— Contextual source documenting lived experiences of formerly enslaved Georgians contemporaneous with Celia Adams's lifetime; used for comparative interpretation rather than direct testimony.

Library of Congress.
Born in Slavery: Slave Narratives from the Federal Writers' Project, 1936–1938.

Manuscript Division, Washington, DC.

— Foundational archive for interpreting memory, trauma, sale, and forced migration patterns similar to those experienced by Celia Adams.

Virginia Slave Trade Records (Richmond).
Shockoe Bottom Jail, Auction, and Trader Records, 19th century.

— Documentary evidence for the Richmond slave trade ecosystem in which Celia Adams and her brothers were sold.

Jefferson County, Georgia, Probate and Sale Records.

19th-century estate and transaction documents.

— Used to contextualize forced sale routes from Virginia to Georgia.

Family and Descendant Sources

Hargrove, Jesse.
The Legacy of Celia Adams.
Unpublished family history manuscript; descendant oral history collection.

— Primary descendant account documenting Celia Adams's birth (1856), sale from Richmond to Louisville, Georgia, and oral memory of the slave market experience.

Oral Histories, Adams–Hargrove Family Collection.

Recorded descendant testimonies, late 20th–early 21st century.

— Multigenerational memory source used with interpretive care and corroboration.

Secondary Scholarship (Contextual & Interpretive)

Baptist, Edward E.
The Half Has Never Been Told: Slavery and the Making of American Capitalism.
New York: Basic Books, 2014.

— Interprets the domestic slave trade system that structured Celia Adams's sale from Richmond.

Berry, Daina Ramey.
The Price for Their Pound of Flesh: The Value of the Enslaved, from Womb to Grave.
Boston: Beacon Press, 2017.

— Essential for understanding bodily valuation, sale rituals, and trauma embedded in slave markets.

Camp, Stephanie M. H.
Closer to Freedom: Enslaved Women and Everyday Resistance in the Plantation South.
Chapel Hill: University of North Carolina Press, 2004.

— Provides interpretive framework for enslaved women's agency, memory, and survival.

Johnson, Walter.
Soul by Soul: Life Inside the Antebellum Slave Market.
Cambridge, MA: Harvard University Press, 1999.

— Definitive study of slave market practices, including public inspection and sale rituals like those remembered in Celia Adams's story.

Schwarz, Philip J.
Slave Laws in Virginia.
Athens: University of Georgia Press, 1996.

— Legal context for enslavement, sale, and family separation in Richmond.

Shockoe Bottom–Specific Scholarship
Campbell, Benjamin, and Maurie McInnis, eds.
Slavery and the University: Histories and Legacies.
Athens: University of Georgia Press, 2019.

— Situates Shockoe Bottom within broader systems of incarceration, education, and memory.

Richmond Slave Trail Commission.
Shockoe Bottom Memorialization Reports.
City of Richmond, Virginia.
— Official documentation linking Shockoe Bottom to national slave trading networks.

Methodological & Museum Practice Sources
National Museum of African American History and Culture.

Talking About Slavery: Interpretive Frameworks.
Smithsonian Institution.

— Guides ethical use of oral history, descendant memory, and traumatic narratives.

Trouillot, Michel-Rolph.
Silencing the Past: Power and the Production of History.
Boston: Beacon Press, 1995.

— Foundational framework for interpreting absence in the archival record, especially relevant where Celia Adams does not appear in WPA interviews.

Chapter 8 B*orn into the Market: Celia Adams, Enslaved Childhood, and Forced Migration in the Domestic Slave Trade*

Notes (Footnotes / Endnotes – Chicago Style)

These may be formatted as footnotes or converted to endnotes without alteration.

Walter Johnson, Soul by Soul: Life Inside the Antebellum Slave Market (Cambridge, MA: Harvard University Press, 1999), 3–6.

Maurie D. McInnis, Slaves Waiting for Sale: Abolitionist Art and the American Slave Trade (Chicago: University of Chicago Press, 2011), 15–42.

Library of Virginia, "The Richmond Slave Trade," Virginia Untold Project, accessed [2026].

Edward E. Baptist, The Half Has Never Been Told: Slavery and the Making of American Capitalism (New York: Basic Books, 2014), 129–162.

Steven Deyle, Carry Me Back: The Domestic Slave Trade in American Life (New York: Oxford University Press, 2005), 21–54.

Tadman, Michael. Speculators and Slaves: Masters, Traders, and Slaves in the Old South (Madison: University of Wisconsin Press, 1989), 112–145.

Alexandria W. Smith and Marie Tyler-McGraw, "Shockoe Bottom: Slavery and Public Memory," Virginia Magazine of History and Biography 123, no. 4 (2015): 364–395.

James Hopkins Adams, "Message to the South Carolina Legislature," 1856, South Carolina Department of Archives and History.

Lacy K. Ford Jr., Deliver Us from Evil: The Slavery Question in the Old South (New York: Oxford University Press, 2009), 256–260.

Daina Ramey Berry, The Price for Their Pound of Flesh: The Value of the Enslaved, from Womb to Grave (Boston: Beacon Press, 2017), 71–98.

Heather Andrea Williams, Help Me to Find My People: The African American Search for Family Lost in Slavery (Chapel Hill: University of North Carolina Press, 2012), 1–27.

U.S. Bureau of Refugees, Freedmen, and Abandoned Lands (Freedmen's Bureau), Georgia Field Office Records, National Archives Microfilm Publication M1903.

U.S. Census Bureau, 1870 and 1880 Census Schedules, Jefferson County, Georgia.

Thavolia Glymph, Out of the House of Bondage: The Transformation of the Plantation Household (Cambridge: Cambridge University Press, 2008), 179–203.

Saidiya Hartman, Lose Your Mother: A Journey Along the Atlantic Slave Route (New York: Farrar, Straus and Giroux, 2007), 17–21.

Tiya Miles, All That She Carried: The Journey of Ashley's Sack, a Black Family Keepsake (New York: Random House, 2021), 201–227.

Michel-Rolph Trouillot, Silencing the Past: Power and the Production of History (Boston: Beacon Press, 1995), 26–30.

National Museum of African American History and Culture, “Domestic Slave Trade Interpretive Framework,” Smithsonian Institution, internal document.

Bibliography

Primary Sources

Adams, James Hopkins. Message to the Legislature of South Carolina. Columbia, SC, 1856.

Freedmen’s Bureau. Records of the Field Offices for the State of Georgia, 1865–1872.

National Archives Microfilm Publication M1903.

Library of Virginia. Virginia Untold: The African American Narrative. Richmond, VA.

U.S. Census Bureau. Population Schedules, 1870 and 1880. Jefferson County, Georgia.

Secondary Sources

Baptist, Edward E. The Half Has Never Been Told: Slavery and the Making of American Capitalism. New York: Basic Books, 2014.

Berry, Daina Ramey. The Price for Their Pound of Flesh: The Value of the Enslaved, from Womb to Grave. Boston: Beacon Press, 2017.

Deyle, Steven. Carry Me Back: The Domestic Slave Trade in American Life. New York: Oxford University Press, 2005.

Ford Jr., Lacy K. Deliver Us from Evil: The Slavery Question in the Old South. New York: Oxford University Press, 2009.

Glymph, Thavolia. Out of the House of Bondage. Cambridge: Cambridge University Press, 2008.

Hartman, Saidiya. Lose Your Mother. New York: Farrar, Straus and Giroux, 2007.

Johnson, Walter. Soul by Soul. Cambridge, MA: Harvard University Press, 1999.

McInnis, Maurie D. Slaves Waiting for Sale. Chicago: University of Chicago Press, 2011.

Miles, Tiya. All That She Carried. New York: Random House, 2021.

Tadman, Michael. Speculators and Slaves. Madison: University of Wisconsin Press, 1989.

Trouillot, Michel-Rolph. Silencing the Past. Boston: Beacon Press, 1995.

Williams, Heather Andrea. Help Me to Find My People. Chapel Hill: University of North Carolina Press, 2012.

Short-Form Exhibition Bibliography (Catalog or Wall Panel)

Walter Johnson, Soul by Soul
Steven Deyle, Carry Me Back
Daina Ramey Berry, The Price for Their Pound of Flesh
Library of Virginia, Virginia Untold
National Archives, Freedmen's Bureau Records
Journal of African American History Adaptation Notes
Footnotes preferred (not endnotes)
Chicago Notes–Bibliography fully acceptable
Emphasis on archival grounding + historiography

Chapter 9 *Slavery in Motion: Shockoe Bottom and the Architecture of the Domestic Slave Trade*

Notes (Footnotes or Endnotes – Chicago Style)
Walter Johnson, Soul by Soul: Life Inside the Antebellum Slave Market (Cambridge, MA: Harvard University Press, 1999), 3–14.

Steven Deyle, Carry Me Back: The Domestic Slave Trade in American Life (New York: Oxford University Press, 2005), 1–32.

Michael Tadman, Speculators and Slaves: Masters, Traders, and Slaves in the Old South (Madison: University of Wisconsin Press, 1989), 9–40.

Library of Virginia, "The Richmond Slave Trade," Virginia Untold Project, accessed [2026].

Maurie D. McInnis, Slaves Waiting for Sale: Abolitionist Art and the American Slave Trade (Chicago: University of Chicago Press, 2011), 17–51.

Alexandria W. Smith and Marie Tyler-McGraw, "Shockoe Bottom: Slavery and Public Memory," Virginia Magazine of History and Biography 123, no. 4 (2015): 364–395.

Edward E. Baptist, The Half Has Never Been Told: Slavery and the Making of American Capitalism (New York: Basic Books, 2014), 121–166.

Daina Ramey Berry, The Price for Their Pound of Flesh: The Value of the Enslaved, from Womb to Grave (Boston: Beacon Press, 2017), 63–99.

Lacy K. Ford Jr., Deliver Us from Evil: The Slavery Question in the Old South (New York: Oxford University Press, 2009), 248–270.

James Hopkins Adams, Message to the Legislature of South Carolina, 1856, South Carolina Department of Archives and History.

U.S. Congress, An Act to Prohibit the Importation of Slaves, 1807.

Thavolia Glymph, Out of the House of Bondage: The Transformation of the Plantation Household (Cambridge: Cambridge University Press, 2008), 156–205.

Heather Andrea Williams, Help Me to Find My People: The African American Search for Family Lost in Slavery (Chapel Hill: University of North Carolina Press, 2012), 1–24.

Michel-Rolph Trouillot, Silencing the Past: Power and the Production of History (Boston: Beacon Press, 1995), 26–30.

National Museum of African American History and Culture, "Domestic Slave Trade Interpretive Framework," Smithsonian Institution, internal document.

Bibliography (Chicago Style)

Primary Sources

Adams, James Hopkins. Message to the Legislature of South Carolina. Columbia, SC, 1856.

Library of Virginia. Virginia Untold: The African American Narrative. Richmond, VA.

South Carolina Department of Archives and History. Legislative Papers, Governor James H. Adams.

U.S. Congress. An Act to Prohibit the Importation of Slaves. 1807.

Secondary Sources

Baptist, Edward E. The Half Has Never Been Told: Slavery and the Making of American Capitalism. New York: Basic Books, 2014.

Berry, Daina Ramey. The Price for Their Pound of Flesh: The Value of the Enslaved, from Womb to Grave. Boston: Beacon Press, 2017.

Deyle, Steven. Carry Me Back: The Domestic Slave Trade in American Life. New York: Oxford University Press, 2005.

Ford Jr., Lacy K. Deliver Us from Evil: The Slavery Question in the Old South. New York: Oxford University Press, 2009.

Glymph, Thavolia. Out of the House of Bondage. Cambridge: Cambridge University Press, 2008.

Johnson, Walter. Soul by Soul. Cambridge, MA: Harvard University Press, 1999.

McInnis, Maurie D. Slaves Waiting for Sale. Chicago: University of Chicago Press, 2011.

Smith, Alexandria W., and Marie Tyler-McGraw. "Shockoe Bottom: Slavery and Public Memory." Virginia Magazine of History and Biography 123, no. 4 (2015): 364–395.

Tadman, Michael. Speculators and Slaves. Madison: University of Wisconsin Press, 1989.

Trouillot, Michel-Rolph. Silencing the Past. Boston: Beacon Press, 1995.

Williams, Heather Andrea. Help Me to Find My People. Chapel Hill: University of North Carolina Press, 2012.

Short-Form Exhibition Bibliography (Catalog / Wall Panel)

Walter Johnson, Soul by Soul
Steven Deyle, Carry Me Back
Daina Ramey Berry, The Price for Their Pound of Flesh
Library of Virginia, Virginia Untold
Alexandria W. Smith and Marie Tyler-McGraw, "Shockoe Bottom

Chapter 10 *Freedom Is Not a Destination: Celia Adams, Emancipation, and Reconstruction Survival*

Primary Sources

U.S. Government & Legal Records

U.S. Constitution. Article I, Section 2; Amendments XIII, XIV, XV.

Congressional Globe. 39th–41st Congresses. Washington, DC.

United States Statutes at Large. Reconstruction Acts, 1867–1868.

Freedmen's Bureau. Records of the Bureau of Refugees, Freedmen, and Abandoned Lands. Record Group 105. National Archives, Washington, DC.

Works Progress Administration

Federal Writers' Project. Slave Narratives: A Folk History of Slavery in the United States from Interviews with Former Slaves. Washington, DC: Government Printing Office, 1941.
– Georgia Narratives
– Virginia Narratives

Judicial Decisions

Dred Scott v. Sandford, 60 U.S. (19 How.) 393 (1857).

The Slaughter-House Cases, 83 U.S. (16 Wall.) 36 (1873).

United States v. Reese, 92 U.S. 214 (1876).

Secondary Sources
Reconstruction & Constitutional History

Du Bois, W.E.B. Black Reconstruction in America, 1860–1880. New York: Free Press, 1935.

Foner, Eric. Reconstruction: America's Unfinished Revolution, 1863–1877. New York: Harper & Row, 1988.

Foner, Eric. The Second Founding: How the Civil War and Reconstruction Remade the Constitution. New York: W.W. Norton, 2019.

Amar, Akhil Reed. America's Constitution: A Biography. New York: Random House, 2005.

Slavery, Geography, and the Internal Slave Trade

Johnson, Walter. Soul by Soul: Life Inside the Antebellum Slave Market. Cambridge, MA: Harvard University Press, 1999.

Baptist, Edward E. The Half Has Never Been Told: Slavery and the Making of American Capitalism. New York: Basic Books, 2014.

Tadman, Michael. Speculators and Slaves: Masters, Traders, and Slaves in the Old South. Madison: University of Wisconsin Press, 1989.

Richmond Slave Trail Commission. Shockoe Bottom Documentation and Public History Reports. Richmond, VA.

Education and Freedom

Anderson, James D. The Education of Blacks in the South, 1860–1935. Chapel Hill: University of North Carolina Press, 1988.

Butchart, Ronald E. Schooling the Freed People: Teaching, Learning, and the Struggle for Black Freedom, 1861–1876. Chapel Hill: University of North Carolina Press, 2010.

Williams, Heather Andrea. Self-Taught: African American Education in Slavery and Freedom. Chapel Hill: University of North Carolina Press, 2005.

Revolutionary War & the Backcountry

Pancake, John S. This Destructive War: The British Campaign in the Carolinas, 1780–1782. Tuscaloosa: University of Alabama Press, 1985.

Buchanan, John. The Road to Guilford Courthouse. New York: Wiley, 1997.

National Park Service. Ninety Six National Historic Site Administrative Histories. Washington, DC.

Biography & Leadership

Mays, Benjamin E. Born to Rebel: An Autobiography. New York: Scribner, 1971.

Fairclough, Adam. To Redeem the Soul of America: The Southern Christian Leadership Conference and Martin Luther King, Jr. Athens: University of Georgia Press, 1987.

Public History & Memory

Trouillot, Michel-Rolph. Silencing the Past: Power and the Production of History. Boston: Beacon Press, 1995.

Levin, Amy K., ed. Defining Memory: Local Museums and the Construction of History in America's Changing Communities. Lanham, MD: AltaMira Press, 2007.

Smithsonian Institution. Framework for African American History and Culture. Washington, DC.

AFRICAN AMERICAN HISTORY & RECONSTRUCTION

Du Bois, W.E.B. Black Reconstruction in America, 1860–1880. Free Press, 1935.

Foner, Eric. Reconstruction: America's Unfinished Revolution. Harper & Row, 1988.

Foner, Eric. The Second Founding: How the Civil War and Reconstruction Remade the Constitution. Norton, 2019.

Hahn, Steven. A Nation Under Our Feet. Harvard University Press, 2003.

Williams, Kidada E. They Left Great Marks on Me. NYU Press, 2012.

EDUCATION, FREEDOM, & BLACK INSTITUTIONS

Anderson, James D. The Education of Blacks in the South, 1860–1935. UNC Press, 1988.

Butchart, Ronald E. Schooling the Freed People. UNC Press, 2010.

Williams, Heather Andrea. Self-Taught: African American Education in Slavery and Freedom. UNC Press, 2005.

Franklin, John Hope. From Slavery to Freedom. McGraw-Hill, multiple editions.

GEOGRAPHY, SLAVERY, & INTERNAL SLAVE TRADE

Baptist, Edward E. The Half Has Never Been Told. Basic Books, 2014.

Johnson, Walter. Soul by Soul. Harvard University Press, 1999.

Tadman, Michael. Speculators and Slaves. Wisconsin Press, 1989.

Richmond Slave Trail Commission, Shockoe Bottom Documentation.

INDIGENOUS & FRONTIER HISTORY

Calloway, Colin G. The American Revolution in Indian Country. Cambridge University Press, 1995.

Perdue, Theda & Green, Michael. The Cherokee Nation and the Trail of Tears. Viking, 2007.

Ethridge, Robbie. From Chicaza to Chickasaw. UNC Press, 2010.

REVOLUTIONARY WAR & NINETY SIX DISTRICT

Buchanan, John. The Road to Guilford Courthouse. Wiley, 1997.

Pancake, John S. This Destructive War: The British Campaign in the Carolinas. University of Alabama Press, 1985.

National Park Service, Ninety Six National Historic Site Administrative Histories.

South Carolina Department of Archives & History, Ninety Six District Records.

BIOGRAPHICAL & LEADERSHIP STUDIES

Mays, Benjamin E. Born to Rebel. Scribner, 1971.

Gates, Henry Louis Jr. The Black Church. Penguin, 2021.

Fairclough, Adam. To Redeem the Soul of America. UNC Press, 1987.

PUBLIC HISTORY, MUSEUMS & INTERPRETATION

National Park Service. Interpretive Development Program (IDP).

Smithsonian Institution. Framework for African American History and Culture.

Levin, Amy K. Defining Memory. AltaMira Press, 2007.

Trouillot, Michel-Rolph. Silencing the Past. Beacon Press, 1995.

DIGITAL HUMANITIES & MAPPING

Bodenhamer, David J. The Spatial Humanities. Indiana University Press, 2010.

Knowles, Anne Kelly. Placing History. ESRI Press, 2008.

Mapbox Documentation (GL JS, Storytelling Frameworks).

CHAPTER NOTES / REFERENCES

Eric Foner, The Second Founding: How the Civil War and Reconstruction Remade the Constitution (New York: W.W. Norton, 2019), 3–28.

U.S. Constitution, art. I, §2; see also Akhil Reed Amar, America's Constitution: A Biography (New York: Random House, 2005), 87–94.

Walter Johnson, Soul by Soul: Life Inside the Antebellum Slave Market (Cambridge, MA: Harvard University Press, 1999), 1–12.

Edward E. Baptist, The Half Has Never Been Told (New York: Basic Books, 2014), 226–260.

Federal Writers' Project, Slave Narratives, Virginia and Georgia volumes.

James D. Anderson, The Education of Blacks in the South, 1860–1935 (Chapel Hill: University of North Carolina Press, 1988), 3–44.

Ronald E. Butchart, Schooling the Freed People (Chapel Hill: University of North Carolina Press, 2010), 67–102.

Benjamin E. Mays, Born to Rebel (New York: Scribner, 1971), 1–22.

W.E.B. Du Bois, Black Reconstruction in America (New York: Free Press, 1935), 120–189.

Michel-Rolph Trouillot, Silencing the Past (Boston: Beacon Press, 1995), 26–50.

Notes

Eric Foner, Reconstruction: America's Unfinished Revolution (New York: Harper & Row, 1988), 44–78.

Leon F. Litwack, Been in the Storm So Long (New York: Knopf, 1979), 221–245.

U.S. Bureau of Refugees, Freedmen, and Abandoned Lands, Georgia Field Office Records, NARA M1903.

Thavolia Glymph, Out of the House of Bondage (Cambridge: Cambridge University Press, 2008), 203–231.

Heather Andrea Williams, Help Me to Find My People (Chapel Hill: UNC Press, 2012), 39–66.

Chapter 11 *Afterlives of the Trade: Memory, Descendants, and the Work of Public History*

Constitutional, Legal, and Federal Sources

U.S. Constitution. Article I, Section 2; Amendments XIII, XIV, XV.

Amar, Akhil Reed. America's Constitution: A Biography. New York: Random House, 2005.

Foner, Eric. The Second Founding: How the Civil War and Reconstruction Remade the Constitution. New York: W.W. Norton, 2019.

Congressional Globe. 39th–41st Congresses.

United States Statutes at Large. Reconstruction Acts, 1867–1868.

Reconstruction, Citizenship, and Democracy

Du Bois, W.E.B. Black Reconstruction in America, 1860–1880. New York: Free Press, 1935.

Foner, Eric. Reconstruction: America's Unfinished Revolution, 1863–1877. New York: Harper & Row, 1988.

Hahn, Steven. A Nation Under Our Feet. Cambridge, MA: Harvard University Press, 2003.

Williams, Kidada E. They Left Great Marks on Me. New York: NYU Press, 2012.

Slavery, Shockoe Bottom, and Forced Migration

Johnson, Walter. Soul by Soul: Life Inside the Antebellum Slave Market. Cambridge, MA: Harvard University Press, 1999.

Baptist, Edward E. The Half Has Never Been Told: Slavery and the Making of American Capitalism. New York: Basic Books, 2014.

Tadman, Michael. Speculators and Slaves. Madison: University of Wisconsin Press, 1989.

Richmond Slave Trail Commission. Shockoe Bottom and the Internal Slave Trade. Richmond, VA.

Education, Freedom, and Reconstruction Networks

Anderson, James D. The Education of Blacks in the South, 1860–1935. Chapel Hill: University of North Carolina Press, 1988.

Butchart, Ronald E. Schooling the Freed People. Chapel Hill: University of North Carolina Press, 2010.

Williams, Heather Andrea. Self-Taught: African American Education in Slavery and Freedom. Chapel Hill: UNC Press, 2005.

Freedmen's Bureau. Education Division Records. RG 105, National Archives.

Revolutionary War, Frontier, and Ninety Six District

Pancake, John S. This Destructive War: The British Campaign in the Carolinas.

Tuscaloosa: University of Alabama Press, 1985.

Buchanan, John. The Road to Guilford Courthouse. New York: Wiley, 1997.

National Park Service. Ninety Six National Historic Site Administrative History. Washington, DC.

South Carolina Department of Archives and History. Ninety Six District Records.

Biography, Leadership, and Intellectual Lineage

Mays, Benjamin E. Born to Rebel: An Autobiography. New York: Scribner, 1971.

Fairclough, Adam. To Redeem the Soul of America. Athens: University of Georgia Press, 1987.

Gates, Henry Louis Jr. The Black Church. New York: Penguin, 2021.

Memory, Public History, and Interpretation

Trouillot, Michel-Rolph. Silencing the Past: Power and the Production of History. Boston: Beacon Press, 1995.

Levin, Amy K., ed. Defining Memory. Lanham, MD: AltaMira Press, 2007.

Smithsonian Institution. Framework for African American History and Culture. Washington, DC.

National Park Service. Interpretive Development Program (IDP) Guidelines.

Primary Oral & Narrative Sources

Federal Writers' Project. Slave Narratives: A Folk History of Slavery in the United States. Washington, DC: GPO, 1941.
– Virginia Narratives
– Georgia Narratives

Notes

Saidiya Hartman, Lose Your Mother (New York: Farrar, Straus and Giroux, 2007), 16–35.

Michel-Rolph Trouillot, Silencing the Past (Boston: Beacon Press, 1995), 26–30.

James Oliver Horton and Lois E. Horton, Slavery and Public History (New York: New Press, 2006), 1–18.

National Museum of African American History and Culture, "Domestic Slave Trade Interpretive Framework," Smithsonian Institution.

Library of Virginia, Virginia Untold Project.

Selected Bibliography (Chapters 5–6)

Foner, Eric. Reconstruction. New York: Harper & Row, 1988.

Glymph, Thavolia. Out of the House of Bondage. Cambridge: Cambridge University Press, 2008.

Hartman, Saidiya. Lose Your Mother. New York: Farrar, Straus and Giroux, 2007.

Horton, James Oliver, and Lois E. Horton. Slavery and Public History. New York: New Press, 2006.

Litwack, Leon F. Been in the Storm So Long. New York: Knopf, 1979.

Williams, Heather Andrea. Help Me to Find My People. Chapel Hill: UNC Press, 2012.

Chapter 12 *From Union Advance to Church-Built Classrooms*

Books & Monographs

"The Education of Blacks in the South, 1860–1935" by James D. Anderson

Comprehensive history of Black education in the South.

"Black Colleges and the African American Experience" edited by Marybeth Gasman

Explores the role of historically Black colleges and universities (HBCUs) in American education.

"American Education: A History" by Wayne J. Urban and Jennings L. Wagoner

Provides context for the evolution of education in the U.S., including the impact on Black communities.

Journal Articles & Papers

"The Role of the Freedmen's Bureau in Establishing Black Schools" by Christopher M. Span

Discusses the direct impact of the Freedmen's Bureau on Black education.

"From Slavery to Freedom: The African American Experience" by John Hope Franklin

A foundational text on the historical journey of African Americans, including education during Reconstruction.

"The Origins of African American Education" in the Journal of Negro Education

Analyzes the early foundations of Black educational institutions.

Primary Sources
Freedmen's Bureau Records (National Archives)

Original documents and reports detailing the establishment of Black schools, teacher assignments, and educational infrastructure.

Church Records and Missionary Archives

Documents from denominations such as the AME, AME Zion, CME, and Baptist archives that detail the founding and growth of Black colleges.

Web Resources

National Park Service – National Historic Landmarks Program

Detailed entries on historically Black colleges and their significance.

Library of Congress – Digital Collections
Access to digitized Freedmen's Bureau records, church archives, and more.
Bibliography, References, and Citations
For "From Union Advance to Church-Built Classrooms"

I. Primary Sources
Freedmen's Bureau Records
Bureau of Refugees, Freedmen, and Abandoned Lands.

Records of the Assistant Commissioner for the State of Georgia, Virginia, North Carolina, South Carolina, Alabama, Mississippi, Tennessee, Louisiana, Texas, and Arkansas.
National Archives Record Group 105.

Washington, DC: National Archives and Records Administration (NARA).

Freedmen's Bureau Education Reports, 1865–1872.
Superintendent of Education Monthly and Annual Reports.
NARA, RG 105.

Civil War Military Records

War of the Rebellion: A Compilation of the Official Records of the Union and Confederate Armies.
128 vols. Washington, DC: Government Printing Office, 1880–1901.

United States Army Chaplaincy Records, Civil War Era.
Library of Congress, Manuscript Division.

II. Church & Denominational Archives

African Methodist Episcopal (AME)

Payne, Daniel Alexander.
History of the African Methodist Episcopal Church.
Nashville: AME Publishing House, 1891.

African Methodist Episcopal Zion (AME Zion)

Hood, James Walker.
One Hundred Years of the African Methodist Episcopal Zion Church.
New York: AME Zion Publishing House, 1895.

Christian Methodist Episcopal (CME)

Phillips, William H.
History of the Colored Methodist Episcopal Church in America.
Jackson, TN: CME Publishing House, 1902.

Baptist

Simmons, William J.
Men of Mark: Eminent, Progressive, and Rising.
Cleveland: George M. Rewell, 1887.

National Baptist Convention Archives, Nashville, Tennessee.

Congregational / American Missionary Association

American Missionary Association.
Annual Reports, 1862–1875.
New York: AMA.

III. Secondary Scholarly Works

Black Education & Reconstruction

Anderson, James D.
The Education of Blacks in the South, 1860–1935.

Chapel Hill: University of North Carolina Press, 1988.

Butchart, Ronald E.
Schooling the Freed People: Teaching, Learning, and the Struggle for Black Freedom, 1861–1876.
Chapel Hill: University of North Carolina Press, 2010.

Span, Christopher M.
From Cotton Field to Schoolhouse: African American Education in Mississippi, 1862–1875.

Chapel Hill: University of North Carolina Press, 2009.

Freedmen's Bureau Studies
Foner, Eric.
Reconstruction: America's Unfinished Revolution, 1863–1877.

New York: Harper & Row, 1988.

Cimbala, Paul A., and Randall M. Miller (eds.).
The Freedmen's Bureau and Reconstruction.
New York: Fordham University Press, 1999.

Black Churches & Institutional Formation
Raboteau, Albert J.
Slave Religion: The "Invisible Institution" in the Antebellum South.
New York: Oxford University Press, 1978.

Lincoln, C. Eric, and Lawrence H. Mamiya.
The Black Church in the African American Experience.
Durham: Duke University Press, 1990.

IV. Institutional & HBCU Histories

Gasman, Marybeth, et al.
Historically Black Colleges and Universities: Triumphs, Troubles, and Taboos.
New York: Palgrave Macmillan, 2010.

Lovett, Bobby L.
America's Historically Black Colleges and Universities: A Narrative History.
Macon, GA: Mercer University Press, 2011.

Wright, Earl, II.
The First Generation of Black College Graduates.
Amherst: University of Massachusetts Press, 2018.

V. Regional & Georgia-Focused Works (Celia Adams Context)

Blight, David W.
Race and Reunion: The Civil War in American Memory.
Cambridge: Harvard University Press, 2001.

Hunter, Tera W.
To 'Joy My Freedom: Southern Black Women's Lives and Labors after the Civil War.
Cambridge: Harvard University Press, 1997.

Berlin, Ira.
Slaves No More: Three Essays on Emancipation and the Civil War.
New York: Cambridge University Press, 1992.

VI. Celia Adams Scholarship

Hargrove, Jesse J.
The Legacy of Celia Adams: From Slavery to Freedom.
Self-published, 2014.

Hargrove, Jesse J.
Testimony before the U.S. Senate Rules and Administration Committee, African American Museum Act, 1992.

Chapter 13 Shockoe Bottom: The Place Where Enslavement Became a Commercial System and the Engine for Profit, and Public Memory

Numbered Footnotes
Edward E. Baptist, The Half Has Never Been Told: Slavery and the Making of American Capitalism (New York: Basic Books, 2014).

Joshua D. Rothman, The Ledger and the Chain: How Domestic Slave Traders Shaped America (New York: Basic Books, 2021).

Walter Johnson, River of Dark Dreams: Slavery and Empire in the Cotton Kingdom (Cambridge, MA: Harvard University Press, 2013).

U.S. Constitution, Article I, Section 2.

Paul Finkelman, "Slavery and the Constitutional Convention," Yale Law Journal 81, no. 1 (1971).

Ira Berlin, Generations of Captivity (Cambridge, MA: Harvard University Press, 2003).

Lacy K. Ford, Deliver Us from Evil (New York: Oxford University Press, 2009).

Elizabeth Brown Pryor, Reading the Man: A Portrait of Robert E. Lee (New York: Viking, 2007).

Charles B. Dew, Apostles of Disunion (Charlottesville: University of Virginia Press, 2001).

Eric Foner, The Second Founding (New York: W.W. Norton, 2019).

U.S. Constitution, Amendments XIII, XIV, XV.

National Park Service, Richmond Slave Trade and African American History Special Resource Study (2016).

James D. Anderson, The Education of Blacks in the South, 1860–1935 (Chapel Hill: UNC Press, 1988).

Heather Andrea Williams, Self-Taught: African American Education in Slavery and Freedom (Chapel Hill: UNC Press, 2005).

Jesse J. Hargrove, The Legacy of Celia Adams: From Slavery to Freedom (Richmond: Hargrove Press, 2014).

Chapter 14 From Coast to Nation: Indigenous People and the Trails Before Shockoe Bottom

Primary & Early Sources

Smith, John. A Map of Virginia. 1612.

Strachey, William. The Historie of Travaile into Virginia Britannia. 1612.

Treaty records between the Virginia Colony and Indigenous nations, 17th–18th centuries.

Secondary Scholarship

Gallay, Alan. The Indian Slave Trade: The Rise of the English Empire in the American South. Yale University Press, 2002.

Hatfield, April Lee. Atlantic Virginia: Intercolonial Relations in the Seventeenth Century. University of Pennsylvania Press, 2004.

Martin, Joel W. Sacred Revolt: The Muskogees' Struggle for a New World. Beacon Press, 1991.

Merrell, James H. The Indians' New World: Catawbas and Their Neighbors from European Contact through the Era of Removal. UNC Press, 1989.

Richter, Daniel K. Facing East from Indian Country. Harvard University Press, 2001.

Public History & Museum Frameworks

Smithsonian National Museum of the American Indian, Native Knowledge 360°

National Park Service, Indigenous Cultural Landscapes guidance

Virginia Indian Heritage Program resources

Selected Bibliography

African Labor, Colonial Expansion, and Revolutionary America

African Arrival, Slavery, and Early Virginia

Berlin, Ira.
Many Thousands Gone: The First Two Centuries of Slavery in North America.
Cambridge, MA: Harvard University Press, 1998.

Horn, James.
1619: Jamestown and the Forging of American Democracy.
New York: Basic Books, 2018.

Morgan, Edmund S.
American Slavery, American Freedom: The Ordeal of Colonial Virginia.
New York: W. W. Norton, 1975.

Rolfe, John.
"Letter to Sir Edwin Sandys, 1619." In The Records of the Virginia Company of London, edited by Susan Myra Kingsbury.
Washington, DC: Government Printing Office, 1906–1935.

Labor, Infrastructure, and Colonial Expansion

Breen, T. H.
Tobacco Culture: The Mentality of the Great Tidewater Planters on the Eve of Revolution.
Princeton: Princeton University Press, 1985.

Foner, Eric.
Give Me Liberty! An American History, Vol. 1.
New York: W. W. Norton, 2019.

Isaac, Rhys.
The Transformation of Virginia, 1740–1790.
Chapel Hill: University of North Carolina Press, 1982.
Kulick, Rebecca J.

"Roads, Rivers, and Slavery in Colonial Virginia."
Journal of Southern History 74, no. 3 (2008): 567–600.

Shockoe Bottom, Richmond, and the Slave Trade

Campbell, Edward L. Jr.
Slavery at the Falls: Richmond, Virginia, 1780–1865.
Charlottesville: University of Virginia Press, 2019.

DeLombard, Jeannine Marie.
"In the Shadow of the Slave Market: Richmond's Shockoe Bottom."
American Quarterly 63, no. 3 (2011): 635–662.

Schwarz, Philip J.
Slave Laws in Virginia.
Athens: University of Georgia Press, 1996.

Wealth, Empire, and the Atlantic World

Beckles, Hilary McD.
The First Black Slave Society: Britain's "Barbarity Time" in Barbados, 1636–1876.
Kingston: University of the West Indies Press, 2016.

Eltis, David, and David Richardson.
Atlas of the Transatlantic Slave Trade.
New Haven: Yale University Press, 2010.

Inikori, Joseph E.
Africans and the Industrial Revolution in England.
Cambridge: Cambridge University Press, 2002.

Slavery and the American Revolution

Dunmore, John Murray, Earl of.
"Dunmore's Proclamation," 1775.
Colonial Williamsburg Foundation Archives.

Holton, Woody.
Forced Founders: Indians, Debtors, Slaves, and the Making of the American Revolution in Virginia.

Chapel Hill: University of North Carolina Press, 1999.

Nash, Gary B.
The Unknown American Revolution.
New York: Viking, 2005.

Somerset v. Stewart, 98 Eng. Rep. 499 (K.B. 1772).

African Americans, Resistance, and Revolutionary Contradictions

Quarles, Benjamin.
The Negro in the American Revolution.
Chapel Hill: University of North Carolina Press, 1961.

Waldstreicher, David.
Slavery's Constitution: From Revolution to Ratification.
New York: Hill and Wang, 2009.

Public History, Memory, and Interpretation

National Museum of African American History and Culture (NMAAHC).

Slavery and Freedom Interpretive Framework.
Washington, DC: Smithsonian Institution, 2018.

PART 3

Deuce Millennium Generation

Promise, Practice, and the Future of Democratic Trust

Introduction

Democracy Promised, Democracy Practiced

Democracy has always lived in the tension between promise and practice. From the founding of the American republic, the language of liberty and equality established a vision of political belonging that was far broader than the nation initially allowed itself to realize. The ideals written into the founding documents declared that all people possessed inherent rights and dignity. Yet the lived experience of democracy—particularly for African Americans—revealed a different reality: one in which participation, citizenship, and trust in institutions had to be fought for, defended, and repeatedly reclaimed.

This tension between democracy promised and democracy practiced has defined the American journey. Across generations, communities that were once excluded from the democratic project became some of its most dedicated architects. Through education, civic engagement, religious leadership, fraternal organizations, and social movements, they insisted that the nation live up to the principles it proclaimed.

The emergence of what may be called the Deuce Millennium Generation represents a new chapter in this legacy. These are the men who came of age at the dawn of the twenty-first century—an era marked simultaneously by unprecedented technological advancement, expanded access to information, and deepening public skepticism about democratic institutions. They inherit a world where the architecture of democracy remains intact, yet public trust in that architecture is increasingly fragile.

For this generation, the question is not simply whether democracy will endure, but how it will be practiced. The challenge before them is both moral and institutional: to renew public confidence in democratic systems while continuing the historic work of expanding participation, protecting rights, and strengthening community life. Their responsibility is not merely to preserve democracy as an abstract ideal, but to demonstrate—through service, leadership, and integrity—that democratic values remain relevant in a rapidly changing world.

In this sense, the Deuce Millennium Generation stands within a long continuum of democratic inheritance. They are heirs to the struggles of those who demanded inclusion in the American experiment and who transformed institutions from within. Their task is to carry forward that inheritance by cultivating trust, strengthening civic participation, and ensuring that the principles of democracy are not only spoken but lived.

Understanding this responsibility requires first examining the deeper historical roots of the democratic tradition itself. The story of democracy in America is neither linear nor complete; it is a contested and evolving narrative shaped by movements, institutions, and individuals who challenged the nation to become more faithful to its own ideals.

It is to those historical foundations—and the long struggle to transform democratic promise into democratic practice—that we now turn.

Deuce Millennium Generation:
Promise, Practice, and the Future of Democracy and Trust

Opening Quotations
"The arc of the moral universe is long, but it bends toward justice."
— Martin Luther King Jr.

"Educate and train the whole man and you cannot help but build the nation."
— Carter G. Woodson

“The price of freedom is eternal vigilance.”
— Thomas Jefferson

“We are not makers of history. We are made by history.”
— Martin Luther King Jr.

“Democracy is not a static thing. It is an everlasting march.”
— Franklin D. Roosevelt

These words remind us that democracy is not self-executing. It must be practiced, defended, expanded, and renewed by each generation that inherits it.

Bridge to the America250 Moment

As the United States approaches the national commemoration of the **United States Semiquincentennial—the 250th anniversary of the nation's founding—Americans are invited to reflect not only on the ideals that shaped the republic, but also on the distance between those ideals and their realization.

The language of liberty announced in the Declaration of Independence proclaimed equality as a universal principle. Yet the early constitutional order defined citizenship in ways that excluded large portions of the population, particularly enslaved African Americans, Indigenous peoples, and women. The American democratic project therefore evolved not simply through institutional development, but through sustained moral and political struggle.

America250 is thus not merely a celebration of national longevity; it is an invitation to examine how each generation has wrestled with the question of belonging.

The Deuce Millennium Generation stands at a pivotal moment in that continuing story.

Chapter 15

Historical Foundations of Democratic Practice

Democracy in the United States did not emerge fully formed in 1776 or 1787. Instead, it developed through a long and often contested process in which ideals of liberty were gradually translated into broader forms of participation and citizenship.

The American Revolution established the foundational claim that legitimate government derives its authority from the consent of the governed. This principle represented a radical departure from monarchical systems in which political power flowed from hereditary authority. Yet even as the revolutionary generation proclaimed liberty as a universal value, the new republic struggled to define who was included within the category of "the governed."

The United States Constitutional Convention of 1787 created the institutional framework that would guide the American political system. The Constitution established mechanisms of representation, separation of powers, and federalism intended to balance liberty with stability. However, the compromises that made the Constitution possible also embedded contradictions within the democratic system itself. Slavery remained protected, and political participation was largely limited to white male property holders.

Throughout the nineteenth century, democratic practice expanded through both reform and conflict. The abolitionist movement, the struggle for women's rights, and the efforts of free Black communities to assert citizenship all challenged the narrow boundaries of early American democracy.

The American Civil War ultimately forced the nation to confront the contradiction between slavery and democratic ideals. The conflict resulted not only in the abolition of slavery through the Thirteenth Amendment, but also in a redefinition of citizenship and rights through the Fourteenth Amendment and the Fifteenth Amendment.

These Reconstruction Amendments represented one of the most significant expansions of democracy in American history. For the first time, the Constitution declared birthright citizenship and sought to guarantee equal protection under the law. African American men briefly exercised political power throughout the South, serving in legislatures and participating in the reconstruction of state governments.

Yet Reconstruction was followed by a period of systematic retrenchment. Through violence, legal manipulation, and segregationist policies, many of the democratic gains of Reconstruction were undermined during the era of Jim Crow laws. Voting rights were suppressed, and racial segregation became institutionalized across large portions of the country.

Despite these barriers, African American communities continued to build institutions that preserved democratic aspirations. Churches, schools, civic associations, and Divine Nine organizations nurtured leadership and cultivated a culture of civic responsibility.

Among these institutions was Omega Psi Phi Fraternity, Inc., founded in 1911 at Howard University. Its founding principles—Manhood, Scholarship, Perseverance, and Uplift—represented not only personal ideals but also civic commitments. Through education, community service, and leadership development, Omega men contributed to the broader struggle to expand democratic participation and opportunity.

The twentieth century witnessed another major transformation of American democracy during the Civil Rights Movement. Activists, scholars, clergy, students, and community leaders mobilized to challenge segregation and voter suppression. Their efforts culminated in landmark legislation such as the Civil Rights Act of 1964 and the Voting Rights Act of 1965, which sought to enforce the constitutional guarantees that had been undermined for nearly a century.

These developments illustrate a central truth about American democracy: its progress has rarely been automatic. Instead, it has required persistent advocacy from citizens who insisted that the nation live up to its professed ideals.

Connecting the Deuce Millennium Generation to Celia Adams

The long arc of democratic struggle is not only a national narrative; it is also a personal one, carried through families and communities whose experiences reveal the lived meaning of constitutional change.

The story of Celia Adams—born in Richmond, Virginia in 1856 and later sold into the slave market in Louisville, Georgia—stands as a powerful reminder of the distance between America's democratic promises and the realities faced by those denied citizenship. Her life unfolded at the threshold of one of the most transformative periods in American constitutional history.

Born before emancipation, she entered a world in which the Constitution recognized enslaved persons primarily as property. Yet within a decade of her birth, the nation would be reshaped by the Civil War and the Reconstruction Amendments, which attempted to redefine the meaning of freedom and citizenship.

For her descendants, this history is not abstract. It represents a living inheritance that connects personal memory with national transformation. The struggles endured by Celia Adams form part of the broader constitutional narrative that expanded the meaning of American democracy.

The Deuce Millennium Generation inherits that legacy.

They are beneficiaries of rights secured through centuries of sacrifice and struggle. Yet inheritance carries responsibility. The democratic gains achieved by earlier generations must be sustained, strengthened, and adapted to new challenges.

In an era marked by declining public trust, political polarization, and rapid technological change, the future of democratic practice will depend heavily on whether emerging leaders can rebuild civic confidence and renew commitment to the common good.

For the Deuce Millennium Generation, the question is not simply whether democracy will endure. The deeper question is whether they will accept the responsibility to practice democracy with the same perseverance that earlier generations demonstrated in demanding it.

The story that began in places like the slave markets of the nineteenth century now continues in classrooms, communities, institutions, and civic organizations across the nation.

The inheritance of freedom is real.

Why Futures Fail Without Education

Futures thinking has long promised societies a way to anticipate change, mitigate risk, and shape desirable outcomes. Yet despite decades of forecasting models, scenario planning, and strategic foresight initiatives, most futures efforts fail to produce durable institutional change. The central reason for this failure is not methodological weakness, technological limitation, or lack of imagination. It is structural. Futures fail because they are rarely anchored to the one institution that reliably spans generations: education.

Education is the only social system designed to operate continuously across time, transmitting knowledge, norms, skills, and values from one cohort to the next. Governments rise and fall, economic systems fluctuate, technologies obsolete themselves, and even cultural institutions

fracture under political pressure. Schools, by contrast, persist. Even when underfunded, segregated, restructured, or contested, education systems endure as generational conveyors. This durability makes education not merely a site of learning, but a form of long-range infrastructure.

Most futures frameworks, however, treat education as a downstream variable—a sector to be "reformed" once futures are imagined elsewhere. Policy futures privilege electoral cycles. Economic futures privilege markets. Technological futures privilege innovation curves. In each case, education is positioned reactively, expected to adjust to futures already defined. This inversion undermines futures planning at its core. Futures that do not originate in education lack continuity, coherence, and transmission.

The Deuce Millennium Generation (DMG) framework begins from a different premise: if futures are to be realized, they must be educated into existence. Futures are not events; they are learned conditions. They emerge when successive generations are prepared, positioned, and empowered to inherit responsibility for time beyond their own lifespan. Education is the only institution capable of cultivating that inheritance.

This chapter argues that the failure of futures thinking is inseparable from the failure to conceptualize education as a generational system rather than a policy sector. By reframing education as the central architecture of long-range planning, the DMG model restores futures thinking to the realm of institutional responsibility rather than speculative abstraction.

Chapter 16

Reconstruction and the Architecture of Delay: From Dr. Carter G. Woodson to the Millennium, A Genealogy of Long Thinking

The Deuce Millennium Generation framework does not emerge in isolation. It is rooted in a distinct African American intellectual tradition that has always understood time differently—less as a linear progression of progress and more as a contested terrain of survival, memory, and obligation. Long before futures studies became a formal field, Black scholars, educators, and institutions were already practicing long thinking.

Dr. Carter G. Woodson's founding of the Association for the Study of Negro Life and History in 1915 was, at its core, a futures intervention. Woodson recognized that a people denied historical memory would be denied a future. His insistence that education must recover, preserve, and transmit Black history was not merely corrective—it was generational. Black History Week, established in 1926, was designed as a recurring educational ritual, embedding long memory into institutional time.

This commitment to continuity extended through figures such as W.E.B. Du Bois, who framed education as racial uplift across generations, and John Hope Franklin, whose scholarship insisted on historical depth as a precondition for democratic participation. For these thinkers,

education was not about individual advancement alone; it was about collective temporal survival.

The DMG framework stands within this lineage but extends it across a millennium horizon. Where earlier Black intellectual traditions fought to secure historical presence within hostile institutions, DMG assumes institutional survival and asks a new question: how do we plan ethically for generations we will never meet?

African American history offers a uniquely qualified answer. A people forced to imagine freedom before it was legally possible developed modes of futures thinking grounded in patience, endurance, and intergenerational responsibility. DMG formalizes this inherited sensibility into a systematic model, translating long thinking from cultural practice into planning architecture.

This genealogy matters. It ensures that DMG is not merely predictive but moral—concerned not only with what futures might occur, but with who bears responsibility for shaping them.

Historical Parallels of Promise, Retrenchment, and Trust Erosion

The erosion of trust experienced by the Deuce Millennium Generation follows a recognizable historical pattern. American democracy has repeatedly expanded its promises—only to retreat from their full implementation. Each retreat has produced not civic collapse, but generational recalibration. Understanding these precedents is essential to interpreting the present moment.

Reconstruction: Rights Without Durable Protection

Reconstruction marked the first major expansion of democratic promise following a period of national crisis. The abolition of slavery and the passage of the Thirteenth, Fourteenth, and Fifteenth Amendments articulated a bold vision of citizenship, political participation, and equal protection. Public education expanded rapidly, particularly for formerly enslaved populations, signaling the federal government's stated commitment to democratic inclusion.

Yet the promise of Reconstruction far exceeded its practice. Federal enforcement proved uneven and temporary. As political will receded, local authorities regained control, often using that authority to undermine newly established rights through violence, intimidation, and economic exclusion. Schools existed but were underfunded. Voting rights existed but were punished. Legal citizenship existed without institutional protection.

The result was an early lesson in democratic inconsistency: rights could be proclaimed without being secured. Trust did not vanish, but it shifted. Black communities invested in churches, mutual aid societies, and historically Black colleges—parallel institutions built to compensate for state retreat. Participation continued, but allegiance to public institutions weakened.

This pattern—formal access paired with material abandonment—reappears in the experience of the Deuce Millennium Generation, particularly in underfunded schools and inequitable civic participation structures.

The Post–Vietnam Era: Authority Without Credibility

The Vietnam War and its aftermath constituted a crisis of institutional truth. Government assurances of progress and necessity were contradicted by evidence revealed in the Pentagon Papers and by the lived experiences of soldiers and civilians. The draft exposed class and racial inequities, while Watergate confirmed that institutional misconduct could reach the highest levels without immediate consequence.

The post–Vietnam generation did not disengage from civic life; it reoriented its relationship to authority. Trust was replaced by skepticism. Journalism became adversarial. Protest supplanted deference. Participation persisted, but it was conditional rather than loyal.

The lesson absorbed was enduring: truth could be managed, withheld, or strategically distorted by institutions charged with public trust.

The Deuce Millennium Generation inherits this skepticism in an era of digital media, algorithmic amplification, and fragmented information ecosystems. For them, truth is not assumed; it must be verified. Institutional narratives are treated as provisional rather than authoritative.

The Post–Civil Rights Era: Equality Without Equity

The legislative victories of the Civil Rights Movement promised a transition from exclusion to inclusion. Legal segregation was dismantled, voting rights expanded, and education was declared the primary engine of opportunity. Yet by the late twentieth century, structural remedies gave way to colorblind frameworks that denied the persistence of inequality.

School funding remained tied to property wealth. Housing segregation endured through market mechanisms. Criminal justice expanded under the guise of neutrality. Inequality persisted, but responsibility for it was increasingly individualized.

The gap between declared equality and lived inequity produced a quiet but corrosive erosion of trust. If systems were fair, persistent disparities had to be framed as personal failure. This reframing absolved institutions while delegitimizing lived experience.

The Deuce Millennium Generation encounters the same logic in achievement gaps explained by effort rather than structure, in access to higher education framed as opportunity despite disproportionate debt burdens, and in civic participation offered without commensurate influence.

The Deuce Millennium Generation in Historical Context

Across Reconstruction, the post–Vietnam era, the post–Civil Rights period, and the present, the pattern is consistent:

Democratic promise expands

Institutional commitment retreats

Responsibility shifts from systems to individuals

Trust erodes cumulatively rather than catastrophically

The Deuce Millennium Generation does not represent a break from American civic tradition. It represents its continuation under new conditions. Their skepticism, selective engagement, and demand for alignment reflect historical learning—not generational deficiency.

Publication-Quality Figures

***Figure 1.* Historical Cycles of Democratic Promise and Retrenchment**

ERA PROMISE PRACTICE RESULT

Reconstruction Citizenship & voting Weak enforcement Parallel institutions

Education for freedmen Federal retreat Distrust of state

Post–Vietnam Truth & accountability Deception, inequity Skeptical engagement

Democratic leadership Adversarial media

Post–Civil Rights Equal opportunity Structural inequality Cynicism about merit

Education as mobility Individualized blame

Deuce Millennium Equity, access, democracy Precarity, opacity Recalibrated trust

Participation & inclusion Alternative systems

Institutional Retrenchment

Historical Era

Core Promise

Generational Response

Reconstruction (1865–1877)

Citizenship, voting, public education

Weak enforcement, federal withdrawal

Parallel institutions, mutual aid

Post–Vietnam (1968–1978)

Truth, accountability, moral authority

Deception, inequitable sacrifice

Skepticism, protest, adversarial media

Post–Civil Rights (1970s–1990s)

Equal opportunity

Structural inequality denied

Cynicism toward merit narratives

Deuce Millennium (2000s–)

Equity, access, participation

Precarity, opacity, performative inclusion

Strategic engagement, alternative systems

Caption: Across eras, unfulfilled democratic promises produce recalibration rather than disengagement.

Figure 2. The Cumulative Model of Trust Erosion

Academic Inequality

(unequal schools, punitive testing)

↓

Educational Access Gap

(debt, conditional inclusion)

↓

Civic Participation Gap

(voice without influence)

↓

Social Support Gap

(punitive or exclusionary systems)

↓

CUMULATIVE OUTCOME:

• Trust becomes provisional

• Engagement becomes strategic

• Institutional legitimacy weakens

Caption: Trust erosion is additive and cross-systemic, not episodic.

Figure 3. Individual Adaptation to Systemic Misalignment

SYSTEM PROMISE LIVED REALITY ADAPTIVE RESPONSE

Merit is rewarded Outcomes stratified Over-credentialing

Education lifts all Debt & instability Selective participation

Civic voice matters. Influence absent Alternative organizing

Support is available Help is punitive Mutual aid, exit strategies

Caption: Adaptive behaviors often misread as disengagement.

Figure 4. Warning–Opportunity Framework

IF MISALIGNMENT CONTINUES:

- Trust erosion deepens
- Institutions hollow out
- Democracy weakens structurally

IF ALIGNMENT IS PURSUED:

- Legitimacy is restored
- Participation becomes durable
- Generation becomes civic anchor

System Behavior

Warning

If Misalignment persists:

Deepening distrust,

Caption: The same generation can signal decline or anchor renewal.

Citations & Historiography (Selected)

Reconstruction

Foner, Eric. Reconstruction: America's Unfinished Revolution, 1863–1877. New York: Harper & Row, 1988.

Du Bois, W.E.B. Black Reconstruction in America. New York: Harcourt, Brace, 1935.

Post–Vietnam / Trust in Government

Schudson, Michael. The Power of News. Cambridge, MA: Harvard University Press, 1995.

Patterson, James T. Restless Giant: The United States from Watergate to Bush v. Gore. Oxford: Oxford University Press, 2005.

Post–Civil Rights / Structural Inequality

Katznelson, Ira. When Affirmative Action Was White. New York: W.W. Norton, 2005.

Alexander, Michelle. The New Jim Crow. New York: The New Press, 2010.

Education, Trust, and Inequality

Ladson-Billings, Gloria. "From the Achievement Gap to the Education Debt." Educational Researcher 35, no. 7 (2006).

Putnam, Robert D. Our Kids: The American Dream in Crisis. New York: Simon & Schuster, 2015.

Civic Trust & Generational Change

Skocpol, Theda. Diminished Democracy. Norman: University of Oklahoma Press, 2003.

Levine, Peter. We Are the Ones We Have Been Waiting For. Oxford: Oxford University Press, 2013.

The Book's Synthesis Line

The Deuce Millennium Generation stands where earlier generations stood when promise exceeded practice. What distinguishes the present moment is not the presence of mistrust, but the scale of alignment now required to reverse it.

Historical Parallels: When Promise Outran Practice

The experience of the Deuce Millennium Generation is not unprecedented. American history shows a recurring pattern: moments of expanded promise followed by institutional retreat, producing generational recalibration rather than collapse.

1. Reconstruction (1865–1877): Citizenship Without Protection

The Promise

Constitutional amendments (13th, 14th, 15th)
Expanded citizenship, voting rights, public education

Federal commitment—at least rhetorically—to equality

The Practice

Uneven enforcement of federal law

Withdrawal of institutional protection

Rise of local control weaponized against newly enfranchised citizens

Schools and civic participation formally open, materially sabotaged

The Resulting Trust Erosion

Formerly enslaved people and their descendants learned a foundational lesson:

Rights on paper do not guarantee rights in practice.

Participation exposed individuals to risk without ensuring protection. Education existed, but underfunded. Voting existed, but was punished. The gap between promise and practice taught communities to rely on mutual aid, churches, and parallel institutions rather than the state.

Parallel to Deuce Millennium Generation:

Formal access without material support
Civic participation without institutional backing
Retreat from federal responsibility framed as "local control"

2. Post–Vietnam Era (late 1960s–1970s): Authority Without Credibility

The Promise

Democratic accountability

Truth from government and media

Moral leadership during global conflict

The Practice

The Pentagon Papers

Watergate

Draft inequities by class and race

Government narratives contradicted by evidence

The Resulting Trust Erosion

A generation learned that official truth could be strategically incomplete or false. Faith in institutions collapsed not because people stopped caring—but because credibility was shattered.

Civic engagement did not disappear. It transformed:

Skepticism replaced deference

Journalism became adversarial

Protest replaced trust-based participation

Parallel to Deuce Millennium Generation:

Truth perceived as negotiable

Institutional narratives contradicted by lived reality

Engagement becomes conditional and skeptical

3. Post–Civil Rights Era (1970s–1990s): Equality Without Equity

The Promise

Legal desegregation

Equal opportunity doctrine

Colorblind policy frameworks

Education as the great equalizer

The Practice

Resegregation through housing and school funding

Unequal enforcement of civil rights protections

Shift from structural remedies to individual responsibility

Criminalization and disinvestment framed as neutrality

The Resulting Trust Erosion

Communities were told the struggle was "over" while outcomes proved otherwise. Inequality persisted, now framed as personal failure rather than systemic design.

The lesson learned:

If inequality is denied, it becomes invisible—and therefore unfixable.

Parallel to Deuce Millennium Generation:

Achievement gaps treated as effort gaps

Access without outcomes

Equity dismissed as favoritism

The Throughline Across Eras

Across Reconstruction, post–Vietnam, post–Civil Rights, and now the Deuce Millennium era, the same mechanism appears:

Expanded promise

Incomplete or withdrawn implementation

Shift of responsibility onto individuals

Generational recalibration of trust and engagement

The Deuce Millennium Generation is not breaking from history.

It is responding exactly as history predicts.

Chapter 17

The Limits of Generational Theory

Modern generational theory is dominated by short-cycle models. The most influential, popularized by William Strauss and Neil Howe, divides history into repeating generational archetypes spanning roughly 20–25 years. While rhetorically compelling, such models suffer from three fundamental limitations: temporal compression, cultural overgeneralization, and institutional irrelevance.

First, short-cycle models compress time into units too small to support meaningful futures planning. A 20-year generation aligns neatly with electoral cycles, marketing cohorts, and media narratives, but it is insufficient for educational systems that require decades to produce outcomes. Education does not operate on generational labels; it operates on cohort flow—the slow movement of learners through institutional pathways.

Second, demographic cohort models overgeneralize cultural experience, flattening differences across race, class, geography, and historical condition. They assume shared consciousness where structural inequality produces radically divergent life chances. Such models are ill-equipped to account for communities whose generational experiences are shaped by exclusion rather than consensus.

Third, and most critically, existing generational theories are largely irrelevant to institutional planning. They describe generations but do not govern transitions between them. Institutions cannot plan based on archetypes; they require frameworks that align time, responsibility, and succession.

The DMG framework rejects generational nostalgia in favor of generational engineering. Rather than asking what defines a generation culturally, DMG asks what each generation must carry forward institutionally. It shifts analysis from identity to obligation.

This chapter argues that generational theory must move beyond description and toward design. Without this shift, generational thinking will remain a rhetorical device rather than a planning tool.

How Gaps Became Breaches: From Inequality to Erosion of Trust

The erosion of trust experienced by the Deuce Millennium Generation did not occur suddenly, nor did it arise from abstract disillusionment. It was built incrementally through repeated encounters with gaps between institutional promise and lived reality. These gaps—academic, educational, civic, and social—functioned as breaches in the social contract. Each unresolved breach compounded the last.

1. Academic Achievement Gaps: When Effort Does Not Equal Outcome

Young people were told—consistently and emphatically—that effort and achievement would be rewarded. Yet academic outcomes remained deeply stratified by race, geography, income, and school funding. High-stakes testing regimes labeled students and schools as "failing" without addressing the unequal conditions under which learning occurred.

For the Deuce Millennium Generation, this produced an early and lasting lesson: **rules are applied uniformly, but conditions are not.**

Students watched peers in under-resourced schools face punitive accountability while wealthier districts absorbed failure through enrichment, remediation, and insulation. Over time, academic metrics came to feel less like measures of learning and more like instruments of sorting.

Trust eroded not because standards existed, but because standards ignored context.

The gap between meritocratic promise and stratified outcomes taught young people that achievement was necessary—but not sufficient—for advancement.

2. Access to Education: When Opportunity Is Conditional

Access to education expanded rhetorically during this period, but it narrowed practically. College was framed as the gateway to mobility even as tuition rose, public funding declined, and student debt became normalized. For many, access came with long-term financial risk rather than security.

Young people learned that access did not equal opportunity—it equaled exposure.

They were invited into institutions without corresponding support, transparency, or protection from structural disadvantage. First-generation and marginalized students encountered bureaucratic opacity, cultural isolation, and uneven advising, reinforcing the sense that inclusion was conditional rather than guaranteed.

When access carries disproportionate cost, it ceases to feel like opportunity and begins to feel like a gamble.

The promise of education as a public good weakened as its delivery became increasingly privatized and transactional.

3. Civic Gaps: When Participation Does Not Produce Influence

The Deuce Millennium Generation was educated in civic ideals while observing their uneven application. Voting rights were praised while access was restricted. Civic engagement was encouraged while institutional responsiveness declined. Young people were urged to participate—yet rarely saw participation translate into policy change.

They learned that being heard is not the same as being heeded.

Civic systems appeared performative: town halls without follow-through, advisory boards without authority, youth councils without power. Accountability flowed downward, but decision-making remained insulated.

This gap between participation and influence taught a crucial lesson: democracy's procedures can exist without democracy's substance.

As a result, many recalibrated engagement—seeking alternative forms of organizing, mutual aid, and digital activism outside formal institutions.

4. Social Inequalities: When Survival Is Individualized

Social systems increasingly framed structural challenges—housing insecurity, healthcare access, mental health, and public safety—as individual responsibility. Young people encountered institutions that punished vulnerability rather than addressed root causes.

They learned that need invites scrutiny more than support.

This produced a quiet but profound shift in trust. Institutions meant to provide protection instead appeared as sites of risk—bureaucratic, financial, or legal. Assistance came with stigma; support with surveillance.

When survival is individualized, solidarity weakens—and so does institutional legitimacy.

5. The Cumulative Effect: From Disappointment to Recalibration

None of these gaps alone would have dismantled trust. It was their accumulation across domains that proved decisive.

Academic inequity taught that fairness was selective.

Educational access taught that opportunity carried hidden cost.

Civic participation taught that voice did not guarantee power.

Social inequality taught that institutions protect themselves first.

Together, these lessons reshaped expectations.

Young people did not abandon engagement; they recalibrated it. They invested selectively. They trusted locally rather than institutionally. They prioritized networks over systems, transparency over tradition, and outcomes over process.

This recalibration is often misread as disengagement. In reality, it is adaptive behavior in response to systemic inconsistency.

The Structural Insight

When institutions ask for trust but fail to earn it, skepticism becomes rational. When values are taught but not practiced, belief becomes provisional. When access is offered without influence, participation becomes strategic rather than loyal.

The Deuce Millennium Generation did not withdraw from civic life.

They learned how to survive it.

The erosion of trust, then, is not a failure of character. It is a record of experience.

And it is reversible—if systems begin to close the gaps they created.

The Deuce Millennium Generation: A Warning and an Opportunity

The Deuce Millennium Generation occupies a rare historical position. It is both a diagnostic generation—revealing what is broken in American systems—and a catalytic generation—capable of helping to repair them. Whether it becomes remembered as a generation of fracture or of renewal depends less on its character than on the choices made by institutions in response to its experience.

The Warning: What Misalignment Produces

When values and systems diverge, trust is the first casualty.

The Deuce Millennium Generation was educated in the language of democracy, equity, and opportunity while living inside systems that routinely contradicted those ideals. They saw schools labeled "failing" long before they themselves had a chance to succeed. They watched institutions demand personal responsibility while avoiding institutional accountability. They encountered a civic culture that celebrated participation rhetorically while restricting it procedurally.

Over time, these contradictions produced not apathy, but disbelief.

Disbelief in the fairness of educational pathways that reward compliance over curiosity.

Disbelief in economic systems that promise mobility while normalizing precarity.

Disbelief in civic institutions that invoke unity while resisting reform.

This erosion of trust is cumulative. Each unaddressed gap between promise and practice widens the distance between citizens and institutions. When young people learn that rules are enforced selectively, that truth is negotiable, and that access does not guarantee influence, they recalibrate their expectations—and their engagement.

The warning embedded in the Deuce Millennium Generation is this:

Democracy cannot survive on inherited legitimacy alone.

If systems remain misaligned with values, disengagement becomes rational, alternative structures replace public ones, and cynicism hardens into detachment. The cost is not merely generational dissatisfaction; it is democratic weakening.

History offers ample evidence. Societies that fail to renew trust across generations experience declining participation, institutional fragility, and vulnerability to authoritarian appeal. The warning is not speculative—it is structural.

The Opportunity: What Alignment Makes Possible

Yet the same conditions that produce warning also create opportunity.

The Deuce Millennium Generation is unusually equipped for renewal precisely because it has lived inside misalignment. Its skepticism is informed, not nihilistic. Its demands are structural, not symbolic. It understands systems because it has had to navigate around their failures.

This generation does not ask institutions to be flawless. It asks them to be coherent.

When systems begin to reflect stated values—when education is funded equitably, when work provides stability, when civic participation carries consequence—trust does not need to be manufactured. It re-emerges organically. Alignment restores legitimacy not through messaging, but through experience.

The opportunity, then, is profound.

If education is reclaimed as a civic institution rather than a marketplace, this generation brings creativity, digital fluency, and historical consciousness into public life.

If economic systems reward contribution with dignity, this generation brings innovation without extraction.

If civic systems expand participation and enforce accountability, this generation brings engagement that is principled, informed, and sustained.

Democratic renewal does not require convincing this generation to care. It requires giving them systems worthy of care.

Renewal Requires Scale and Seriousness

Alignment cannot be incremental or cosmetic. The Deuce Millennium Generation is acutely attuned to performative reform. Pilot programs without permanence, inclusion without power, and rhetoric without resources deepen skepticism rather than repair it.

Renewal requires seriousness—policies that redistribute opportunity, enforce accountability, and invest in public goods at scale. It requires institutions willing to change how they operate, not merely how they communicate.

Most importantly, renewal requires shared responsibility. The burden of fixing misaligned systems cannot be placed on the very generation harmed by them. Leadership, investment, and reform must come from those who control institutional levers.

The Choice Before Us

Every generation presents a question to the society that precedes it. **The Deuce Millennium Generation's question is unambiguous:**

Will values finally govern systems—or will systems continue to hollow out values?

If misalignment persists, this generation will adapt elsewhere—outside traditional institutions, outside civic trust, and eventually outside democratic participation. That is the warning.
But if alignment is pursued with seriousness and scale, this generation can become a cornerstone of democratic renewal—rebuilding trust, revitalizing civic life, and carrying democratic ideals forward with renewed credibility. That is the opportunity.
History will not ask whether the Deuce Millennium Generation was patient enough, resilient enough, or optimistic enough.
History will ask whether institutions were honest enough to change.

Tell It From the Mountaintop: Is Anyone Listening in Congress and Communities?

Congressional / Legislative Testimony

Chairperson, Members of the Committee, thank you for the opportunity to testify.

I am here to speak about the Deuce Millennium Generation—not as a cultural curiosity, but as a policy signal.

This generation did not disengage from American institutions by choice. They encountered systems that no longer behaved as promised. Across education, the economy, and civic life, they experienced a widening gap between stated values and operational reality. That gap is not abstract. It is measurable, cumulative, and consequential.

We tell young people that education is the great equalizer. Yet we fund schools inequitably, reduce learning to test performance, and treat education as a private commodity rather than a public good. We celebrate work ethic while normalizing wage instability, debt dependency, and credential inflation. We teach democracy while constraining participation and avoiding institutional accountability.

The response of the Deuce Millennium Generation—skepticism, alternative organizing, and demand for transparency—is rational. It reflects civic awareness, not civic failure.

This generation is asking for alignment.
They are asking that equity be more than rhetoric; that truth be more than selective history; that participation carry real power; that accountability apply to institutions as well as individuals; and that intergenerational responsibility guide policy choices whose costs are deferred to the future.

From a policy standpoint, the implications are clear:

Education must be treated as nation-building infrastructure

Workforce policy must prioritize dignity and stability

Civic systems must expand access and enforce accountability

Social systems must be designed for well-being, not punishment

Resilience cannot substitute for justice. Innovation cannot replace investment. And adaptation cannot excuse abandonment.

The Deuce Millennium Generation represents both a warning and an opportunity. If systems remain misaligned with values, trust will continue to erode. If alignment is pursued with seriousness and scale, this generation can become a cornerstone of democratic renewal. History will measure not what we said about them—but what we changed because of them.

Op-Ed - Community / National / Regional Press

The Generation Isn't Broken. Our Systems Are.

Every generation inherits the consequences of decisions it did not make. But the Deuce Millennium Generation inherited something more corrosive than economic hardship or social change: misalignment.

They were raised on the language of opportunity, equity, and democracy—while living inside systems that often delivered the opposite. Schools preached fairness while operating under unequal funding. Employers praised ambition while offering instability. Civic leaders invoked participation while constraining access and accountability.

Predictably, trust eroded.

Too often, this erosion is misread as apathy or entitlement. In reality, it is evidence of discernment. Young people noticed that the values America claims are not consistently reflected in how its institutions behave.

This generation is not demanding perfection. They are demanding coherence.

They are asking why education is celebrated as a public good but financed like a private luxury. Why democracy is revered rhetorically but narrowed procedurally. Why labor is deemed essential yet treated as disposable. Why history is invoked but not taught honestly.

These are not cultural complaints. They are policy indictments.

The systems most visibly out of alignment—*education, the economy, civic institutions, information platforms,* and social supports—share a common flaw: they ask individuals to compensate for structural failure. Resilience becomes a requirement. Debt becomes a bridge. **Silence becomes the price of belonging.**

That bargain is no longer holding.

The Deuce Millennium Generation has responded not by withdrawing from public life, but by reimagining it—through new forms of organizing, cultural production, and civic participation that bypass institutions they no longer trust.

The danger is not their skepticism. The danger is our refusal to listen.

Alignment is possible. It requires treating education as nation-building infrastructure, not a marketplace. It requires economic policy that rewards contribution with stability. It requires civic systems that expand participation and enforce accountability upward. And it requires acknowledging that intergenerational responsibility is not sentimental—it is ethical.

History shows that when a generation insists that systems match values, reform follows. The only question is whether leaders respond with structural change—or cosmetic language.

The generation is not broken.

The systems are.
And repair is still possible.

Listening From the Mountaintop Experience: Curriculum Module

For High School (Grades 11–12), Undergraduate, or Graduate Courses

Module Title

Values, Systems, and the Deuce Millennium Generation

Learning Objectives

Students will be able to:

Identify core democratic values and compare them to real-world institutional practices

Analyze how policy decisions shape generational experience

Evaluate claims about generational disengagement using historical and structural evidence

Propose reforms that align values with systems

Key Concepts

Values vs. Systems

Structural vs. Individual Responsibility

Intergenerational Equity

Civic Trust and Legitimacy

Education as a Public Good

Core Values Discussed

Equity

Truth and Transparency

Dignity of Education and Labor

Participation with Power

Accountability

Intergenerational Responsibility

Belonging

Systems Analyzed

Education (K–12, Higher Education)

Economic and Workforce Systems

Civic and Political Institutions

Media and Information Systems

Social Support Systems

Discussion Questions

How can a society claim to value equity while maintaining unequal systems?

Is skepticism toward institutions a sign of civic decline or civic awareness? Why?

Where do you see misalignment between values and systems in your own experience?

What would "alignment" look like in one specific system (education, labor, voting)?

Applied Activity (Policy Lab or Writing Assignment)

Assignment:

Choose one system (education, labor, civic participation).

Identify the stated values

Identify current system behaviors

Analyze the gap

Propose one policy reform that improves alignment

Assessment Options

Reflective essay

Policy memo

Debate or mock testimony

Community-based project

Core Takeaway for Students

Generations do not fail in isolation. They respond to the systems they inherit. *Civic responsibility includes not only participation—but reform.*

A Policy Framework from the Mountaintop

Aligning Values and Systems for the Deuce Millennium Generation

Purpose

To realign American public systems with the democratic, educational, and economic values consistently articulated—but inconsistently practiced—across the early twenty-first century. This framework responds directly to the lived experience of the Deuce Millennium Generation.

Core Premise

The Deuce Millennium Generation does not suffer from disengagement; it suffers from misalignment. Public systems profess equity, opportunity, and participation while operating

through exclusion, precarity, and opacity. This framework identifies the values at stake, the systems responsible, and the policy direction required.

Guiding Values (What Must Be Honored)

4. Equity Over Rhetoric

Fair outcomes that account for historical and structural disadvantage.

5. Truth and Transparency

Honest history, clear data, and visible accountability.

6. Dignity of Education and Labor

Human development over extraction and sorting.

7. Participation With Power

Engagement that shapes outcomes, not optics.

8. Accountability With Consequences

Responsibility applied upward as well as downward.

9. Intergenerational Responsibility

Stewardship that protects the future from present neglect.

10. Belonging Without Erasure

Full inclusion without cultural or civic penalty.

Key Systems Requiring Alignment (Where Policy Must Act)

Education (K–12 and Higher Education)

Economic and Workforce Systems

Civic and Political Institutions

Cultural and Information Systems

Social Support and Public Well-Being Systems

Policy Direction (What Must Change)

Treat education as nation-building infrastructure, not a consumer product

Replace symbolic inclusion with structural equity measures

Design economic policy around stability, dignity, and contribution

Expand civic participation through access, transparency, and trust

Shift from punishment-based social systems to well-being-centered design

Outcome Goal

Restore institutional legitimacy by achieving value–system coherence, thereby rebuilding public trust and unlocking the full civic, economic, and intellectual capacity of the Deuce Millennium Generation.

Side-by-Side Table for Lawmakers
Values vs. Systems: Where Alignment Breaks—and How to Repair It

Policy Realignment Needed
Stated Value
Current System Behavior
Resulting Impact
Equity
Equal language, unequal funding
Persistent racial & economic gaps
Equity-based funding formulas; targeted investment
Truth
Sanitized history; selective data
Distrust, misinformation
Truthful curricula; transparent reporting
Dignity of Education
Test-driven compliance
Disengagement, burnout
Whole-child, civic-centered education
Dignity of Labor
Precarious wages; debt dependency
Economic instability
Living wages; debt reform; workforce pathways
Participation
Performative engagement
Civic withdrawal
Binding participatory mechanisms
Accountability
Consequences for individuals only
Institutional impunity

Oversight with enforcement authority
Intergenerational Care
Short-term policymaking
Climate, debt, civic erosion
Long-horizon policy metrics
Belonging
Conditional inclusion
Alienation
Power-sharing, representation reforms
(My Chart is ready to be clipped and pasted)

Key Legislative Insight:
Trust cannot be restored through messaging alone. It is restored when systems behave as promised.

Chapter 18

Civil Rights and the Limits of Declaration:

The Deuce Millennium Generation Model

The Deuce Millennium Generation (DMG) model introduces a 300-year generational architecture spanning from 1997 to the year 3000. It is composed of 53 sequential generational cohorts, each representing approximately 18 years—the length of time required for an individual to move through formal education and into society.

These cohorts are organized into larger epochal groupings, culminating in the Third Millennium Generation (3MG) horizon. Unlike traditional generational models, DMG is not designed to label people but to map institutional responsibility across time.

Each DMG cohort represents a transfer point: a moment when education systems hand societal stewardship to a new generation. By extending this logic across centuries, DMG enables institutions to visualize continuity rather than rupture. The model asks planners to consider not only immediate outcomes, but second-, third-, and fourth-order generational effects.

The power of DMG lies in its scalability. It can be applied at the level of a single school district or across national and global systems. It accommodates technological change without being

driven by it. Most importantly, it insists that no generation acts alone—each is a steward of futures it will not inhabit.

The 3MG horizon functions not as a prediction but as an ethical boundary. It marks the point at which planning exceeds personal interest and enters moral obligation. To plan to 3000 is to accept responsibility for continuity beyond recognition.

This chapter establishes DMG as both a conceptual model and a practical instrument—one capable of transforming how institutions understand time, succession, and purpose.

This model is a visionary, and distinctly original submission style—part manifesto, part exhibit caption, part time-map—while preserving the DMG framework

Figure 1. The Hargrove Deuce Millennium Map (DMG → 3MG)

Charting Fifty-Three Generations of Human Passage

The Hargrove Deuce Millennium Map is not a forecast—it is a long view of responsibility.

Stretching across more than a thousand years, **the Map** traces 53 **distinct Deuce Millennium Generations (DMGs),** each representing a cohort of students who will enter P–12 education, mature into civic life, and ultimately shape society's moral, intellectual, and institutional character. Together, these generations **form a continuous human relay—from DMG-1 (1997) to the threshold of 3MG (Year 3000).**

This framework insists on a radical premise:

Education is not episodic; it is civilizational.

Each DMG spans approximately 18 years, aligning with the developmental arc from birth to adulthood. The Map therefore functions simultaneously as:

a pedagogical timeline,

a societal accountability chart, and

a moral ledger of intergenerational stewardship.

Figure 1 The Hargrove Deuce Millennium Map From DMG 1 to 3MG

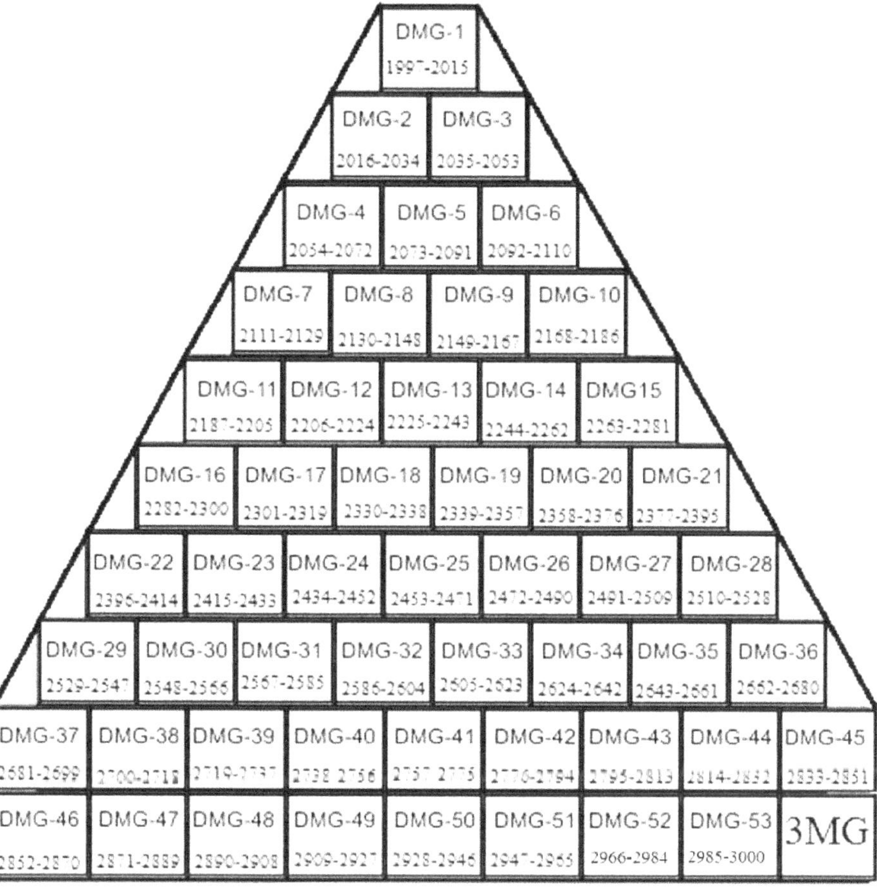

The DMG outlines the 53 generations of student cohorts who will journey through P-12 schools to society until 3MG.

"Chart 2 The Hargrove Deuce Millennium Chart From DMG-1 to 3MG"

DMG-1 (1997-2015)	DMG-2 (2016-2034)	DMG-3 (2035-2053)	DMG-4 (2054-2072)	DMG-5 (2073-2091)
DMG-6 (2092-2110)	DMG-7 (2111-2129)	DMG-8 (2130-2148)	DMG-9 (2149-2167)	DMG-10 (2168-2186)
DMG-11 (2187-2205)	DMG-12 (2206-2224)	DMG-13 (2225-2243)	DMG-14 (2244-2262)	DMG-15 (2263-2281)
DMG-16 (2282-2300)	DMG-17 (2301-2319)	DMG-18 (2320-2338)	DMG-19 (2339-2357)	DMG-20 (2358-2376)
DMG-21 (2377-2395)	DMG-22 (2396-2414)	DMG-23 (2415-2433)	DMG-24 (2434-2452)	DMG-25 (2453-2471)
DMG-26 (2472-2490)	DMG-27 (2491-2509)	DMG-28 (2510-2528)	DMG-29 (2529-2547)	DMG-30 (2548-2566)
DMG-31 (2567-2585)	DMG-32 (2586-2604)	DMG-33 (2605-2623)	DMG-34 (2624-2642)	DMG-35 (2643-2661)
DMG-36 (2662-2680)	DMG-37 (2681-2699)	DMG-38 (2700-2718)	DMG-39 (2719-2737)	DMG-40 (2738-2756)
DMG-41 (2757-2775)	DMG-42 (2776-2794)	DMG-43 **(2795-2813)**	DMG-44 (2814-2832)	DMG-45 (2833-2851)
DMG-46 (2852-2870)	DMG-47 (2871-2889)	DMG-48 (2890-2908)	DMG-49 (2909-2927)	DMG-50 (2928-2946)
DMG-51 (2947-2965)	DMG-52 (2966-2984)	DMG-53 (2985-3000)	**3MG**	

Note: Hargrove DMG Millennium Map, Charts 53 Generations, Jlanuary 12, 20:16.

The Third Millennium Generation: Arrival, Reckoning, Renewal

Interpretive Note

The Deuce Millennium framework reframes time not as destiny, but as duty. **Each DMG inherits the unfinished work of the last**—educationally, ethically, and structurally. The question posed by the Map is simple and unsettling:

What kind of world are we preparing for people we will never meet—but are fully responsible for?

Policy-Facing Conclusion

For Legislators, Education Leaders, Foundations, and Civic Institutions

The Deuce Millennium Generation represents a decisive policy inflection point. Their experiences reveal not isolated shortcomings, but systemic fractures across education, workforce development, civic engagement, and social trust. These fractures are measurable, cumulative, and consequential. They demand response—not rhetoric.

Decades of policy choices have reshaped education into a narrow instrument of compliance rather than a broad engine of democratic preparation. Accountability regimes emphasized testing over teaching, efficiency over equity, and short-term outcomes over long-term civic capacity. As a result, institutions designed to cultivate opportunity increasingly function as filters that reproduce inequality.

The Deuce Millennium Generation did not disengage from civic life; they encountered civic systems that failed to engage them meaningfully. Declining trust in public institutions, skepticism toward political leadership, and alternative forms of organizing should be understood as rational responses to lived experience. Policy must begin from this reality rather than mischaracterize it as generational deficiency.

A policy reset is required—one grounded in historical awareness and forward responsibility. Education policy must be reframed as nation-building policy. This includes sustained investment in early childhood education, equitable school funding, teacher development, culturally grounded curricula, and pathways that link education to meaningful economic participation. Workforce policy must recognize the dignity of labor alongside innovation. Civic policy must restore participation through transparency, accountability, and inclusion.

The central lesson of the Deuce Millennium Generation is clear: resilience cannot substitute for justice. Innovation cannot replace investment. And adaptation cannot excuse abandonment.

If policymakers are serious about democratic renewal, this generation offers both warning and opportunity. The choice is whether to respond with incremental adjustment—or with structural commitment equal to the moment. History will measure the difference.

Public Lecture / Keynote Address

"The Deuce Millennium Generation: Reckoning and Renewal"

Good evening.
We often talk about generations as if they appear out of nowhere—fully formed, fully responsible for the world they inherit. But history tells a different story. Generations are shaped long before they take their first steps—by the policies we pass, the schools we fund, the truths we teach, and the promises we keep—or break.

The Deuce Millennium Generation came of age in a world of contradiction. They were told education was the great equalizer—then watched schools struggle for basic resources. They were promised opportunity—then handed debt. They were taught democracy—then witnessed distrust replace dialogue.

And still, they adapted.
Not by withdrawing, but by questioning.
Not by surrendering, but by reimagining.
Not by waiting for permission, but by building new pathways where old ones failed.

This generation's skepticism is not apathy. It is evidence. Evidence that young people notice when institutions say one thing and do another. Evidence that they understand history—even when we pretend it doesn't matter anymore.

The Deuce Millennium Generation is asking us a simple but unsettling question:

Will we finally align our values with our systems?

They are not asking for rescue. They are asking for honesty.

They are not asking for charity. They are asking for investment.

They are not asking for nostalgia. They are asking for courage.

Education must once again be about more than survival—it must be about possibility. Civic life must be more than performance—it must be participatory. And leadership must be more than authority—it must be accountable.

Every generation is judged by what it passes forward. The question before us is whether we will leave behind patched systems and borrowed solutions—or whether we will do the harder work of renewal.

The Deuce Millennium Generation stands ready—not as a problem to be solved, but as partners in rebuilding. The future they inherit will reflect the choices we make now.

History is watching.
And so are they.

Thank you.

Summary: The Deuce Millennium Generation

The Deuce Millennium Generation traces the emergence of a cohort born into contradiction: unprecedented technological power alongside deep structural inequality; expanded global awareness paired with eroding civic trust; and cultural visibility without corresponding institutional equity. Across the chapters, the narrative establishes that this generation did not fail systems of education, governance, and opportunity—those systems failed them.

The book situates the Deuce Millennium Generation within a long arc of American history, particularly the unfinished struggle for educational justice, racial equity, and democratic participation. Drawing from historical precedents, policy analysis, lived experience, and intergenerational comparison, the chapters demonstrate how the promises of the late twentieth century gave way to the precarity of the early twenty-first. Schools became testing grounds rather than incubators of imagination. Civic institutions retreated from moral leadership. Economic mobility narrowed while expectations expanded.

Yet the narrative resists despair. The Deuce Millennium Generation is portrayed not as disengaged, but as discerning; not apathetic, but skeptical of systems that have repeatedly broken faith. The chapters reveal how this generation redefines leadership, community, and knowledge production—through digital fluency, cultural entrepreneurship, grassroots organizing, and a renewed insistence that education must be both practical and humane.

By grounding contemporary challenges in historical continuity, the book reframes the Deuce Millennium Generation as inheritors of struggle rather than anomalies of decline. Their story is not one of collapse, but of reckoning.

Conclusion: Reckoning, Responsibility, and Renewal

The story of the Deuce Millennium Generation is ultimately a test—not of youth, but of society. It asks whether institutions will continue to extract resilience from young people without offering restoration, or whether the nation will finally confront the consequences of deferred justice in education, economics, and civic life.

History teaches that generations do not fail in isolation. They respond to the conditions they inherit. When education is underfunded, when truth is politicized, when opportunity is rationed, young people adapt in ways that unsettle older assumptions. The Deuce Millennium Generation has done precisely that—exposing the fragility of systems long assumed to be permanent.

This generation's defining contribution may not be technological innovation alone, but moral interrogation. They demand coherence between rhetoric and reality. They question why democracy feels distant, why education feels transactional, and why progress remains unevenly distributed. In doing so, they echo earlier reformers who insisted that the future is not something we enter—it is something we build.

The responsibility, therefore, does not rest solely with the Deuce Millennium Generation. It rests with educators willing to teach beyond metrics; policymakers willing to invest beyond election cycles; elders willing to mentor without nostalgia; and institutions willing to reform rather than rebrand.

If this generation is to be remembered not as a "lost" cohort but as a transformational one, the reckoning must give way to renewal.

Education must reclaim its role as a public good. Civic life must restore trust through accountability. And history must be taught not as distant memory, but as instruction.

The Deuce Millennium Generation stands at the threshold of that possibility. Whether society meets them there will determine not only their legacy—but our own.

Chapter 19

DMG as Educational Infrastructure

Education is often described metaphorically as a "pipeline," a "ladder," or a "system." Each metaphor implies movement, progression, and structure, yet none adequately captures education's most consequential function: its role as generational infrastructure.

Infrastructure is not defined by efficiency or innovation alone; it is defined by durability. Roads, water systems, and power grids matter because they persist beyond any single generation. Education, uniquely among social institutions, performs this same infrastructural role for knowledge, values, and civic capacity.

The Deuce Millennium Generation (DMG) model reframes education not as a sector responsive to social change, but as the primary mechanism through which societies stabilize continuity across time. Each DMG cohort represents the predictable movement of learners through institutional pathways—from early childhood education through formal schooling and into civic participation. This flow is not incidental; it is the backbone of social reproduction.

Most education reforms fail because they treat schools as sites of intervention rather than as long-duration systems. Reforms are introduced on timelines misaligned with generational reality. Leaders expect measurable outcomes within electoral or funding cycles, ignoring the fact that educational impact unfolds over decades. The

DMG framework corrects this misalignment by synchronizing policy imagination with cohort progression.

By mapping cohorts across 53 DMGs, the model enables planners to visualize education as a relay rather than a race. Each generation inherits unfinished work and incomplete futures. Infrastructure thinking requires humility: one builds not for immediate reward, but for reliability across time. DMG positions education squarely within this ethic, insisting that institutional success be measured not by disruption, but by intergenerational handoff.

This chapter argues that once education is understood as infrastructure, futures planning becomes less speculative and more accountable. Infrastructure demands stewardship. DMG supplies the temporal map that stewardship requires.

The framework's focus on long-range educational planning, policy horizons, and intergenerational accountability.

The Deuce Millennium Generation Framework:

An Intergenerational Model for Educational Policy and Long-Term Planning (1997–3000)

Author Note
Jesse J. Hargrove, Ph.D., earned his doctorate in Interdisciplinary Studies in Multicultural Education from the University of Illinois at Urbana–Champaign. He is the author and creator of the Deuce Millennium Generation (DMG) Framework and the Hargrove Deuce Millennium Map, a long-range model for understanding education as a civilizational system across generations.

Abstract
Educational policy is typically designed within short temporal horizons, such as electoral cycles, budget periods, or decade-long reform initiatives. This article introduces the Deuce Millennium Generation (DMG) Framework, a long-range intergenerational model that reconceptualizes education as a civilizational system extending from

1997 to the year 3000. The framework identifies 53 Deuce Millennium Generations, each spanning approximately 18 years and corresponding to the human developmental passage from birth through formal education and entry into civic life. Grounded in generational theory, multicultural education, and futures studies, the DMG Framework offers policymakers a tool for evaluating educational decisions through the lens of intergenerational equity, ethical responsibility, and long-term societal sustainability. The article argues that policy coherence across generations—not short-term performance optimization—must become a central objective of educational governance.

Keywords: educational policy, generational theory, futures studies, intergenerational equity, long-term planning, multicultural education

The Problem of Short-Termism in Educational Policy

Educational policy in the United States and globally is overwhelmingly shaped by short-term incentives and constraints. Reform initiatives are often evaluated within narrow windows defined by election cycles, standardized testing regimes, or funding timelines. While such approaches may yield measurable short-term gains, they frequently fail to account for the cumulative effects of educational decisions across generations.

Scholars in policy studies and futures research have warned that short-termism undermines institutional sustainability and ethical governance (Slaughter, 1995; UNESCO, 2015). Education, by its very nature, produces outcomes that unfold over decades rather than years. Yet policy structures rarely reflect this temporal reality.

The Deuce Millennium Generation (DMG) Framework responds to this structural mismatch by offering a generational model that aligns educational policy with the full arc of human development and societal inheritance.

Theoretical Foundations of the DMG Framework

Generational Theory and Social Time

Karl Mannheim's (1952) foundational work on generational consciousness emphasized the role of shared historical experience in shaping cohort identity. Subsequent generational models have often narrowed this concept, emphasizing cultural consumption patterns or labor-market characteristics (Howe & Strauss, 1991). While influential, such models are poorly suited for long-range educational policy analysis.

The DMG Framework departs from trend-based generational labeling and instead anchors generations in biological and educational time—approximately 18 years, reflecting the period during which individuals typically move from birth through compulsory education and into civic participation.

Multicultural Education and Intergenerational Equity

Multicultural education scholarship emphasizes the structural and historical dimensions of inequality embedded within educational systems (Banks, 2006; Ladson-Billings, 1995). The DMG Framework extends this analysis temporally, arguing that inequities are not only reproduced across social groups but also transmitted across generations.

From this perspective, educational policy becomes an ethical project of intergenerational justice, echoing Rawls's (1971) principle that social arrangements must be just not only for present populations but for future ones.

Futures Studies and Long-Range Governance

Futures studies scholars argue that institutions must cultivate the capacity to think beyond immediate crises and political cycles (Inayatullah, 2008; Slaughter, 1995). The DMG Framework operationalizes futures thinking by embedding it within a concrete generational structure that policymakers and institutions can use for long-term planning.

The Deuce Millennium Generation Framework

Structure and Scope

The DMG Framework spans 53 generations, beginning with DMG-1 (1997–2015) and concluding with DMG-53 (2985–3000). Each generation represents a cohort that passes through P–12 education and enters broader social, economic, and civic life.

The framework culminates in 3MG (The Third Millennium Generation), a symbolic and analytical threshold representing the long-term consequences of educational decisions made across the preceding centuries.

The Hargrove Deuce Millennium Map

The Hargrove Deuce Millennium Map visually represents the framework as a horizontal timeline, enabling policymakers, educators, and the public to conceptualize education as a continuous intergenerational process rather than a series of isolated reforms. The Map is designed for use in policy analysis, institutional planning, and public humanities contexts.

Education as a Civilizational System

Central to the DMG Framework is the assertion that education functions as a civilizational inheritance system. Each generation inherits not only knowledge and skills, but also institutional strengths, structural inequities, and unresolved policy failures. Educational policy therefore shapes conditions for generations far beyond those directly served.

Implications for Educational Policy

Policy Evaluation Across Generations

The DMG Framework encourages policymakers to assess reforms based on their projected intergenerational impact rather than short-term outcomes alone. This shift supports policies oriented toward sustainability, equity, and institutional resilience.

Strategic Institutional Planning

School systems, universities, and government agencies can use the framework to align mission statements and strategic plans with long-range societal goals, reducing policy volatility caused by leadership turnover.

Public Accountability and Democratic Discourse

By making generational time visible, the DMG Framework enhances public understanding of educational responsibility, fostering democratic dialogue about the kind of society current policies are creating for future generations.

Limitations and Future Research

The DMG Framework is not predictive. It does not forecast specific social or technological outcomes, nor does it prescribe uniform policy solutions. Rather, it provides a conceptual scaffold for future empirical research, comparative policy analysis, and scenario modeling. Future studies may explore applications of the framework in climate education, global governance, and international development policy.

Conclusion

Educational policy is among the most consequential forms of governance precisely because its effects extend far beyond the present. The Deuce Millennium Generation Framework offers a model for aligning educational policy with this reality, reframing education as a civilizational project that unfolds across generations. By extending the policy horizon to the year 3000, the framework challenges policymakers to confront their ethical responsibility to people they will never meet—but whose lives are already being shaped by today's decisions.

References

Banks, J. A. (2006). Cultural diversity and education: Foundations, curriculum, and teaching (5th ed.). Pearson.

Howe, N., & Strauss, W. (1991). Generations: The history of America's future, 1584 to 2069. William Morrow.

Inayatullah, S. (2008). Six pillars: Futures thinking for transforming. Foresight, 10(1), 4–21. **https://doi.org/10.1108/14636680810855991**

Ladson-Billings, G. (1995). Toward a theory of culturally relevant pedagogy. American Educational Research Journal, 32(3), 465–491.

Mannheim, K. (1952). Essays on the sociology of knowledge. Routledge & Kegan Paul.

Rawls, J. (1971). A theory of justice. Harvard University Press.

Slaughter, R. A. (1995). The foresight principle: Cultural recovery in the 21st century. Adamantine Press.

UNESCO. (2015). Rethinking education: Towards a global common good? UNESCO.

Chapter 20

Epochs as Decision Windows: Education, Debt, and the Illusion of Access

Time is not uniform. Certain moments carry disproportionate weight, shaping outcomes long after the moment itself has passed. In futures studies, these moments are often described as "critical junctures" or "decision points." The DMG framework formalizes this insight by identifying each generational cohort as a decision window—a bounded period during which institutional choices echo forward across multiple generations.

Traditional planning models assume continuity unless disrupted. DMG assumes the opposite: that continuity must be actively constructed, generation by generation. Each DMG cohort represents a window during which societies choose—explicitly or implicitly—what knowledge will be prioritized, what histories will be transmitted, and what futures will remain imaginable.

Educational institutions sit at the center of these decisions. Curriculum adoption, teacher preparation, governance structures, and resource allocation all occur within generational windows. Yet these decisions are rarely framed as futures choices. DMG recontextualizes everyday institutional actions as epochal acts.

By clustering DMGs into larger epochs, the model allows planners to distinguish between incremental adjustment and structural transformation. Some epochs stabilize systems; others reorient them. The model does not predict which epochs will be transformative, but it makes visible the consequences of neglect when decision windows are ignored.

Below is a critical claim with conceptual clarity, scholarly grounding, and alignment to the DMG arc.

Decision Windows and Institutional Inertia
Futures Are Lost Less by Catastrophe than by Drift

History often narrates the loss of futures through catastrophe—wars, depressions, pandemics, revolutions. Yet most educational futures are not destroyed in dramatic rupture. They are diminished through institutional inertia.

This chapter advances a central claim of the Deuce Millennium Generation (DMG) framework: futures are lost less often through visible crisis than through the quiet failure to act during bounded periods of possibility. These bounded periods are decision windows—moments when institutional choices reverberate forward across multiple generations. When such windows close without deliberate intervention, the default outcome is not neutrality. It is the reproduction of inequality, fragmentation, and short-termism.

DMG formalizes this insight by identifying each generational cohort as a decision window—a structured opportunity for redirection. In this sense, generational time is not merely descriptive. It is normative. It places moral weight on institutional action.

Institutional Inertia as Democratic Risk

Institutional inertia does not require malicious intent. It often emerges from procedural stability, bureaucratic complexity, political compromise, and what Hannah Arendt described as the routinization of action in administrative systems (Arendt 1958). Institutions continue to function, but they cease to imagine.

Educational systems are particularly vulnerable to this form of drift. Curricula persist. Funding formulas roll forward. Accountability mechanisms calcify. Reform cycles repeat familiar patterns. Yet demographic realities shift, technological landscapes evolve, and democratic expectations transform. The structure remains; the world moves.

John Dewey warned that democracy depends upon education's capacity to reconstruct experience in light of changing conditions (Dewey 1916). When education fails to reconstruct itself, it becomes archival rather than generative. It preserves past arrangements without preparing future citizens.

DMG interprets this drift through temporal structure. Every DMG epoch contains a decision window—approximately one generational span—during which policymakers, educators, and civic leaders can redirect long-term trajectories. When those windows close without structural reform, inequality hardens into legacy.

The failure is rarely explosive. It is incremental.

Decision Windows: Bounded Possibility

A decision window is not merely a reform moment. It is a generational threshold when institutional imagination is both possible and necessary.

Decision windows often open under three conditions:

Demographic transition (population shifts, migration, generational turnover)

Technological transformation (printing press, industrialization, digital revolution)

Political realignment (constitutional change, civil rights movements, new policy regimes)

When these conditions converge, institutional architecture becomes malleable. At such moments, deliberate educational design can interrupt inherited inequities.

But when reform is deferred, diluted, or narrowed to short-term metrics, the window closes.

The DMG model maps these windows across long arcs of time. Rather than focusing on five- or ten-year reform cycles, it situates education within century-scale continuity. Each DMG epoch thus becomes a structured moment of accountability: What was possible? What was done? What was deferred?

The Default Setting: Reproduction of Inequality

The absence of deliberate action does not produce stasis. It produces patterned reproduction.

Policy Memory as Guardrail

demonstrates that inequality reproduces itself through institutional continuity—through funding formulas tied to property wealth, selective admissions mechanisms, cultural capital distribution, and differential access to advanced curricula. Without interruption, these systems stabilize stratification.

Rawls's intergenerational thought experiment asks institutions to design principles behind a veil of ignorance extended across time (Rawls 1971). DMG extends that logic historically. If we evaluate each generational window from the perspective of those not yet born, institutional inertia appears not as neutrality but as ethical failure.

Inertia allows:

Short-term political cycles to dominate long-term educational planning

Fiscal expediency to override structural investment

Policy fatigue to dilute reform energy

Crisis response to replace preventive design

The result is fragmentation—unequal districts, polarized narratives, and declining civic trust.

Interrupting the Default: The DMG Intervention

DMG offers a structural interruption.

It does so in three ways:

1. Temporal Expansion

DMG expands policy imagination beyond electoral cycles. By situating each cohort within a 2,000-year horizon and projecting toward a 3MG framework (three millennia), it forces institutions to ask: What will this decision mean two generations from now? Five? Ten?

Temporal expansion disciplines urgency. It reframes educational investment as democratic infrastructure rather than discretionary spending.

2. Ethical Accountability Across Generations

DMG embeds moral continuity within policy analysis. Each decision window becomes an ethical threshold. Leaders must ask not only what is efficient but what is sustainable across cohorts.

Dr. Martin Luther King Jr.'s moral arc metaphor—"the arc of the moral universe is long, but it bends toward justice"—is not a passive assurance. It is a call to generational practice (King 1963). The arc bends only through deliberate institutional effort.

DMG transforms that metaphor into structural expectation.

3. Policy Memory as Guardrail

Institutional inertia thrives when systems forget. DMG creates policy memory by mapping reforms onto generational timelines. Instead of evaluating policy solely by immediate outcomes, it examines longitudinal consequences.

Policy memory reduces repetition. It documents how previous windows were opened or squandered. It restores historical consciousness to reform discourse.

Carter G. Woodson warned that miseducation occurs when institutions sever communities from historical continuity (Woodson 1933). DMG answers Woodson by embedding education within extended historical awareness.

Case Illustration: Civil Rights as a Decision Window

The Civil Rights Movement represented a major decision window in American education. Legal segregation was dismantled. Federal enforcement expanded. Higher education access broadened.

Yet subsequent decades reveal how partial implementation allowed inertia to reassert itself. Re-segregation, funding inequities, and policy retrenchment illustrate how a window, once partially closed, permits the reconstitution of inequality

DMG does not dismiss progress. It asks whether progress was institutionally anchored across multiple generations.

A window can open. It can even produce reform. But unless embedded in structural continuity, the default setting returns.

Futures Planning as Institutional Design

Futures scholarship often focuses on technological foresight or speculative modeling. DMG re-centers education as the only institution guaranteed to span generations. Markets fluctuate. Governments reconfigure. Educational systems persist.

Therefore, futures planning without educational design becomes fragile.

To design educational futures across decision windows requires:

Intergenerational fiscal planning Curriculum that integrates historical continuity with emerging competencies Democratic participation structures that persist beyond electoral cycles Archival preservation of reform memory Without these, institutional inertia becomes destiny.

From Drift to Design

The DMG framework advances a disciplined optimism. It does not deny catastrophe. It recognizes that crises accelerate or compress decision windows. But the greater danger lies in drift—when institutions continue without imagination.

Drift normalizes inequality. Drift fragments civic identity. Drift shortens policy horizons.

DMG interrupts drift by rendering time visible.

When time is mapped, windows become legible. When windows are legible, responsibility becomes measurable. When responsibility becomes measurable, design becomes possible.

Futures are not secured through prediction. They are secured through deliberate institutional action during bounded moments of possibility.

Conclusion: The Moral Weight of Timing

Institutional inertia is rarely dramatic. It is procedural, incremental, and often defended as stability. Yet stability without reconstruction becomes stagnation.

DMG reframes generational cohorts as structured opportunities. Each cohort is a decision window. Each window carries moral weight.

If action is delayed, the system defaults toward inherited patterns. If action is deliberate, trajectories shift.

The question, then, is not whether the future will arrive. It is whether institutions will act before their window closes.

The following chapter turns from diagnosis to design. If decision windows exist, how should educational systems intentionally structure reform across three generations? What principles can anchor policy beyond electoral cycles? How might institutions cultivate memory strong enough to resist drift?
Chapter 21 begins that constructive turn.

References

Arendt, Hannah. 1958. The Human Condition. Chicago: University of Chicago Press.

Dewey, John. 1916. Democracy and Education. New York: Macmillan.

King, Martin Luther Jr. 1963. "I Have a Dream." Speech delivered August 28, 1963, Washington, DC.

Rawls, John. 1971. A Theory of Justice. Cambridge, MA: Harvard University Press.

Woodson, Carter G. 1933. The Mis-Education of the Negro. Washington, DC: Associated Publishers.

This chapter advances a critical claim: futures are lost less often through catastrophe than through institutional inertia. When decision windows close without deliberate action, futures default to the reproduction of inequality, fragmentation, or short-termism. DMG offers a means of interrupting that default.

Chapter 21

Civil Inclusion Without Influence:

Planning Across Centuries

Most institutions struggle to plan beyond five years. Some manage ten. Very few attempt to imagine responsibility beyond a generation. This limitation is not simply a failure of imagination; it is a failure of temporal design. Institutions lack tools that make century-scale thinking operational rather than aspirational.

The DMG framework addresses this gap by extending planning horizons without demanding predictive certainty. Planning across centuries does not require knowing what the future will be; it requires knowing who will inherit it. DMG shifts the focus of planning from outcomes to succession.

Century-scale planning is not about permanence. It is about resilience—the capacity of institutions to adapt while maintaining continuity of purpose. Education systems already operate at this scale implicitly, as each cohort moves through them regardless of policy instability. DMG makes this implicit continuity explicit, enabling institutions to plan responsibly rather than reactively.

This chapter demonstrates how DMG can be used to align long-range vision with short-term action. Policies enacted today are framed not as endpoints, but as contributions to a chain of generational stewardship. Planning documents become intergenerational letters rather than administrative artifacts.

Chapter 21 deepens the theoretical clarity of Epochs 1–3, sharpens the philosophical claim about succession over prediction

Planning Without Prophecy: Succession, Epochs, and the Ethics of Long Design

I. The Problem of Predictive Planning

Modern futures discourse is often trapped in a paradox. Institutions are asked to "plan for the future," yet they are cautioned not to pretend to predict it. The result is paralysis disguised as prudence. Policymakers shorten timelines to what can be measured. Reformers narrow goals to what can be forecast. Educational planning becomes a sequence of short-cycle adjustments rather than a long-horizon design.

The Deuce Millennium Generation (DMG) framework intervenes precisely at this impasse. It advances a disciplined alternative: planning across centuries does not require predictive certainty. It requires succession certainty.

We do not need to know what the year 2300 will look like.

We need to know that someone will be there.

Futures fail when planning confuses uncertainty with impossibility. The inability to predict becomes an excuse not to prepare. DMG reframes the task. The central question is not: What will happen? The central question is: Who will inherit what we build?

Planning shifts from outcome prediction to generational succession.

II. From Outcomes to Inheritance

Most educational reforms are outcome-centered. They ask:

What scores will improve?

What graduation rates will rise?

What metrics will demonstrate success?

While important, such questions remain temporally narrow. They focus on deliverables within a single political or administrative cycle. They assume that planning success can be measured within the lifespan of the planner.

DMG replaces this logic with an inheritance-centered framework. It asks:

What institutional structures will the next generation receive?

What cultural memory will be preserved?

What democratic capacities will endure?

What inequities will harden if left unattended?

In this shift, the planner becomes a steward. The task becomes ethical before it becomes predictive.

Rawls (1971) argued that justice requires consideration of future generations under a "veil of ignorance." Arendt (1961) framed education as the act through which adults assume responsibility for a world they introduce to the young. Dewey (1916) insisted that democracy survives only through reconstruction across time. DMG operationalizes these philosophical commitments by structuring time itself into visible generational epochs.

III. The Three Epochs of the DMG Arc

The Deuce Millennium Generation framework is organized into three macro-epochs spanning 1997–3000:

Epoch 1 (DMG-1 to DMG-17): Stabilization and Structural Equity

Epoch 2 (DMG-18 to DMG-35): Institutional Maturation and Democratic Durability

Epoch 3 (DMG-36 to DMG-53): Civilizational Stewardship and Intergenerational Ethics

These epochs do not predict events. They establish stewardship horizons.

Epoch 1: Stabilization and Structural Equity

Epoch 1 is concerned with correcting inherited inequalities. It spans the generations immediately adjacent to our present decision windows.

This epoch demands:

Infrastructure repair

Equity-driven resource allocation

Protection of democratic norms

Preservation of public education as a shared good

Its central ethical task is interruption: preventing the reproduction of entrenched inequality. If Epoch 1 fails, later epochs inherit instability.

This is the most politically volatile epoch because it confronts existing arrangements. It requires institutional courage.

Epoch 2: Institutional Maturation and Democratic Durability

Epoch 2 assumes that stabilization has occurred sufficiently to allow refinement. Here the focus shifts from repair to resilience.

Key questions include:

How do institutions outlast partisan cycles?
How do educational systems embed civic memory?

How do public schools function as long-term democratic anchors?

In this epoch, the risk is complacency. Once crises recede, systems may drift. Institutional inertia returns in subtle form. DMG's generational mapping ensures that maturation does not devolve into stagnation.

Epoch 2 is about strengthening democratic muscle memory.

Epoch 3: Civilizational Stewardship

Epoch 3 extends beyond ordinary policy cycles into civilizational ethics. It confronts the moral imagination of institutions.

By this stage, planners will not know the technologies, climate realities, or geopolitical conditions of the year 2900. But they will know that:

Human beings will inherit educational systems.

Democratic stability will still require transmission.

Cultural memory will still anchor survival.

Epoch 3 reframes education as humanity's long-term continuity mechanism.

It asks not what outcomes will be achieved, but what ethical posture will endure.

IV. Planning Without Knowing

Critics may argue that planning across centuries risks abstraction. DMG answers that abstraction is avoided precisely by anchoring planning in succession rather than speculation.

We do not design the future by predicting its content. We design it by structuring its handoffs.

Consider a cathedral built over generations. The original architects knew they would not see its completion. Their plans included room for unknown craftsmen. Their designs allowed adaptation without collapse.

Education is that cathedral.

DMG transforms generational cohorts into architectural phases. Each cohort is a decision window. Each epoch is a structural layer. The planner's responsibility is not omniscience but continuity.

V. Interrupting the Default

Without intervention, institutions default toward:

Short-termism

Fragmentation

Inequality reproduction

Political volatility

These are not catastrophic failures. They are accumulative drifts.

DMG interrupts this default by making time visible. When policymakers can see their actions located within Epoch 1, 2, or 3, they are forced to confront scale. Decisions gain temporal weight.

A funding cut is no longer a line-item adjustment. It becomes an intergenerational inheritance decision.

A curriculum revision is no longer a political compromise. It becomes a memory transfer.

DMG does not demand prophecy. It demands accountability across succession.

VI. The Ethical Reorientation of Futures

Martin Luther King Jr. spoke of the "long arc of the moral universe" bending toward justice. That arc does not bend automatically. It bends through practice.

Planning across epochs is a form of moral practice.

Carter G. Woodson understood that memory determines survival. When institutions fail to preserve historical consciousness, communities must carry it themselves. DMG extends Woodson's insight into structural time. It embeds memory within planning itself.

To plan without predicting is to trust that the future belongs to inheritors, not forecasters.

VII. Conclusion: From Prediction to Promise

The DMG framework advances a critical reorientation:

Planning is not prediction.

Planning is succession design.

Futures are not forecasts.

Futures are inheritances.

Epoch 1 stabilizes. Epoch 2 matures. Epoch 3 stewards.

Together, they transform educational planning from short-term management into civilizational continuity.

We may not know what the year 3000 will look like.

But we know it will belong to someone.

By normalizing century-scale thinking, DMG challenges institutions to confront ethical questions they often avoid: What obligations do we have to future learners? What knowledge must survive us? What failures are we willing to pass forward?

Chapter 22

Public Humanities and the Deuce Millennium Generation: Inheriting the Gap

Public humanities institutions—museums, archives, cultural centers—are often treated as repositories of the past. Yet their most powerful function is future-facing. They shape collective memory, define cultural inheritance, and signal what stories matter enough to preserve. In this sense, public humanities institutions are educational futures infrastructure.

The DMG framework positions public humanities as essential partners in generational planning. Exhibitions, oral histories, and interpretive programs are not supplemental to education; they extend it across lifespan and community. When aligned with DMG epochs, public humanities initiatives can reinforce generational continuity beyond formal schooling.

This chapter explores how DMG translates into exhibition design, curriculum alignment, and digital interpretation. By anchoring public narratives to generational cohorts, institutions can move beyond commemorative cycles toward long-range cultural stewardship.

The Smithsonian-affiliated DMG exhibits, curricula, and digital companions exemplify this approach. QR-linked learning, audio narration, and interactive timelines do not merely disseminate information; they model how knowledge travels across generations. The medium becomes the message: continuity is intentional.

Public humanities, when aligned with DMG, become spaces where futures literacy is practiced collectively. Visitors encounter not only what has been, but what must be carried forward.

The Race for the Future: Promise, Practice, and the Design of the Track

The race had been announced years in advance.

It would take place in a global city in 2028, before a vast international audience, and it would be called The Race for the Future. Its purpose, according to the organizers, was simple: to demonstrate that talent, preparation, and determination would determine who crossed the finish line first.

Two competitors were introduced.

One was named Promise.

The other was named Practice.

From the beginning, the crowd's attention gravitated toward Promise. He spoke confidently, eloquently, and often. He made declarations about what he would do once the race was over. He assured everyone that his victory was inevitable. He did not train in public, nor did he feel compelled to explain how he would prepare. "Preparation," he said, "is not the same as destiny."

Practice, on the other hand, trained every day.

He ran in heat and rain. He studied the track. He adjusted his stride when conditions changed. He learned how to pace himself when the ground shifted beneath his feet. No cameras followed him. No speeches announced his progress. His preparation was quiet, disciplined, and constant.

The crowd noticed the contrast.

Many admired Practice's work ethic. Others pitied him. A few questioned why he needed to train so hard if the race was truly fair.

Promise, after all, seemed so certain. “Let Practice do the practicing,” Promise said with a smile. “I promise I will win.”

When race day arrived, both runners took their places in the starting blocks.

The gun fired.

And Promise surged ahead.

The crowd erupted—not in surprise, but in recognition. Some said they had expected it. Others said it simply proved what they had always believed.

Only a few noticed what actually happened.

Promise had started closer to the finish line.

The surface beneath his feet was smooth and carefully maintained. Practice’s lane was uneven, patched together from older materials, marked by inclines and sudden drops that demanded constant adjustment. Promise carried nothing. Practice ran with weight—expectations, debts, histories—added incrementally over time, never acknowledged as part of the race.

The rules, though printed uniformly, were enforced selectively. When Promise stumbled, it was called strategy. When Practice slowed to regain balance, it was called deficiency. Officials praised Promise’s confidence and questioned Practice’s discipline.

Promise had not outrun Practice.

Promise had been advantaged by the design of the track.

The crowd, however, was told they had witnessed merit.

The First Time the Race Was Run: Reconstruction

This was not the first time such a race had been held.

After the Civil War, a race much like it was announced. Newly freed citizens were told they were full participants now—runners at last. Constitutional amendments were passed. The language of citizenship, voting rights, and education filled the air with optimism.

But the track was never rebuilt.

Practice trained. Black communities built schools, churches, businesses, and civic organizations with extraordinary discipline and urgency. They ran despite violence, intimidation, and economic exclusion. Promise, meanwhile, rested on declarations. Federal commitment weakened. Enforcement retreated. The finish line remained visible but unreachable.

When Practice fell behind, observers blamed effort rather than terrain.

The lesson was devastating and enduring: **rights proclaimed without protection become burdens rather than guarantees.**

Trust recalibrated. Participation continued, but allegiance shifted. Parallel institutions emerged—not out of separationist desire, but out of necessity. The race continued, but faith in its fairness did not.

The Second Time the Race Was Run: Civil Rights

A century later, the race was announced again.

This time, the promise was equality. Laws changed. Segregation was dismantled on paper. Education was heralded as the great equalizer. The finish line was described as finally attainable.

Once again, Practice trained.

Families integrated schools under threat. Students endured hostility for the chance to run on a different track. Communities complied with new rules, believing alignment between promise and practice had finally arrived.

But the track adjusted itself quietly.

School funding remained unequal. Housing patterns hardened. Economic opportunity stratified itself behind race-neutral language. When disparities persisted, officials declared the race fair and blamed the runner.

Equality had been promised.

Equity had not been engineered.

The crowd was told the race was over. Practice was told to stop complaining. And yet, the distance to the finish line had not meaningfully changed.

The Current Race: The Deuce Millennium Generation

The Deuce Millennium Generation was born into the longest version of this race.

They were trained from childhood to believe that preparation was the answer. Test scores would unlock doors. Degrees would secure stability. Participation would yield influence. They practiced relentlessly—credentialing themselves, adapting to shifting rules, absorbing costs previously carried by institutions.

Meanwhile, Promise spoke constantly.

Promise promised innovation without investment. Access without support. Participation without power. Promise promised the future while deferring responsibility for the present.

When the gun fired for this generation, the pattern repeated.

Those who prepared most often faced the greatest precarity. Access arrived bundled with debt. Participation arrived without authority. Truth became negotiable. Rules changed mid-race, then were declared neutral.

The Deuce Millennium Generation noticed.

They did not stop running.

They stopped believing the race was honest.

So they recalibrated.

They trained outside the stadium. They built new lanes. They formed networks rather than waiting for invitations. Their skepticism was not laziness—it was literacy. They had learned how the track worked.

What the Allegory Reveals

Promise wins when systems reward declaration over discipline.

Practice loses when effort is asked to compensate for design.

This is not a story about individual failure. It is a story about institutional responsibility. When societies confuse intention with outcome, confidence with competence, and promise with practice, trust erodes—not suddenly, but structurally.

The erosion is cumulative.

Each unfair race teaches runners to expect less.

Each shifted rule teaches them to invest elsewhere.

Each denied reality teaches them to trust provisionally.

The Choice Still Before Us

The race can be redesigned.

Promise can be required to practice.

Practice can be rewarded rather than burdened.

Starting lines can be equalized.

Tracks can be rebuilt.

Rules can be enforced consistently.

If that happens, the Deuce Millennium Generation will not need persuasion. They are already prepared. They are already trained. They have been running under conditions that demanded more of them than of those ahead.

But if the race continues as designed, history will record another generation that understood the truth too well to pretend otherwise.

Promise will keep winning applause.

Practice will keep carrying the cost.

And democracy will keep mistaking advantage for merit.

Closing Line

The future does not belong to Promise or Practice alone.

It belongs to whoever finally has the courage to rebuild the track.

Descriptive Analysis

This story lands because the answer isn't athletic—it's structural.

When the gun fired, Promise outran Practice not because Promise was stronger, faster, or better prepared, but because the race itself was never neutral.

Here's what caused Promise to win:

What Actually Happened in the Race for the Future

Promise started closer to the finish line.

Promise ran on a smoother track while Practice ran on uneven ground.

Promise had rules rewritten mid-race to his advantage.

Promise was cheered as inevitable, while Practice was scrutinized, timed, and penalized.

Promise carried no extra weight, while Practice ran with historical burdens strapped to his back.

Promise didn't train—because the system was already trained to carry him.

Practice trained every day—because the system required him to.

The Deeper Meaning of the Analogy

The crowd believed they were watching a fair competition between Promise and Practice.

They were not.

They were watching what generations have watched before:

Promise rewarded for intention

Practice burdened with proof

Outcome mistaken for merit

Advantage mistaken for excellence

Promise did not win because he practiced less.

Promise won because the race was designed to reward promise without practice.

Why This Matters for the Deuce Millennium Generation

The Deuce Millennium Generation has been running this race their entire lives.

They were told:

"If you work hard, you'll succeed."

"If you prepare, opportunity will follow."

"If you believe in the promise, the future is yours."

But what they observed was different:

Those who practiced the most were asked to wait

Those who promised the most were allowed to leap ahead

Those who followed the rules were told the rules had changed

Those who questioned the race were accused of lacking discipline

So they stopped cheering the starting gun.

Not because they don't believe in effort—but because they finally understood the design of the track.

The Warning Embedded in the Story

If society continues to celebrate Promise while neglecting Practice:

Trust erodes

Effort feels naïve

Preparation feels unrewarded

Participation feels performative

Young people don't stop running because they're lazy.

They stop believing because they keep losing races they trained to win.

The Opportunity the Story Reveals

The race does not have to be this way.

Alignment means:

Promise must practice

Practice must be rewarded

Starting lines must be equal

Rules must apply to everyone

The finish line must be real

If that happens, the Deuce Millennium Generation will not need to be motivated.

They are already trained.

They are already prepared.

They are already running.

What they are waiting for is a race worthy of their effort.

Closing Line (Book / Keynote Ready)

Promise keeps winning because we let it.

Practice keeps training because it has no choice.

Democratic renewal begins when we finally make them meet on the same track.

Footnotes and Historical Anchors

11. Reconstruction (1865–1877): The allegory's first race corresponds to the post–Civil War constitutional moment—13th, 14th, and 15th Amendments—followed by federal retreat, the Compromise of 1877, Black Codes, and Jim Crow. See Eric Foner, *Reconstruction: America's Unfinished Revolution.*

12. Civil Rights Era (1954–1975): The second race reflects desegregation after Brown v. Board of Education, the Civil Rights Act of 1964, and the Voting Rights Act of 1965, alongside unequal school funding, housing segregation, and deindustrialization. See Thomas Sugrue, *Sweet Land of Liberty.*

13. Deuce Millennium Policy Failures (2000–2025): The current race maps onto neoliberal education reform, student debt expansion, erosion of labor protections, voter suppression, and declining institutional trust among Millennials and Gen Z. See Jacob Hacker & Paul Pierson, *Winner-Take-All Politics;* Pew Research Center on generational trust.

Full-Page Visual Race Diagram (Facing Page)

Figure X.1 – The Race for the Future: Designed Inequality

16. Two parallel lanes labeled Promise and Practice
17. Promise's lane begins 30% closer to the finish line
18. Promise's surface: smooth, maintained, unburdened
19. Practice's lane: uneven terrain, added weights labeled *Debt, History, Selective Enforcement*
20. Officials positioned unevenly, signaling rule discretion
21. Finish line labeled *Democratic Legitimacy & Trust*

Chapter 23

Technology, Memory, and Continuity

Technological change is often treated as the primary driver of the future. Educational institutions are routinely urged to "keep up" with innovation, adapt to emerging platforms, and prepare learners for jobs that do not yet exist. Yet technology alone does not determine futures. Without memory, technology accelerates fragmentation rather than continuity. The critical question is not how fast technology changes, but what knowledge survives those changes.

The Deuce Millennium Generation (DMG) framework reframes technology as a carrier, not a driver, of generational continuity. Digital tools—QR codes, interactive timelines, audio narration, and microsites—are not futures in themselves. They are vessels through which memory is stabilized across cohorts. When designed intentionally, technology becomes a bridge between generations rather than a rupture.

Education systems have historically struggled with technological transitions precisely because they lacked long-range frameworks. New tools are layered atop old structures without attention to generational handoff. DMG corrects this by embedding technology within cohort progression. Each DMG epoch inherits not only tools, but interpretive responsibility—the obligation to curate what is passed forward.

This chapter argues that the true risk of technological change is not obsolescence, but amnesia. Societies that innovate without memory lose continuity of purpose. DMG positions digital infrastructure as a means of preserving intergenerational coherence, ensuring that futures remain intelligible to those who inherit them.

Up to this point, this chapter has traced the distance between democratic ideals and institutional outcomes. History has shown where the gaps emerged, how they widened, and whom they burdened. Yet analysis alone cannot fully capture the moral clarity of this divide. What follows is not a departure from policy analysis, but its distillation. Through allegory, the contradictions of democratic promise and democratic practice become visible at once—compressed into a single race whose outcome has been centuries in the making.

This following shares four key points why this chapter is of critical importance:

Theoretical legitimacy → protects against “just a story” critique

Pedagogical utility → increases classroom and museum adoption

Policy clarity → makes abstraction actionable

Press alignment → appropriate framing

The writer made a great analogy when he told the story at a banquet in his keynote speech:

There was great track meet scheduled to take place. It was plan in an international city in the year 2028. The two competitors named "Promise" and the other was named "Practice." The crowd was anxious as they awaited the history making Race for the Future. They has seen how Mr. Practice dedicated his prior four years to practicing daily. However, the crowd has never seen Mr. Promise doing any preparation for the big Race for the Future. Mr. Promise was so confident that he would win that he never practiced. He said let Mr. Practice do the practicing. I promise that I will win, and my win will put him in his place. On the day of the race, they were in their starting blocks. When the gun was fired to start the race, what caused Promise to outrun Practice?

Yet, there were several other versions.

Below are versions of the story, each designed for a different moment and audience. All three answer the central question—what caused Promise to outrun Practice?

Version 1: The Keynote Banquet Version

(Elevated, vivid, and ceremonial)

Dr. Jesse Hargrove once shared an analogy at a major banquet during a keynote address that brought the room to a hush.

He asked the audience to imagine a great international track meet, scheduled to take place in a global city in the year 2028. The event was called The Race for the Future, and the world had gathered to witness history.

There were two competitors.

One was named Practice.

For four long years, the crowd had watched Practice train. Every morning. Every season. Rain or shine. He studied the track. He strengthened his stride. He learned from failure. No one questioned his preparation—only whether preparation would be enough.

The other competitor was named Promise.

Curiously, no one had ever seen Promise train. Not once. He never practiced publicly, never broke a sweat, never appeared concerned. When asked about it, Promise would smile and say, "Let Practice do the practicing. I promise I will win."

He was confident. Assured. Untouched by doubt.

On the day of the race, the stadium was electric. The runners stepped into their starting blocks. The crowd leaned forward. The gun fired.

And Promise surged ahead.

The question Dr. Hargrove posed to the audience was simple—but unsettling:

What caused Promise to outrun Practice?

It wasn't speed.

It wasn't discipline.

It wasn't effort.

Promise won because he started closer to the finish line.

The race itself had been designed that way.

Version 2: The Policy & Civic Version

(Sharper, explicit, ideal for lawmakers or public forums)

At a large public gathering, Dr. Jesse Hargrove once told a story that sounded like sports—but was really about systems.

He described a highly anticipated track meet, set in an international city in 2028. The event was called The Race for the Future, and it featured two runners: Promise and Practice.

Practice had done everything right.

For four years, Practice trained daily. He followed every rule. He trusted the system. He believed that preparation would be rewarded.

Promise, on the other hand, never trained at all.

When questioned, Promise laughed. "Why should I practice?" he said. "I promise I'll win. And when I do, it will put Practice in his place."

The crowd assumed confidence would eventually meet reality.

Race day arrived. The runners took their places. The gun sounded.

Promise won.

Not because he ran harder.

Not because he ran smarter.

But because the system gave him a head start.

Different starting lines.

Different standards.

Different rules are quietly enforced.

Dr. Hargrove turned to the audience and said:

“When we reward promise more than practice, we should not be surprised who wins—or who stops believing in the race.”

Version 3: The Commencement / Youth-Facing Version

(Direct, moral, and resonant)

Dr. Jesse Hargrove once told a story that speaks especially to young people.

He said: imagine a race called The Race for the Future, scheduled in 2028, in front of the whole world.

There are two runners.

One is Practice. Practice trains every day. He sacrifices. He studies. He prepares because he believes the rules are real.

The other is Promise. Promise doesn’t train. He doesn’t need to. He says, “I promise I’ll win. That’s enough.”

People laugh—but they also believe him.

On race day, both runners crouch in their starting blocks. The gun goes off.

Promise wins.

Not because Practice failed.

Not because effort didn’t matter.

But because Practice was running uphill, carrying weight, and being timed differently.

Promise had a smoother track.

Promise had fewer barriers.

Promise had the benefit of belief.

Dr. Hargrove ended the story by saying:

"This generation isn't tired of running. They're tired of races where preparation isn't rewarded. **Fix the track**—and watch how fast Practice can go."

Hargrove's story functions as an allegory of Promise versus Practice because every element in it operates on two levels at once: a simple, accessible narrative and a deeper structural critique of democratic systems. Here's what makes it an allegory—rather than just a parable or anecdote.

1. The Characters Are Abstractions, Not Individuals

Promise and Practice are not people; they are principles.

Promise represents declarations: laws passed, speeches made, rights announced, anniversaries celebrated.

Practice represents implementation: enforcement, investment, accountability, and time-bound follow-through.

Because the competitors are named for concepts, the story immediately signals allegory. The race is not about who runs faster—it's about which principle actually governs outcomes.

2. The Race Is a System, Not an Event

The "Race for the Future" mirrors democracy itself:

It has rules (laws and institutions)

A starting line (formal equality)

A finish line (justice, opportunity, legitimacy)

An audience (the public)

And an official gun (policy action)

Allegory emerges because the race appears fair on the surface, yet its outcome depends on preconditions established long before the gun fires—just as democratic outcomes depend on historical investment, not last-minute declarations.

3. Preparation Equals Policy

Practice trains for years. Promise does not.

This reflects a central truth of governance:

Rights without infrastructure do not produce results.

Reconstruction promised citizenship without protection.

Civil Rights promised equality without full enforcement.

The Deuce Millennium promised access without affordability or influence.

Practice's daily preparation symbolizes sustained policy, budgeting, oversight, and enforcement—the unglamorous work democracy requires.

4. The Surprise Outcome Exposes the Illusion of Confidence

The audience expects Promise to win because:

It sounds good

It speaks confidently

It carries symbolic authority

This mirrors public life, where rhetoric often substitutes for readiness. When Promise "outruns" Practice, the allegory reveals how systems can be engineered to reward promise even when practice is weak—through shortcuts, rule changes, or selective enforcement.

The question “What caused Promise to outrun Practice?” is the allegorical pivot. The answer is not speed—it is structural advantage.

5. Time Collapses Into One Moment

By placing the race in 2028, the story collapses centuries of policy history into a single event. This is classic allegory: long-term consequences made visible in one decisive scene.

Reconstruction, Civil Rights, and the Deuce Millennium are all “pre-race conditions” that shape the outcome—whether acknowledged or not.

6. The Moral Is Systemic, Not Personal

The story does not blame Practice for losing or praise Promise for winning. Instead, it asks:

Who set the rules?

Who controlled the starting conditions?

Who decided what counts as winning?

That shift—from character to structure—is what makes the story an allegory of democracy itself.

7. Why This Allegory Resonates Now

For the Deuce Millennium Generation, the story names a lived reality:

They were promised access

They practiced compliance

Yet outcomes remained uneven

The allegory explains why trust erodes: not because people reject democracy, but because they experience the gap between what is promised and what is practiced.

In One Sentence

Hargrove's story is an allegory of Promise versus Practice because it transforms democratic failure from a matter of intention into a question of structure, preparation, and alignment, revealing that democracy succeeds not when it is promised—but when it is practiced.

Promise vs. Practice: Allegory as Democratic Diagnosis

Allegory has long functioned as a method for exposing systemic contradictions that cannot be fully apprehended through empirical description alone. In the tradition of Plato's Allegory of the Cave, George Orwell's Animal Farm, Ralph Ellison's Invisible Man, and James Baldwin's moral essays on American innocence, allegory renders structural power visible by transforming abstraction into lived narrative.[1]

The allegory of Promise versus Practice operates within this lineage. It does not accuse individuals of moral failure; instead, it interrogates systems that reward declaration over discipline, rhetoric over readiness, and symbolism over sustained investment. The "Race for the Future" dramatizes a central democratic paradox: equality is proclaimed at the starting line, yet outcomes are determined by preparation, rule design, and historical advantage established long before the race begins.

In this framing, Promise represents the declarative state—laws announced, rights named, anniversaries celebrated—while Practice represents the administrative state—budgets, enforcement, oversight, and time. The allegory exposes how democratic legitimacy erodes when promises accumulate faster than practices capable of honoring them.

For the Deuce Millennium Generation, this allegory is not metaphorical but experiential. They inherit a democracy rich in language and thin in follow-through. The allegory therefore functions as both warning and diagnostic tool: warning that misalignment produces cynicism, and diagnostic in revealing where policy repair must occur.

Footnotes (for this subsection)

Plato, Republic, Book VII; George Orwell, Animal Farm (1945); Ralph Ellison, Invisible Man (1952); James Baldwin, The Fire Next Time (1963). Each uses allegory or moral abstraction to reveal systemic contradictions masked by dominant narratives of progress.

Teaching Guide / Policy Explainer

Teaching the Allegory: Promise vs. Practice

Learning Objectives

Distinguish between symbolic policy commitments and structural implementation

Understand how historical inequities shape present outcomes

Analyze trust erosion through systemic misalignment

Discussion Questions

Why does Practice train while Promise does not?

What historical "pre-race conditions" affect the outcome?

How do systems reward Promise even when Practice is stronger?

Where do we see this dynamic today in education, voting, housing, or labor?

Policy Translation

Promise without funding = unmet rights

Practice without visibility = undervalued governance

Alignment = democratic maturity

Assessment Activity

Ask students or policymakers to redesign the race:

Move the starting line?

Standardize rules?

Invest in training?

Redefine the finish line?

Chapter 24

The Race for the Future: Promise vs Practice

Training Futures Literacy

If futures are to be planned responsibly, futures literacy must be taught. Yet futures thinking remains marginal in educator preparation, leadership training, and policy education. When it appears at all, it is treated as an elective or enrichment rather than as a core civic competency. The DMG framework insists that futures literacy is an educational obligation, not a speculative exercise.

Futures literacy, as defined here, is the capacity to understand one's actions as part of a generational sequence. It requires the ability to locate oneself within time—not merely historically, but prospectively. DMG offers a concrete structure for cultivating this capacity by anchoring futures thinking to cohort movement and institutional succession.

Teacher education programs, leadership academies, and policy institutes can use DMG as a scaffolding device. Rather than asking participants to imagine abstract futures, the model asks them to consider who follows them, what those successors will inherit, and what responsibilities remain unfinished. Futures literacy thus becomes relational rather than predictive.

This chapter positions DMG as a training framework for educators, administrators, and docents. By integrating DMG into professional development, institutions move beyond reform cycles toward stewardship cultures. Futures literacy becomes less about anticipation and more about accountability.

Global Adaptability and Comparative Futures

Although the DMG framework emerges from U.S. educational history, its structure is not nationally bound. All education systems, regardless of context, confront the same challenge: transmitting knowledge and responsibility across generations under conditions of uncertainty. DMG offers a comparative futures framework adaptable to diverse cultural, political, and institutional settings.

Global education systems differ in governance, curriculum, and scale, yet cohort progression remains universal. DMG's emphasis on generational flow rather than demographic labeling allows it to be translated across contexts without imposing cultural uniformity. The model does not prescribe content; it structures temporal responsibility.

This chapter explores how DMG can be adapted for international education planning, development initiatives, and global policy coordination. It aligns particularly well with long-term sustainability goals, postcolonial education reform, and intergenerational justice frameworks. By extending planning horizons beyond donor cycles and political transitions, DMG offers a counterweight to short-term development logic.

Global futures demand models that honor difference while sustaining continuity. DMG provides a shared temporal language without erasing local meaning.

Production-ready digital/audio infrastructure is within the Global Adaptability and the Futures Grasp

Audio Script Templates

DMG Cluster Narration (5-Generation / Century Groupings)

(Designed for QR-triggered audio, docent playback, or app-based tours)

Audio Template A: Standard DMG Cluster (2–3 minutes)

Tone: Calm, authoritative, reflective

Audience: General public, museum visitors, educators

You are standing before a cluster of five Deuce Millennium Generations—roughly one century of educational time.

In the Deuce Millennium Generation framework, education is not a reform cycle or a policy moment. It is a relay across generations. What is learned, preserved, interrupted, or neglected in one generation shapes the conditions of learning for the next.

This cluster represents a period in which schools, families, institutions, and cultures carried knowledge forward under changing political and social conditions. Policies shifted. Technologies evolved. But education remained the one institution that never reset.

As you move along this timeline, consider this question: What responsibilities do we inherit from past learners—and what obligations do we owe to learners not yet born?

The Deuce Millennium Map invites us to plan not for the next election or reform, but **for the next century.**

Audio Template B: Policy-Focused Variant (2 minutes)

Audience: Policymakers, civic leaders, students of governance

This DMG cluster reveals a core tension in modern governance: policy moves quickly, while education unfolds slowly.

Laws are passed, repealed, and replaced within years. Yet students remain in classrooms for decades, and educational consequences echo for generations.

The Deuce Millennium Generation model asks policymakers to locate their decisions within a much longer horizon—one where accountability is measured not in outcomes this year, but in conditions inherited one hundred years from now.

In this cluster, short-term decisions produced long-term consequences. The question before us is whether future decisions will do the same—or do better.

Audio Template C: Cultural Memory & Survival Variant (2–3 minutes)

Audience: Public humanities, African American history contexts

Across centuries, communities have survived not only through policy, but through memory—through teaching, storytelling, ritual, and the quiet work of transmission.

This cluster reflects generations who learned under unequal conditions, yet carried knowledge forward anyway. Education here is not only schooling; it is survival infrastructure.

The Deuce Millennium Map draws from African American traditions of long thinking—where time is measured not in decades, but in endurance.

These generations remind us that education is how cultures remember themselves into the future.

Figure Insertion for Book

(Global–ready)

Figure 1. The Hargrove Deuce Millennium Map

Figure Caption (book-ready):

Figure 1. The Hargrove Deuce Millennium Map.

The Deuce Millennium Generation (DMG) Map represents education as a continuous intergenerational process spanning fifty-three generations (DMG-1 to DMG-53) across approximately one thousand years. Displayed as a horizontal timeline with vertical overlays—education, policy regimes, and cultural memory—the model enables policymakers, educators, and scholars to conceptualize long-term responsibility beyond short-cycle reforms. Developed by Jesse J. Hargrove, Ph.D., the DMG framework positions education as the only institution that reliably spans centuries and therefore must anchor futures planning.

In-text callout (example):

As illustrated in Figure 1, the DMG framework reframes generational analysis by extending the planning horizon from decades to centuries.

Touring Exhibit Panel Layouts

Using the Stacked DMG Model

Option 1: 3-Panel Core Exhibit (Small Venues)

Panel 1 — "Seeing Time Differently"

Intro to DMG concept

Partial timeline (DMG-1 to DMG-15)

Education overlay emphasized

Panel 2 — "Institutions Across Generations"

Full stacked model (education / policy / memory)

Century clustering visually highlighted

One QR code per cluster

Panel 3 — "Responsibility to the Long Future"

3MG horizon

Visitor reflection prompts

Audio station or listening bench

Option 2: 6-Panel Traveling Exhibit (Medium Galleries)

Origins of Long Thinking (Woodson → DMG)

Limits of Generational Theory

DMG Timeline + Century Clusters

Vertical Overlays Explained

Policy Consequences Across Time

Education as Stewardship of the Future

Each panel:

One visual anchor

120–150 words max

One QR/audio interaction

Option 3: 12-Panel Immersive Exhibit (Flagship Install)

One panel per thematic chapter cluster

Alternating visual rhythm:

Timeline panel

Interpretation panel

Multiple audio voices:

Scholar

Educator

Student / descendant

This version mirrors the book's intellectual arc, allowing the exhibit and manuscript to reinforce each other.

Why this matters

You now have:

A repeatable audio system that scales from museums to classrooms

A theoretically precise figure anchoring the book's argument

A modular exhibit architecture funders and institutions immediately understand

The Deuce Millennium Generation now has a Theory, a book, and an exhibit that speak the same language of time.

Chapter 25

Letter Looking at America250 Through the Eyes of Celia Adams

Two hundred-fifty years after Independence, the United States stands at a familiar crossroads—invoking democracy while struggling to fulfill its promise. Still Chasing Democracy reframes the American story through the life of Celia Adams, a Black woman born into slavery in Richmond, Virginia, whose forced journey through the domestic slave trade and lifelon commitment to education reveal the nation's deepest contradictions and its most enduring hopes.

Drawing on archival records, oral history, and public memory, Dr. Jesse J. Hargrove traces how Adams's life intersected with the rise of American institutions—from slave markets and church basements to Reconstruction classrooms and the foundations of historically Black education. Her story illuminates how democracy in America was not granted but pursued—carried forward by those denied its protections yet determined to claim its meaning.

Blending family history with national narrative, Still Chasing Democracy challenges celebratory accounts of the American experiment and insists on a fuller reckoning at the nation's semiquincentennial. Through Celia Adams's eyes, democracy emerges not as a settled achievement, but as an unfinished project—shaped by memory, resistance, faith, and the quiet labor of generations who believed America could become what it promised.

At once intimate and expansive, this book offers a vital contribution to American history, African American studies, and public discourse—reminding us that the pursuit of democracy has always depended on those most often excluded from it.

Optional short back-cover blurb (for presses that prefer tighter copy)

At America's 250th anniversary, Still Chasing Democracy tells the nation's story through the life of Celia Adams, a woman born into slavery whose journey exposes the distance between democratic ideals and lived reality. Grounded in archival research and public memory, this book reveals democracy not as inheritance, but as pursuit—shaped by those who were forced to demand what the nation promised but withheld.

Reasons Why the Celia Adams story works

Centers Celia Adams as historical witness, not symbol

Signals scholarly credibility without academic heaviness

Positions the book squarely in the America 250 moment

Aligns with museum, university press, and serious trade readers

1. Reason One

Academic/Regional Focus:

In Still Chasing Democracy, Dr. Jesse J. Hargrove intertwines the life of Celia Adams with the broader American narrative, revealing how democracy was both a promise and a pursuit. This compelling blend of regional history and personal journey offers new insights into the legacy of African American resilience and the unfinished work of democracy in the heart of America.

2. Reason Two

Educational/Scholarly Focus:

Still Chasing Democracy offers a profound exploration of American democracy through the lived experience of Celia Adams. By weaving her journey from slavery to the foundations of Black education, Dr. Hargrove illuminates the complex interplay of history, memory, and identity. This narrative is an essential read for those examining the ongoing quest for equality and justice in American history.

3. Reason Three

Innovative/Interdisciplinary Focus:

In Still Chasing Democracy, Dr. Jesse J. Hargrove transcends traditional historical narrative by placing Celia Adams at the heart of America's democratic journey. This richly layered work intertwines biography, public history, and social justice, offering a fresh perspective on the ongoing struggle for equality. Ideal for readers seeking a dynamic, interdisciplinary approach to American history and the human experience.

4. Reason Four

Global/Trade Focus:

Still Chasing Democracy presents a compelling, human-centered lens on America's quest for equality. Through the life of Celia Adams, Dr. Jesse J. Hargrove explores the enduring tension between America's democratic ideals and its historical realities. This narrative, rich in archival depth and reflective insight, offers readers a global perspective on the unfinished journey toward true democracy.

Narrative Address:

In Still Chasing Democracy, Dr. Jesse J. Hargrove explores the life of Celia Adams, a woman born into slavery who became a silent witness to America's evolving democracy. From the brutal realities of the slave trade to the foundations of Black education, Adams's journey is a powerful testament to resilience, faith, and the unfulfilled promises of democracy.

A Legacy Endures:

Dr. Jesse J. Hargrove is a historian and public scholar whose work bridges the gap between personal narratives and national history. With a focus on African American experiences, Hargrove's scholarship has been instrumental in shaping our understanding of the past and its implications for the present.

Inside Connection:

As America commemorates its 250th anniversary, Still Chasing Democracy offers a timely reflection on the enduring struggle for equality. Through Celia Adams's eyes, the book unpacks the complexities of America's democratic ideals and the lived realities of those who shaped them.

Book's 1–2 Line Hooks:

"A riveting journey through America's unfinished democracy, seen through the eyes of Celia Adams."

"Uncovering the soul of American democracy through the powerful legacy of Celia Adams."

Still Chasing Democracy: America at 250 Through the Eyes of Celia Adams

Exhibit Companion / Trade Crossover

Retracing America's Unfinished Work
What does American democracy look like when seen from the margins rather than the center? Still Chasing Democracy invites readers to experience the nation's history through the life of Celia Adams, a Black woman born into slavery in Richmond, Virginia, whose forced journey through the domestic slave trade and lifelong commitment to education illuminate the distance between America's ideals and its lived reality.

Told with clarity, empathy, and narrative force, this book moves from slave markets and church sanctuaries to classrooms and communities where freedom was imagined, taught, and protected. Through Celia Adams's eyes, democracy appears not as a finished achievement, but as a fragile and ongoing pursuit—carried forward by ordinary people whose lives rarely appear in textbooks, yet shaped the nation in lasting ways.

Back Story

As the United States marks its 250th anniversary, Still Chasing Democracy offers a timely and deeply human reckoning with the American experiment. Blending family history, public memory, and historical research, Dr. Jesse J. Hargrove shows how democracy has been sustained by those most often denied its protections—women, educators, faith leaders, and formerly enslaved people who built institutions of hope in the shadow of exclusion.

Designed to accompany exhibitions, classrooms, and public conversations, this book invites readers to slow down, look closely, and listen—to the stories that reveal not only where America has been, but where it is still trying to go.

Author's Connection

Dr. Jesse J. Hargrove is a historian, public scholar, and descendant of Celia Adams. His work has contributed to national conversations on African American history, education, and public memory, including testimony that helped lay the groundwork for the Smithsonian's National Museum of African American History and Culture. He lives and works at the intersection of scholarship, storytelling, and civic remembrance.

1–2 Line Hooks Trade / Exhibit Ready

"A powerful American story told from the ground up—where democracy was tested, taught, and reimagined."

"At 250 years old, America is still chasing democracy. This is what that pursuit looked like through one woman's life."

"Part family history, part national reckoning—an intimate guide to America's unfinished democratic promise."

"An exhibit in book form: vivid, human, and essential to understanding who built American democracy."

1. Wall-Label-Length Micro Copy (Exhibit Panels)

(50–75 words each; readable in 20–30 seconds)

Panel 1: Still Chasing Democracy

Two hundred and fifty years after its founding, the United States continues to wrestle with the meaning of democracy. This exhibition tells that story not through presidents or monuments, but through the life of Celia Adams—a woman born into slavery whose journey reveals how democracy was built, contested, and carried forward by those excluded from its promises.

Panel 2: Celia Adams

Born in Richmond, Virginia, Celia Adams was sold as a child through the domestic slave trade and forced south. Her life unfolded across enslavement, emancipation, and Reconstruction—eras that shaped the nation while denying her full citizenship. Through faith, education, and endurance, Adams helped build the foundations of freedom where democracy had failed to reach.

Panel 3: Democracy from the Ground Up

For generations of African Americans, democracy was not inherited—it was pursued. In church basements, classrooms, and communities, people like Celia Adams taught literacy, organized care, and imagined futures beyond bondage. These spaces became laboratories of democracy, sustaining hope when laws and institutions refused to do so.

Panel 4: An Unfinished Project

This exhibition asks visitors to consider democracy not as a completed achievement, but as an ongoing responsibility. Celia Adams's story reminds us that the nation's ideals have always

depended on the courage, labor, and vision of ordinary people who believed America could become what it promised.

2. QR Audio Narration Scripts (Aligned to Flaps)

(60–90 seconds each; warm, reflective, invitational tone)

Audio Stop 1: Welcome

Welcome. As America marks 250 years, this exhibition invites you to look at democracy from a different vantage point—not from the halls of power, but from lived experience. Through the life of Celia Adams, you will encounter a story of survival, faith, and education that challenges us to ask not only what democracy claims to be, but who it has served—and who has carried it forward when it fell short.

Audio Stop 2: Celia Adams's Journey

Celia Adams was born into slavery in Richmond, Virginia, and sold as a child through the domestic slave trade. Her journey south was not just a movement across geography—it was a passage through the deepest contradictions of American freedom. Yet Adams's life did not end in captivity. Through education and community-building, she helped shape spaces where freedom could grow, even when democracy remained incomplete.

Audio Stop 3: Education as Democracy

After emancipation, education became one of the most powerful tools for freedom. In classrooms built by churches and communities, people like Celia Adams taught literacy, history, and dignity. These were not simply schools—they were acts of democracy. Long before equality was written into law, it was practiced here, lesson by lesson.

Audio Stop 4: Still Chasing

This exhibition does not offer easy conclusions. Instead, it asks a question: If democracy has always relied on those denied its protections, what does that mean for us today? Celia Adams's story reminds us that democracy is not static. It must be carried, protected, and renewed—generation after generation.

3. Museum Shop Back-Cover Copy (Short, Punchy)

(75–100 words)

At America's 250th anniversary, Still Chasing Democracy tells the nation's story through the life of Celia Adams—a woman born into slavery whose journey reveals how freedom was pursued long before it was protected by law. Blending family history, public memory, and national reckoning, this book offers an intimate, powerful look at democracy as lived experience. An essential companion to the exhibition—and a reminder that America's democratic promise remains unfinished.

4. Smithsonian-Style Exhibition Catalog Language

(Formal, reflective, authoritative—but human)

Still Chasing Democracy situates the life of Celia Adams within the broader arc of American history, using biography as a lens through which to examine the nation's evolving democratic ideals. Rather than centering institutions alone, this exhibition foregrounds lived experience—revealing how enslaved and formerly enslaved individuals shaped democracy through education, faith, and community-building.

By connecting personal narrative to national transformation, the exhibition challenges visitors to reconsider democracy not as a static inheritance, but as a dynamic process sustained by those most often excluded from its protections. In the story of Celia Adams, the American experiment appears unfinished—yet enduring, shaped by resilience, memory, and the pursuit of justice across generations.

Chapter 26

Systems Alignment and the 3MG Horizon: Planning for Generations We Will Never Meet

The Third Millennium Generation (3MG) horizon marks the ethical boundary of the DMG framework. It is not a prediction, nor a target. It is a moral commitment: to plan for a future beyond personal recognition, institutional legacy, or historical memory. To plan to the year 3000 is to accept that the most important beneficiaries of today's decisions will never know our names.

Modern institutions rarely operate under such conditions. Incentives reward visibility, immediacy, and attribution. DMG disrupts this logic by redefining success as continuity without authorship. The 3MG horizon demands humility. It reframes planning as an act of care rather than control.

This final chapter argues that the true measure of a society is not what it builds, but what it sustains. Education, as the longest-lasting institution humans have devised, carries the burden of that sustainability. DMG does not promise certainty; it offers responsibility.

To plan for generations we will never meet is not idealism. It is realism at scale. Futures do not belong to those who predict them, but to those who prepare others to inherit them wisely.

What the Deuce Millennium Generation is asking for is not abstract morality; *it's alignment between professed values and operating* *systems*. Below is a clear, policy-literate framing that is able to be used in testimony, or in a policy public address.

The Values the Deuce Millennium Generation Is Asking for alignment to be Honored:

These are not "new" values. They are long-stated American and democratic ideals that this generation has seen violated in practice.

1. Equity Over Rhetoric

Value: Fairness that accounts for history and starting conditions—not equal language masking unequal outcomes.

This generation rejects symbolic inclusion without structural change. They expect systems to correct disparities, not merely acknowledge them.

Equity means the system works for those historically excluded—not just those already advantaged.

2. Truth and Transparency

Value: Honest narratives, accurate history, and clear accountability.

They have lived in an era of misinformation, selective history, and institutional spin. As a result, they demand truth—about history, outcomes, and intent.

Transparency is not a public relations strategy; it is a democratic obligation.

3. Dignity of Education and Labor

Value: Learning and work as sources of human dignity, not merely economic throughput.

The Deuce Millennium Generation resists systems that reduce people to test scores, productivity metrics, or disposable labor.

Education is formation, not sorting. Work is contribution, not exploitation.

4. Participation Over Performance

Value: Real voice in decisions—not performative engagement.

They expect civic and institutional participation to be consequential, not ceremonial.

Being invited to the table means nothing if decisions are already made.

5. Accountability With Consequences

Value: Responsibility that applies upward—not just downward.

They have watched individuals be punished while institutions evade responsibility.

Rules that only apply to the powerless are not rules—they are control mechanisms.

6. Intergenerational Responsibility

Value: Long-term stewardship over short-term gain.

Climate, debt, education, and democracy itself are inherited conditions. This generation expects ethical stewardship, not extraction.

The future is not a line item to be deferred.

7. Belonging, Not Conditional Inclusion

Value: Full membership without cultural erasure.

They want systems that do not require assimilation, silence, or self-betrayal to succeed.

Belonging is measured by power, not proximity.

The Systems That Must Align With These Values

These are the institutional arenas where misalignment is most visible—and most damaging.

1. Education Systems

Includes: K–12 schools, higher education, accreditation, assessment, curriculum, funding formulas.

Misalignment:
Value equity, fund inequality
Praise critical thinking, reward compliance
Teach democracy, practice exclusion

Required Shift:
Education as a public good and civic institution, not a marketplace or sorting mechanism.

2. Economic and Workforce Systems

Includes: Labor markets, wages, debt structures, internships, gig economy, credentialing.

Misalignment:
Celebrate merit, ignore inherited advantage
Demand productivity, withhold stability
Promise mobility, deliver precarity

Required Shift:
Economic systems that reward contribution, provide stability, and honor labor dignity.

3. Civic and Political Systems

Includes: Voting, representation, policymaking, courts, public trust institutions.

Misalignment:
Promote participation, restrict access
Invoke democracy, resist accountability

Call for unity, avoid justice

Required Shift:
Civic systems that expand participation and restore legitimacy through fairness and transparency.

4. Cultural and Information Systems

Includes: Media, technology platforms, historical narratives, public memory institutions.

Misalignment:
Monetize attention, degrade truth
Celebrate diversity, sanitize history
Amplify voices, ignore accountability

Required Shift:
Truth-centered systems that value context, history, and responsible storytelling.

5. Social and Support Systems

Includes: Healthcare, housing, mental health, public safety, social services.

Misalignment:
Treat survival as individual failure
Criminalize vulnerability
Privatize risk, socialize blame

Required Shift:
Systems designed for human well-being, not punishment or exclusion.

The Central Claim of the Deuce Millennium Generation
This generation is not demanding perfection.
They are demanding coherence.
They are asking a simple question with profound implications:

If these are our values, why don't our systems behave as if they matter?

Until values and systems align, trust will remain fractured—and reform will remain cosmetic.

But alignment is possible.

And history suggests that *when a generation insists on coherence, transformation follows.*

Integrated Book Conclusion

Alignment as the Measure of Renewal
The Deuce Millennium Generation has surfaced a truth that can no longer be avoided: societies are judged not by the values they proclaim, but by the systems they sustain.

This generation was educated in the language of equity while living within structures of inequality. They were taught civic ideals while witnessing institutional avoidance of accountability. They were encouraged to prepare for the future while inheriting debt—financial, environmental, and democratic. Their response has not been withdrawal, but interrogation.

What they are asking for is coherence.
They are asking why education is celebrated as a public good but funded as a private commodity. Why democracy is praised while participation is constrained. Why labor is essential yet treated as expendable. Why history is invoked but not taught honestly. These questions do not signal cynicism; they signal civic literacy.

The misalignment between values and systems has consequences. It erodes trust, weakens participation, and transfers the cost of institutional failure onto individuals least able to bear it. Resilience has become a substitute for justice, adaptation a cover for abandonment.

Yet history suggests that moments of misalignment are also moments of possibility. When a generation insists that systems match values, reform becomes unavoidable. The Deuce Millennium Generation stands at such a threshold—not as a problem to be corrected, but as a mirror held up to the nation itself.

The responsibility for alignment does not rest with youth alone. It rests with educators who must teach beyond metrics, policymakers who must govern beyond election cycles, and institutions willing to reform rather than rebrand. Alignment requires investment, truth, and the courage to confront structural inheritance.

If education is to reclaim its civic purpose, if democracy is to regain legitimacy, and if the future is to be something more than deferred responsibility, then values must once again govern systems.

The Deuce Millennium Generation has made the demand plain.

History will record how we responded.

Freedom in Law and in Practice

When my great-grandmother Celia Adams was sold from Richmond, Virginia, to Louisville, Georgia, she was forced to walk around a slave market three times before purchase. The law recognized her not as a person but as property. After the Civil War, the Constitution changed. The Thirteenth Amendment abolished slavery. The Fourteenth granted citizenship. Freedom, at last, was written into law.

But writing freedom and living it are not the same.

In the decades after Reconstruction, Southern states passed vagrancy laws that criminalized unemployment. Black men who could not prove labor contracts were arrested and leased to private employers. Courts narrowed the reach of the Reconstruction Amendments. Segregation became constitutional under "separate but equal." My great-grandmother's generation was free in theory yet constrained in practice.

Today, the United States faces heated debates over immigration enforcement, deportation policy, and the power of federal agencies such as ICE and Customs and Border Protection. These debates are not about slavery; history does not repeat itself so neatly. But they do raise a familiar American question: When the law promises rights, how faithfully does enforcement honor them?

The Supreme Court has affirmed that noncitizens physically present in the United States are "persons" under the Constitution. They are entitled to due process. Courts have ruled against indefinite detention and struck down vague deportation statutes. And yet, immigration enforcement operates largely within an administrative system where arrests may rely on executive warrants rather than judicial ones, and expedited removal can limit access to full hearings.

Supporters argue that these tools are necessary to enforce federal law and secure the border. Critics argue that some tactics test the boundaries of constitutional protections, particularly when families are separated before judicial review occurs.

What binds the nineteenth century to the twenty-first is not identical injustice but a recurring tension: the gap between constitutional ideals and enforcement practices.

My family's history is a reminder that freedom is not only declared—it is administered. After emancipation, Black Americans were citizens. But citizenship did not prevent incarceration under discriminatory laws. It did not prevent segregation. It did not prevent the narrowing of constitutional promises by courts and local officials.

Similarly, today's immigration system exists within constitutional boundaries. But whether those boundaries are robustly protected or administratively compressed is an ongoing national debate.

Family separation is one of the most painful intersections of law and enforcement. Under slavery, families were separated by sale. During Reconstruction, incarceration and labor exploitation fractured households. In recent years, immigration detention has again raised questions about how enforcement affects children and parents. The Constitution recognizes family integrity as a liberty interest. The challenge is ensuring that enforcement mechanisms respect that principle.

My great-grandmother was what I call a "Freedom Seeker" before emancipation and a "Freedom Dweller" after it. She sought liberty before the law recognized it. She attempted to dwell securely in it once it was proclaimed.

America continues to wrestle with who may dwell securely within its borders. Immigration enforcement is a legitimate function of government. But legitimacy depends on fidelity to constitutional protections—due process, equal protection, and freedom from unreasonable seizure.

History teaches that rights are strongest not when proclaimed, but when protected in practice.

Celia Adams's descendants would one day testify before the United States Senate in support of establishing the National Museum of African American History and Culture. That arc—from slave market to Senate chamber—reflects the nation's capacity for growth. Yet growth requires vigilance.

The enduring American question is simple but profound: Will our enforcement systems reflect our constitutional ideals, or quietly narrow them?

Freedom written in law is aspiration. Freedom honored in practice is democracy.

The epilogue and historiographical paragraph below situates this work within Reconstruction and immigration scholarship

Epilogue

Freedom in Law and in Practice: From Reconstruction to the Present

The Legacy of Celia Adams is, at its foundation, a genealogical recovery. Yet genealogy in the American context is never merely familial; it is constitutional. The life of Celia Adams—enslaved in Virginia, sold into Georgia, emancipated yet constrained—unfolded within a nation that declared liberty universal while administering it selectively. Her story, extended through four generations, reveals a recurring tension in American history: the distance between constitutional promise and enforcement practice.

The Reconstruction Amendments sought to redefine American citizenship. The Thirteenth Amendment abolished slavery "except as a punishment for crime."[1] The Fourteenth guaranteed birthright citizenship and equal protection of the laws.[2] The Fifteenth prohibited racial discrimination in voting.[3] On paper, Celia Adams's generation entered constitutional modernity. Freedom was no longer aspirational; it was textual.

In practice, however, freedom was narrowed almost as swiftly as it was proclaimed.

Black Codes and vagrancy statutes criminalized unemployment and mobility, funneling freedpeople into convict leasing systems that reconstituted coerced labor under penal authority.[4] The Supreme Court's restrictive reading of the Reconstruction Amendments in The Slaughter-House Cases (1873) limited federal protection of civil rights,[5] while Plessy v. Ferguson (1896) constitutionalized segregation under the doctrine of "separate but equal."[6] Constitutional amendments remained intact; their enforcement was diluted.

Celia Adams's post-emancipation life thus unfolded within a paradox. She was legally free yet economically tethered. She possessed nominal citizenship yet lived under regimes that surveilled mobility and restricted opportunity. The generation that followed her inherited not simply freedom, but freedom conditioned by administrative discretion and local enforcement.

This pattern—rights articulated expansively and applied narrowly—has reappeared in other domains of American law, including immigration enforcement.

Immigration regulation lies within Congress's plenary power over naturalization and border control.[7] Yet the Supreme Court has long affirmed that noncitizens physically present within the United States are "persons" under the Constitution and therefore entitled to due process.[8] In Zadvydas v. Davis (2001), the Court held that indefinite detention of removable noncitizens raised serious constitutional concerns.[9] In Sessions v. Dimaya (2018), it invalidated a vague statutory provision used to justify deportation.[10] And in Department of Homeland Security v. Regents of the University of California (2020), the Court ruled that rescission of the Deferred Action for Childhood Arrivals (DACA) program was arbitrary and capricious under administrative law.[11]

These decisions reaffirm that constitutional constraints apply even within immigration enforcement. Yet the structure of the immigration system—administrative warrants issued by executive officers, expedited removal procedures, civil detention without the full panoply of criminal procedural safeguards—has generated ongoing debate about the scope of Fourth and Fifth Amendment protections. Equal protection principles, applied to the federal government

through the Fifth Amendment, prohibit discriminatory enforcement,[12] but allegations of racial profiling and unequal application persist in litigation and scholarship.

The comparison to Reconstruction does not rest on equivalence of suffering or historical context. Slavery was a system of racialized chattel bondage unparalleled in its brutality. Immigration enforcement is a federal regulatory regime operating within constitutional boundaries. The connection lies instead in structure: both eras demonstrate how legal status shapes lived freedom.

During Reconstruction's aftermath, citizenship existed on paper while vagrancy laws and convict leasing constrained Black autonomy. In the modern immigration context, constitutional personhood exists in doctrine while administrative enforcement tests procedural boundaries. In both instances, mobility, labor, and family integrity become sites where law and power converge.

Family separation provides a particularly stark lens. Under slavery, families were divided by sale. After emancipation, incarceration and labor exploitation fractured households. In the contemporary immigration system, detention and deportation may separate parents and children before judicial review is complete. The Supreme Court has recognized family integrity as a protected liberty interest under the Due Process Clause,[13] yet enforcement practices often precede adjudication.

The Adams family story demonstrates that constitutional development is not linear. It is iterative. Celia Adams was denied legal personhood. Her descendants would later participate in shaping national memory, including advocacy contributing to the establishment of the National Museum of African American History and Culture.[14] That arc reflects both progress and persistence.

Historiographical Context

This work enters into conversation with leading scholars of Reconstruction and American state formation, including Eric Foner's analysis of the unfinished revolution of citizenship,[15] and the scholarship of Steven Hahn, who emphasizes grassroots Black political mobilization in the postbellum South.[16] It also engages the literature on carceral continuity and convict leasing explored by Douglas A. Blackmon and Khalil Gibran Muhammad.[17] In the field of immigration history and law, it intersects with the constitutional analyses of Hiroshi Motomura and Gerald Neuman, who examine the tension between plenary power doctrine and constitutional personhood.[18] By placing a multigenerational African American genealogy in dialogue with constitutional doctrine and administrative enforcement, The Legacy of Celia Adams bridges social history and legal history. It contributes to a growing body of scholarship that treats family narrative not as anecdotal supplement but as evidentiary archive—demonstrating how constitutional interpretation is experienced at the level of lived life.

Celia Adams sought freedom before the Constitution recognized her claim to it. After emancipation, she attempted to dwell within a constitutional order that only partially secured her rights. Her descendants inherited both the promise and the fragility of that order.

The enduring American question is not whether rights are declared. It is whether enforcement honors them.

Freedom in America has always been both articulated and administered. The distance between those two realities—between text and practice—is where constitutional memory resides.

Footnotes

U.S. Const. amend. XIII.

U.S. Const. amend. XIV, §1.

U.S. Const. amend. XV.

Douglas A. Blackmon, Slavery by Another Name (New York: Anchor Books, 2008).

The Slaughter-House Cases, 83 U.S. (16 Wall.) 36 (1873).

Plessy v. Ferguson, 163 U.S. 537 (1896).

Chae Chan Ping v. United States (The Chinese Exclusion Case), 130 U.S. 581 (1889).

Yick Wo v. Hopkins, 118 U.S. 356 (1886).

Zadvydas v. Davis, 533 U.S. 678 (2001).

Sessions v. Dimaya, 138 S. Ct. 1204 (2018).

Department of Homeland Security v. Regents of the University of California, 591 U.S. ___ (2020).

Bolling v. Sharpe, 347 U.S. 497 (1954).

Meyer v. Nebraska, 262 U.S. 390 (1923); Troxel v. Granville, 530 U.S. 57 (2000).

S. 523, National African American Museum Act, 102nd Cong. (1992).

Eric Foner, Reconstruction: America's Unfinished Revolution, 1863–1877 (New York: Harper & Row, 1988).

Steven Hahn, A Nation under Our Feet (Cambridge, MA: Harvard University Press, 2003).

Blackmon, Slavery by Another Name; Khalil Gibran Muhammad, The Condemnation of Blackness (Cambridge, MA: Harvard University Press, 2010).

Hiroshi Motomura, Americans in Waiting (New York: Oxford University Press, 2006); Gerald L. Neuman, Strangers to the Constitution (Princeton: Princeton University Press, 1996).

References

Bell, Wendell. 1997. Foundations of Futures Studies: Human Science for a New Era. New Brunswick, NJ: Transaction Publishers.

Dewey, John. 1916. Democracy and Education. New York: Macmillan.

Du Bois, W. E. B. 1935. Black Reconstruction in America. New York: Harcourt, Brace and Company.

Franklin, John Hope. 1947. From Slavery to Freedom: A History of African Americans. New York: Knopf.

Freire, Paulo. 1970. Pedagogy of the Oppressed. New York: Continuum.

Illich, Ivan. 1971. Deschooling Society. New York: Harper & Row.

Mead, Margaret. 1970. Culture and Commitment: A Study of the Generation Gap. Garden City, NY: Doubleday.

Miller, Riel. 2018. Transforming the Future: Anticipation in the 21st Century. Paris: UNESCO.

Schwartz, Peter. 1991. The Art of the Long View. New York: Doubleday.

Strauss, William, and Neil Howe. 1991. Generations: The History of America's Future, 1584–2069. New York: William Morrow.

Toffler, Alvin. 1970. Future Shock. New York: Random House.

UNESCO. 2015. Rethinking Education: Towards a Global Common Good? Paris: UNESCO Publishing.

Woodson, Carter G. 1933. The Mis-Education of the Negro. Washington, DC: Associated Publishers.

Historical Anchors

1. Reconstruction (1865–1877): The allegory's first race corresponds to the post–Civil War constitutional moment—13th, 14th, and 15th Amendments—followed by federal retreat, the

Compromise of 1877, Black Codes, and Jim Crow. See Eric Foner, Reconstruction: America's Unfinished Revolution.

2. Civil Rights Era (1954–1975): The second race reflects desegregation after Brown v. Board of Education, the Civil Rights Act of 1964, and the Voting Rights Act of 1965, alongside unequal school funding, housing segregation, and deindustrialization. See Thomas Sugrue, Sweet Land of Liberty.

3. Deuce Millennium Policy Failures (2000–2025): The current race maps onto neoliberal education reform, student debt expansion, erosion of labor protections, voter suppression, and declining institutional trust among Millennials and Gen Z. See Jacob Hacker & Paul Pierson, Winner-Take-All Politics; Pew Research Center on generational trust.

Bibliography

(Extended historiography and recommended readings, including Reconstruction, Civil Rights, and Deuce Millennium policy literature.)

Biography of the Author

Dr. Jesse J. Hargrove is a retired educator, historian, poet, and public scholar whose work explores African American historical memory, constitutional belonging, and intergenerational narratives rooted in family history. After more than 45 years in education, he retired in 2025 following 26 years at Philander Smith University in Little Rock, Arkansas, where he served as a tenured Associate Professor of Spanish and Art and as an administrator. During his tenure, he taught courses in Spanish language, art, and social justice while mentoring students and encouraging them to develop critical intellectual frameworks for understanding history, culture, and civic responsibility.

Born in Gough, Georgia, a rural agricultural community historically associated with large cotton production, Dr. Hargrove traces his lineage to his great-grandmother Celia Adams, a formerly enslaved woman born in Richmond, Virginia, in 1856. After emancipation, Adams became a respected midwife and community leader who strongly advocated education for African American children during the Reconstruction era. Family history recounts that when a training school serving formerly enslaved students was displaced from Springfield Baptist Church in Augusta, Georgia, Adams helped shelter the effort within her church community. That school would later become part of the early institutional history of Morehouse College, reflecting the broader post–Civil War movement to establish educational institutions for newly freed people.

This multigenerational story forms the foundation of Dr. Hargrove's historical and scholarly work. His research examines how family histories intersect with national constitutional developments,

particularly the evolving meaning of citizenship, education, and belonging in the United States. His book project, **Freedom's Inheritance During America250: Celia Adams and the Long Struggle for Constitutional Belonging,** situates one family's experience within larger cycles of American legal and social transformation.

Dr. Hargrove's commitment to historical preservation and public memory also extends to national cultural institutions. On March 12, 1992—the birthday of Celia Adams—he testified before the United States Senate Committee on Rules and Administration at the invitation of Senators John McCain and Paul Simon in support of legislation that would ultimately contribute to the creation of the Smithsonian National Museum of African American History and Culture, dedicated in Washington, D.C., in 2016.

A lifetime member of Omega Psi Phi Fraternity, Inc., Dr. Hargrove has also played an important role in documenting African American institutional history. He served as the first Co-Chair of the fraternity's Artifacts and Memorabilia Committee within its History and Archives Committee. Currently, he serves as Co-Chair of the Ninth District digital museum initiative, which seeks to document and preserve the historical contributions of distinguished African American leaders in Arkansas, Louisiana, Texas, and Oklahoma. This effort is part of a broader initiative to develop a national digital repository—the Omega Index—cataloguing the historical contributions of fraternity members worldwide.

Dr. Hargrove has also been deeply involved in public service and historical preservation within Arkansas. He worked seven (7) years with the Arkansas State Archives and the Black History Commission of Arkansas, and previously served 11 years on the Arkansas Commission on Closing the Achievement Gap. His research interests include documenting overlooked individuals and institutions in African

American history, tracing migration and forced labor routes across the American South—including those connected to the historical origins of Juneteenth—and studying the cultural symbolism embedded within African American quilting traditions.

Dr. Hargrove is also a poet and author whose writings reflect the intersection of history, culture, and education. His works include Closing the Achievement Gap in America: A National Imperative for a Super Man, a Super Woman, and a Superintendent, which outlines educational strategies aimed at empowering future generations. He has also written poetry reflecting on the historical experiences and cultural resilience of African Americans.

He earned his undergraduate degree from Dillard University, where he credits his education with shaping his intellectual development. During the 1973–1974 academic year, he was selected as one of ten scholars from historically Black colleges and universities to study at University of California, Berkeley as part of the Crown Zellerbach Foundation Scholars program. The program was designed to challenge controversial theories advanced by Arthur Jensen and William Shockley, who claimed that African American students could not compete academically at elite institutions. The success of the participating scholars—including physicians, professors, and community leaders—demonstrated the fallacy of those claims.

Through scholarship, teaching, archival research, and public history work, Dr. Hargrove continues to document the long struggle for education, citizenship, and belonging that defines the African American experience.

www.ingramcontent.com/pod-product-compliance
Ingram Content Group UK Ltd.
Pitfield, Milton Keynes, MK11 3LW, UK
UKHW062259290726
14090UKWH00017B/786

9 798901 244449